Decoding Abortion Rhetoric

DECODING ABORTION RHETORIC

Communicating Social Change

CELESTE MICHELLE CONDIT

UNIVERSITY OF ILLINOIS PRESS
Urbana and Chicago

First Illinois paperback, 1994
© 1990 by the Board of Trustees of the University of Illinois

1 2 3 4 5 C P 6 5 4 3 2

Library of Congress Cataloging-in-Publication Data

Condit, Celeste Michelle, 1956-
Decoding abortion rhetoric : communicating social change / Celeste
Michelle Condit.
p. cm.
Includes index.
ISBN 0-252-01647-5 (alk. paper)/ISBN 978-0-252-01647-6
1. Abortion—Moral and ethical aspects. 2. Pro-choice movement—United States. 3. Pro-life movement—United States. I. Title.
363.4'6—dc20   89-33469
                      CIP

Paperback ISBN 978-0-252-06403-6

Printed and bound in Great Britain by
Marston Book Services Limited, Oxford

for my sister,
Deirdre Moira Condit,
at whose expense I have gained much:
a little interest on the loan of your life

CONTENTS

ACKNOWLEDGMENTS

Unlike so many books these days, this work was not supported by foundations or time off from teaching or other outside aid. As a consequence, the extra effort had to come out of the lives of my friends, colleagues, and family. I am, therefore, more than usually indebted to others for their heroic efforts or heroic tolerance. Most centrally, my spouse, Loren Bruce Railsback, has not only edited my work and provided photographs, he has tolerated a cranky, single-minded eccentric as a life partner and discussed these issues beyond all reasonable expectations (especially for a geologist, who finds our human traumas rather short-lived and small-scale). I am also indebted to John Louis Lucaites for his thoughtful "academic" reading of the manuscript. I owe my sister for providing a "non-academic" reading along with permanent support and inspiration. I thank my mother and father for teaching me to care and to argue. I thank Michael Calvin McGee for inspiring me to write a book on this topic, in this way. I thank Paula Treichler for helping me to negotiate the mine field of feminist academic politics. In addition, I want to thank Lawrance Bernabo for providing the materials that made chapter 7 possible, and Sally Kenney for her reading of chapter 6.

I must also acknowledge John Lyne and Samuel Becker, members of my dissertation committee, and Bruce Gronbeck, my adviser. Chapters 2 and 4 overlap with that dissertation. I express thanks to the many other scholars in the field of rhetorical criticism and communication studies who have provided feedback on portions of this work, including Elizabeth Nelson, Tom Duncanson, James Hay, Susan Owen, Karlyn Kohrs Campbell, Cheris Kramerae, Joe Wenzel, Larry Grossberg, Dean Hewes, Bernard Brock, Ellen Wartella, Donovan Ochs and the many others of you whose important suggestions and responses I have woven into this discourse while ungratefully forgetting the sources. I am grateful to Katrina Maxtone-Graham for her permission to use her interviews in chapter 9 and for her assistance in making sure I have done so accurately. I am indebted to Cynthia Mitchell for her thoughtful editing.

I also thank the Speech Communication Association for permission to use material overlapping with my essay "The Contemporary Abortion Controversy: Stages in the Argument," *Quarterly Journal of Speech*

70 (November 1984), 410–24; the *Journal of Communication Inquiry* for permission to use material from "Abortion on Television: The 'System' and Ideological Production" 11 (Summer 1987), 47–60, that overlaps with chapter 7; and the *Pensacola News-Journal* for permission to use the letter which appears in Appendix B.

Finally, I express my gratitude to all of the women scholars who have fought so many battles and crafted so many examples for me and others: they have made this work possible in a dozen hidden ways. In spite of its flaws, I hope this discourse contributes in some manner toward the collective craft of women's scholarship as well as to our understanding of rhetoric, social systems, and abortion in America.

The Politics of Abortion Study

The practice of abortion has always been politically charged and morally problematic because abortion allows power over a central arena of social life; abortion provides the most effective control over human reproductive labor. Consequently, different historical groups, differently situated, have held diverse positions on abortion. Passionate disagreement has prevailed, even among women. The first wave of American feminist social reformers used opposition to abortion as a reason to support birth control.[1] Even though the second wave of American feminists evolved a consensus in favor of legalized abortion as a major component of "reproductive freedom," they did so only gradually. In the early years of the second movement, struggles over abortion were extremely divisive for groups like the National Organization for Women.[2] Even in the seventies and eighties the consensus was not complete; a small group calling themselves Feminists for Life continuously seconded a much larger group of homemakers in opposing abortion.

By the 1980s, controversy over abortion had also spread throughout the academic realm. In the law journals, scholars and lawyers argued about the fitness of the "privacy" doctrine (see chapter 6). In journals and books in women's studies, academics began extensive explorations of a wide range of issues relating to "mothering" and reproduction, and this work had profound implications for the issue of abortion.[3] Simultaneously, some cultural feminists suggested that the abortion "choice" might be wrong when it involves eliminating deformed fetuses (disvaluing disabled persons) or females.[4] Feminist scholars with socialist beliefs indicated that the choices of individual women might be less important than the outcomes for women as a class.[5]

To write a book about abortion rhetoric in the midst of such controversial argument is challenging and, perhaps, risky. Partisans of various positions may resent even the portrayal of their arguments as "rhetoric," for the term has taken on the connotations of "empty deceit." However, I use the word in the academic sense, to mean persuasion (by argument and other means). Rhetoric is not necessarily bad: arguments can be either sound or unsound; styles of presentation, either attractive or unattractive. Moreover, rhetoric is essential to a democracy.

This book's primary goal is not to buttress any particular political position but to describe the way in which legal and cultural consensus was molded through the public interactions between the various partisans. Because it offers detailed analysis of the development and functioning of opposing positions, it may be of use or interest to persons from a wide range of perspectives. To add increased understandings of the shape and depth of a controversy, and of how one's rhetoric functions, is to gain power to further the argument. The political issue, nonetheless, returns at a second level. In order to assess the effects of various persuasive strategies and arguments, I have often had to assess the kinds of strengths and weaknesses these rhetorics feature. Partisans tend to be embarrassed as much by having the strategic elements of their discourse openly identified and labelled "persuasive" as by having their arguments labelled incomplete. These assessments on my part, therefore, have unavoidable political implications.

Further, despite the traditional canons of objectivity thought necessary for scholarly work, I do not claim to be a "disinterested" observer.[6] I am fully aware that my choice of this topic as well as the ways in which I have put the issues together are influenced by my position as a career woman (not solely a homemaker) who has never faced an unwanted pregnancy and who has adequate resources to insure a relatively high degree of control over her fertility.[7] I nonetheless claim academic objectivity for this work, according to a standard of objectivity that is sounder than that of "disinterest."[8] Because I address a divided audience of both rhetorical theorists and feminist scholars, I have not adopted the feminist approach to objectivity elucidated by Mary O'Brien, who argues that because male scholarship is one-sided, one-sided female scholarship is needed to balance it.[9] Although I would defend that standard as appropriate for many kinds of academic work, in this book I have applied a standard that derives from the problems raised by the investigation of discourse. This standard proposes that studying meaning-laden human activities requires not detachment from competing sides but full empathetic engagement with all positions. In order to understand how a series of public rhetorics functioned to shape law and culture, one ought to try to live fully—emotionally and logically—in the broad range of discourses produced on the controversy. Such "recreation of situations" is a standard practice in traditional rhetorical criticism.[10] It is, further, as Douglas Ehninger has noted, necessarily an enterprise requiring self-risk.[11] If one authentically engages life-worlds different from one's own, there is a good chance one's views will be substantially altered.

In order to present an account of the abortion controversy, I have had to risk myself in this way, and I have indeed come through this surprisingly painful process changed. At the least, I am more committed to the need for better public policies on reproductive issues because I now understand more fully both the crucial role of abortion in some women's lives *and* the substantiality of the later-term fetus. The process of coming to understand the development of the controversy, as opposed to the process of forming one's opinion on its issues, requires the additional intellectual skill of separating what a principle or statement means as a guide for policy in one's present context from the impact of that "same" principle, value, story, or statement in a different historical context. Discourses that one might not wish to endorse as "equipment for living" today may nonetheless have served useful social functions in a different historical context.[12] This entails treating discourse as "rhetoric"—historically situated empirically real communicative events which have identifiable effects— rather than treating words as "ideas" or philosophic principles—transcendent statements made about ideals or future policies. That kind of separation does not negate politics; it may help to manage the tricky balance between "mere" politics and "mere" scholarship: if humanist scholarship is inevitably political, it must have a politics that learns.

Academic work on important issues—be it foreign policy, international trade, pollution control, or criminology—inevitably entails value judgments and political consequences. Such political dimensions do not negate the worth of such human science but rather indicate quite clearly its potential for worth to the human species. It is only in the execution of a particular work that it will become clear whether the politics of the scholar have been managed to produce something of interest and value to others who do not necessarily share those politics or whether the academic has succeeded only in generating material that will hearten compatriots. I hope I have achieved the broader standard.

NOTES

1. This anti-abortion stance was not by any means uniform among early feminists and birth control advocates. A variety of works deal directly and

indirectly with this issue. See Colin Francone, *Abortion Freedom: A Worldwide Movement* (London and Boston: George Allen and Unwin, 1984), esp. pp. 60–61; Carl Degler, *At Odds: Women and the Family in America* (New York: Oxford University Press, 1980), esp. p. 243; Linda Gordon, *Woman's Body: Woman's Right* (New York: Grossman, 1976); Carol Smith-Rosenberg, *Disorderly Conduct: Visions of Gender in Victorian America* (New York: Alfred A. Knopf, 1983); Eleanor Flexner, *Century of Struggle* (1959; rpt. Cambridge, Mass.: Belknap Press, 1968).

2. See "NOW Bill of Rights," "Letters to Our Sisters in Social Work," and "Redstockings Manifesto" in *Sisterhood Is Powerful: An Anthology of Writings from the Women's Liberation Movement*, ed. Robin Morgan (New York: Random House, 1970); also The Boston Women's Health Book Collective, *Our Bodies, Ourselves: A Book By and For Women* (New York: Simon and Schuster), pp. 138–53; "Jane," photocopy reprinted from *Voices*, June-November 1973.

3. See, for example, Adrienne Rich, *Of Woman Born: Motherhood as Experience and Institution* (New York: W. W. Norton, 1976); Nancy Chodorow, *The Reproduction of Mothering* (Berkeley: University of California Press, 1978); Mary O'Brien, *The Politics of Reproduction* (Boston: Routledge and Kegan Paul, 1983); Germaine Greer, *Sex and Destiny: The Politics of Human Fertility* (New York: Harper Colophon Books, 1984); Shulamith Firestone, *The Dialectic of Sex* (London: Paladine, 1972). The *Feminist Dictionary* (ed. Cheris Kramarae and Paula A. Treichler [London: Pandora Press, 1985]) defines abortion as "termination of pregnancy prior to about twenty weeks gestation," suggesting another ground of difference in perspectives.

4. Helen B. Holmes and Betty B. Hoskins, "Prenatal and Preconception Sex Choice Technologies: A Path to Femicide?" in *Man-Made Women: How New Reproductive Technologies Affect Women*, ed. Gena Corea et al. (Bloomington: Indiana University Press, 1987), pp. 15–30; Robyn Rowland, "Motherhood, Patriarchal Power, Alienation and the Issue of 'Choice' in Sex Preselection," in Corea et al., p. 84; Madhu Kishwar, "The Continuing Deficit of Women in India and the Impact of Amniocentesis," in Corea et al., pp. 30–37; Viola Roggencamp, "Abortion of a Special Kind: Male Sex Selection in India," in Rita Arditti, Renate Duelli-Klein and Shelley Minden, eds. *Test-Tube Women: What Future for Motherhood?* (London: Pandora Press, 1984), pp. 213–34, but consider Gayatri Chakravorty Spivak, "Let the Subaltern Speak," in *Marxism and the Interpretation of Culture*, ed. Cary Nelson and Lawrence Grossberg (Urbana: University of Illinois Press, 1986), pp. 271–313; Ann Finger, "Claiming All of Our Bodies: Reproductive Rights and Disabilities," in Arditti, Duelli-Klein, and Mindern, pp. 281–97.

5. See Rowland; for a recent description of the disagreements among feminists see Catharine R. Stimpson, "Nancy Reagan Wears a Hat: Feminism and Its Cultural Consensus," *Critical Inquiry* 14 (Winter 1988), 223–44.

6. The masculinist version of "objectivity" is revealed, not only in the originating documents of fathers of the scientific revolution like Bacon and Descartes (see Sandra Harding, *The Science Question in Feminism* [Ithaca: Cornell University Press, 1986]) but also in textbooks that purport to teach

young scholars how to practice their trade. Consider, for example, the admonitions of Savoie Lottinville to young historians: "In historical writing you must exercise the severest possible detachment." The writer should "imagine himself a man 'on a peak in Darien,' surveying his episode with the eyes of a visitor of another land, undisturbed by national interests or fate." Lottinville, *The Rhetoric of History* (Norman: University of Oklahoma Press, 1976), pp. 8, 9.

7. The phrase "only a homemaker" has generated an unfortunate confusion. That statement tends to disvalue the important work of housekeeping and child-rearing and to ignore the fact that most career women are also homemakers. To be a homemaker is important work, but for a person who has a career outside the home *and* is a homemaker, those who do not work outside the home are "only" homemakers, not taking on *two* different jobs.

8. See note 6.

9. O'Brien says: "Feminist theory has to be biased because it is anti-bias. We have to correct a profound and long-sustained imbalance, and this cannot be done without jumping rather brutally and without invitation on the end of the philosophical seesaw which has lingered too long in the rarefied heights of the complacent taken-for-grantedness of male conceptions of the nature of man" (p. 12).

10. Robert L. Scott and Bernard L. Brock, "The Traditional Perspective," in *Methods of Rhetorical Criticism: A Twentieth Century Perspective*, ed. Scott and Brock, 1st ed. (New York: Harper and Row, 1972), pp. 29–37.

11. Douglas Ehninger, "Argument as Method: Its Nature, Its Limitations and Its Uses," *Speech Monographs* 37 (June 1979), esp. p. 104.

12. Kenneth Burke, *Permanence and Change: An Anatomy of Purpose*, 3rd ed. (Berkeley: University of California Press, 1984).

DECODING ABORTION RHETORIC

CHAPTER ONE

The Social Force of Rhetoric

The practice and meaning of abortion in the United States of America underwent stunning changes between 1960 and 1985. In the previous century abortions had been done primarily "underground." The term itself had been a whisper-word, not to be spoken in polite company or in public. Beginning in the sixth decade of the twentieth century, however, major social changes brought abortion within routine institutional medicine, reconfigured its public meanings, and dramatically altered both the private practices of women with regard to abortion and their relationship to "motherhood." These tumultuous revisions were negotiated within a heated, continuing public controversy.

The breadth and depth of the impacts of this singular, contested, and rapid change can hardly be underestimated: the meaning and practice of abortion is central to the reproduction of the human species, to our understandings of gender, and to our life ethics. Because of its pivotal role in our national and personal lives, scholars have begun to tie the contemporary controversy over abortion into a wide range of social forces.[1]

This book attempts something different: it examines the path taken by the developing *public discourse* that constituted the most visible element of that controversy. The story told here is not a conventional history, for histories usually focus on the people and events that "cause" social changes, relegating public discourse to a supporting role in the story.[2] In contrast, this account focuses directly on the American *argument* about abortion, describing the vast flows of public discourse that spread across America to shift the meaning of abortion and of related terms, practices, and laws. Chapter 2 begins the tale in the early sixties when the persuasive power of a plaintive story about women's experiences made illegal abortion a *public* concern for the first time in many years. This compelling story drew forth powerful histories (chapter 3), which escalated the controversy to a battle over

1

constitutive values (chapter 4) and dramatic visual images (chapter 5). The Supreme Court addressed the constitutional issue thereby raised through modification and legal instantiation of the vocabularies offered by the activists on both sides (chapter 6). The new law and legitimated public vocabulary were then simultaneously both integrated into the popular culture (chapter 7) and violently rejected by some groups (chapter 8). In the end, women's lives and stories, which had generated the controversy, came to reflect and be revised by the new public discourse (chapter 9).

To expend effort describing "what people have said" to the extent this book does is not yet a familiar practice in the intellectual community (those unconcerned about the theoretical support of this approach may prefer to skip to the beginning of the abortion issue itself at chapter 2). The prevailing approaches to the study of social change in America have dismissed the words of social activists as quickly as has the American "common sense," which dictates that "actions speak louder than words."[3] After all, individuals may lie to us, their intentions may be hard to determine from their language, and they probably do not fully understand their own reasons for acting. Consequently, scholars have tended to submerge description and analysis of public discourse, studying instead the "framework of social forces" behind those words, the actors and events surrounding the discourse, or the private communication contained in letters and diaries.[4]

The majority of studies of changes in American abortion laws have shared important elements of this non-discursive approach. Kristin Luker's excellent and important book on the controversy provides a clear example. In spite of the fact that she directs a great deal of her own attention to the discursive *content* of the social change processes, Luker advances this justification for preferring studies of economic forces to analysis of the persuasion *process:* "It is tempting to argue that the pro-Choice people simply 'persuaded' a great many fellow Americans to accept their point of view. To some extent, they probably did; certainly the mere fact that they made the abortion issue a subject for public debate allowed many more people to become familiar with it and to form personal opinions about the merits of their case. It seems likely, however, that American public opinion was shaped more significantly by the large-scale social changes going on at the same time."[5]

Luker believes that the work lives of women activists provide the central large-scale force. Consequently, she collapses the "framework of understanding" that has guided their activism into a static set of beliefs and values devolving from these life issues, ignoring the discourse as a change agent in itself.[6]

Luker's assumptions have been widely shared. Rosalind Pollack Petchesky's rich analysis of current abortion policies and practices emphasizes the improved economic position of women as the central causal factor in the recent changes. In doing so, Petchesky omits serious consideration of the pro-Life argument in defense of the fetus.[7] Additionally, she provides no explanation of *how* American public discourse arrived at the liberal phrase "right to choice," instead of her preferred phrase "control of our own bodies," as a justification for current abortion practices. Such gaps in explanation suggest that, however vital the knowledge provided by studies of "social forces" that do not focus on public discourse, they have not yet provided us complete understandings.

The other major branch of scholarship about abortion has focused not on material forces but on abstract ideas, preferring a philosophical, ethical, or moral bent. These articles and books feature explorations of the moral and political concerns involved in ethically sound abortion policies. They employ history, at most, as a backdrop for their formulations.[8] As vital as these works are for helping us sort out where we ought to go in abortion policies and practices, they provide little explanation for how we got where we are.

Explanations of the path through which America has arrived at its current abortion laws, practices, and understandings must include the study of discursive forces because only through public discourse can material realities be expressed and ideas materialized. Public discourse serves as such a bridge because it is both a concrete material practice and the bearer of ideas. It becomes, therefore, vital to any understanding of the evolution of material practices and ethics. Unfortunately, the few studies that have taken serious account of the *discourse* of the abortion controversy have lacked methodological sophistication or have taken a static, ahistorical perspective. They have not, therefore, produced *explanations* of the functioning of the public argument in the revision of widely shared meanings.[9] For activists as well as scholars, this limitation on our understanding is a significant one.

There have been serious reasons for the absence of such scholarship. In order to chart broad-scale social changes of this nature, academics have had to develop ways of seeing discourse as an empirical entity operating through multiple voices across the social scale, rather than as the intentions of individual speakers. Fortunately, most of the barriers to such an approach are falling. Most centrally, the maturation of the American school of rhetorical criticism has provided a way for scholars to avoid examining public discourse solely on the authors' terms—for intended meaning. Instead, current approaches favor studying discourse obliquely, through rhetorical structure.[10] In addition, a wide range of theoretical work in several fields has begun to indicate both the importance of ideology and its partial independence from the means of economic production, political demographics, social institutions, and other such super-structural factors.[11]

My particular version of these theoretical and methodological orientations are likely to be unfamiliar to many readers, so I wish to sketch the outlines of a model indicating how public discourse functions in American society. I cannot provide a complete theoretical argument here, but will merely summarize the position (I include references to fuller theoretical elaborations). I have provided a glossary for the few technical terms you will need and marked words appearing in the glossary with an asterisk (e.g., *narratives) at their first use or, later, for emphasis.

The Force of Rhetoric in Society

Public discourse is constituted of *rhetoric. That word carries negative connotations that provide a useful reminder: those who speak in public have their own agendas; they seek to persuade us of something that is in their interest. However, those negative connotations, and our tendency to treat the phrase "mere rhetoric" as a single, inseparable unit, should not disguise the fact that rhetoric has important social functions.

The social role of rhetoric is perhaps best indicated through the Greek root of the term. The verb *rheo* originally meant "to flow" or "to gush forth." As the verb became a noun denoting a particular type of speech, it captured the way in which the flow of meaning is constituted through persuasive public discourse (i.e., "rhetoric"). As its root suggests, therefore, public rhetoric is important because it is the most immediate source of the flow of social meanings, and all persons, as social beings, are destined to live in the world through meaning.

Even those who take a determinist position, declaring every rhetorical statement to be a simple product of a particular condition, recognize that the *articulation of social conditions *through rhetoric* is a substantively different artifact than those supposedly primary social conditions themselves. Large-scale social forces cannot be directly

dealt with or even experienced by governments, politicians, bu-
reaucrats, or individuals. They can be dealt with only through understandings of them, which are predominantly carried through a shared
*public vocabulary. Thus, in the abortion controversy, the competing
concerns of professional women, the Catholic church, high-tech busi-
nesses seeking well-educated workers, etc., cannot be directly
weighed, or even mathematically calculated, by the people who construct and operate nation-states. They must be *addressed* through a
complex network of meanings about the role of government, about
what is good for "the people," and about the particular character of
particular situations. The complexities of the production and use of
meanings make it necessary for scholars and politicians alike to add
detailed understandings of rhetorical processes to conventional studies of the underlying social forces to which they are linked.

The full determinist position, however, is probably neither the
most popular position nor the most accurate, and for those who admit
that public discourse may have some independence from its economic
roots, the social force of rhetoric appears even greater.[12] A broad
range of studies have begun to join rhetorical criticism and public
address in taking seriously public and popular discourse. The majority of these studies have been focused on *culture in such a way as to
emphasize the private or sub-cultural responses of individuals, families, or classes.[13] While these works share important alliances with
my own endeavors, this volume focuses on the *public impact of
political and cultural discourses, rather than upon their direct ramifications in the personal realm, and so the findings and orientations are
quite different.

Most notably, a study of public, political discourse must be quite
explicit about providing a model of governance that presumes the
possibility of social change through the social process of rhetoric. This
requires the fusion of the three dominant theories of representative
government. While it would require an entire volume to accurately
trace these theories and their multiple transformations, it is enough
for present purposes to sketch a set of caricatures.

The "conservative" position on representative government pro-
claims that, through a marketplace of ideas, rational argumentation by
individuals produces policies that serve the general interests of all of
the people. The "liberal" realist replies that, in fact, partisan interest
groups use a range of persuasive devices to convince politicians and
citizens to enact policies that favor partisan interests under the guise
of general interests. The "leftist" denounces even that account, indicating that the disproportionate power of elites allows them to circum-

vent any true clash with other groups, maintaining power directly, behind a veil of false consciousness.

Each of these positions offers important components of a more complete account. The conservatives are correct in suggesting that it is only through the attempt to use rational argumentation to make government serve the public interest that legitimacy, and hence survival, of this form of government can be maintained. Moreover, I believe that they are correct, that sometimes that goal is achieved. However, the liberals offer important correctives. Because the process of public argumentation is conducted through interest groups, there is always the potential for the public interest to be hijacked, via persuasion, into serving some partisan interests. Finally, the leftists are correct in noting that, in fact, the disproportionate power of some groups allows them disproportionate influence in the public discourse and thereby results in a general tendency that favors elites repeatedly.

A comprehensive model of mass-mediated representative government presumes, then, that a large number of competing groups seek to control the available resources and practices to their own advantage. These groups vary in size, influence, and degree of organization, and membership in them overlaps. Some groups and individuals have incredible and disproportionate power (e.g., the ruling elites serving as directors of major corporations or the 1 percent of the populace holding a third of the national wealth, or males as a class), but they must wield this power by gaining public assent for the policies and practices they prefer (at least on major issues).[14] This public assent (active or passive) is achieved through the rhetorical process, whether deliberative, forensic, or *epideictic.

In public arenas of discourse—such as newspapers, magazines, the floor of Congress, presidential speeches, television programs, or bureaucratic hearings—rhetors advance claims on "the nation" couched in terms of major values, suggesting that particular sentiments, policies, or laws are in the general interest. To the extent that they are successful at convincing the *public of this potential for general good, they are able to enact their will. However, the process of convincing requires not only that a given policy be accepted but also that a given vocabulary (or set of understandings) be integrated into the public repertoire. Thus, for example, "protective" legislation for women was passed by employing and simultaneously strengthening a definition of all women as weak, vulnerable, and worthy of protection because of their inherent reproductive role—*motherhood.[15] These meanings are reflected, reproduced, and revised throughout the social formation at various levels—in the law, in cultural artifacts, in social and economic practices, and in individual lives (and that is why "the personal is political"). Over time, a powerful social group's way of describing the general interest may become embedded within the public vocabularies and practices. Future arguments for that group's interests are then easier to make, because supporting practices and the *warrants for the arguments are already in place. Even when a subject is lobbied privately rather than debated publicly, this public repertoire of meanings exerts influences on the outlines of policies.

Eventually, this rhetorical process might result in a near-monolithic control by a few powerful groups. However, at least as this nation has been constituted, there have always been crucial issues over which major groups were at odds with each other (e.g., farmers vs. industrialists and unions, importers vs. exporters, slave owners vs. employers of free labor, and, today, multi-nationals and nationals, high-tech industry and service industry).[16] This has resulted in continual disputes about meanings and vocabularies, and these disputes have kept open possibilities for less powerful, less well-organized groups to influence the public repertoire of meanings as well.

Hence, terms such as "shared meanings," a "dominant *ideology," or a *hegemony of understandings locate a concrete, identifiable set of discourses that have identifiable effects because they are shared by an identifiable public. The characters of ideology and the public, however, are different from what has often been presupposed. The dominant ideology, materialized in a wide range of public discourse, contains conflicting beliefs and values—for example, a preference for individual *liberty* to accumulate wealth at the cost of others and also a commitment to *equality* and even compassion. The distribution of resources and power is therefore determined both by the relative dominance of the favored terms of some groups over others and by the practical application of those terms in particular areas. This mechanism allows the rhetorical process at any given historical instance to shape and alter public discourse about particular issues in ways that make it, in its own right, a creative contributor to the distribution of power through law, institutions, and social practices.[17]

Similarly and crucially, "the public" is not a simple entity, including all the people of the nation equally; it is rather the *articulated element of the populace—dominated by national politicians, journalists, and big-business leaders but also including, at lower amplification, organized classes and interest groups—e.g., women's groups, representatives of the elderly, or unionized workers. The public thus includes a wide array of groups and individuals who are simultaneously at odds with each other and in league together against other disempowered or empowered groups. In practice the public does not necessarily include everyone equally, even though American ideology holds that it should do so. This is why opinion polls are not accurate indicators of "public opinion" or predictors of public policy. On numerous issues, ranging from the Equal Rights Amendment to the Panama Canal to gun control to aid for the Nicaraguan Contras, the polls show the beliefs of the populace to be at odds with the dominant meanings being conveyed in the public realm and with public policies. The opinion polls count all the people more or less equally, rather than reproducing the covert weightings that result from access to influence over public discourse, which is held by powerful agents (the "publicly articulate agents").

Several factors preserve and sustain the discrepancy between what the people want and what the public wants and often gets. In the first place, the demands and pleasures of everyday life and the complexities of modern politics impose real limits on the political energies of the populace. Additionally, legislators and interest groups make real attempts to obscure the acts of legislation. Further, access to political resources (including both information and civic skills) is limited. Additionally, the relative wealth and satisfaction of a sizable portion of the populace generates an inertia, and, finally, the force of *epideictic—ritualized, patriotic, aesthetic, reassuring discourse—encourages satisfaction and passivity regardless of real political conditions. All these factors are fluid, however, allowing shifts in the groups who constitute the public and in the power of the public itself.

Public argument, therefore, is the process through which the underlying interests of rhetorically organized and differently empowered *groups or *classes contest against and with each other for particular policies and practices through the negotiation of persuasive meanings. The process is drastically skewed by the superior access to articulation held by powerful groups and by the encrustations of a history of such skewing that embeds those distortions in the public vocabulary.[18] Nonetheless, to describe these distorting forces is not to describe the public discourse as fully determined by the underlying sources of power. Rhetoric, as a central and unique node in the social system, is a process with its own impacts, influences, or consequences. Understanding how rhetoric functions would enable understandings of these discursive inputs on the political system.

Rhetorical processes are, however, tied to social conditions in another way—not through the links between message sources and their social conditions but through the links between audiences and their social experiences. Rhetoric materializes ideas through the distribution of compelling vocabularies to large numbers of potent audience members or institutions. Rhetoric therefore may communicate social change to people by using language as a medium that negotiates a collective "expression" of social conditions and social interests. No idea can have force of its own. Only if that idea is convincing to a large number of people will it carry social force and gain materiality. Ideas can be convincing for two reasons—through sheer repetition (historical instantiation by dominant groups in near-complete control of the communication media) or through effective expression of the conditions of an audience member's world ("effective" here means aesthetically pleasing or pragmatically useful). This will occur on a large scale only if a large number of individuals share similar social conditions and/or discursive histories. Hence, ideas come to have social force when they are persuasive to a large number of individuals. The battle between social forces of change and of stability is therefore often a battle between the high-frequency messages reflective of the interests of powerful groups and those less-amplified, indigenous codes reflective of the interests of various segments of the populace.

This account allows us to deal with the dominant controversy in contemporary social theory—the characterization of the contents of public discourse. One school of theorists, led by social critics such as Jürgen Habermas and rhetorical theorists such as Douglas Ehninger, can be read as arguing that public consensus through rational argumentation processes is the necessary end goal of public deliberation and that it is, ultimately, a largely achievable goal.[19] Political theorists such as Murray Edelman and social theorists such as Anthony Giddens scoff at such "naive idealism," suggesting that, in seeking to "universalize" or call up "condensation symbols," public discourse necessarily seeks to get a particular interest misidentified as a general interest.[20] Given the account of representative government as a rhetorical process, the former school provides a necessary ideal and the latter an equally necessary restraint. Ultimately, because of the social characteristics of argumentation and persuasion, most discourse must deal with both dimensions—this *double articulation of rhetoric— simultaneously, *not* with one to the exclusion of the other.

To the extent that rhetoric is a social process undertaken by interest groups, public rhetoric will always be constituted by spokespersons for particular interests, who recognize that getting those interests legitimated through public acceptance of their vocabulary is advantageous, even essential, to their interests; they will recognize that representing their partisan interests as universal is an essential rhetorical move. However, they will also always be constrained by the fact that they must be *convincing*: they must find "good reasons" (according to the judgment of their audiences, as based on their social experiences, influenced by indigenous codings of those experiences) that demonstrate that, in fact, their partisan interests *are* in the general interest.[21] This interplay between particular and general interests works because, in practice, rhetorically generated "universals" may be genuinely in the general interest at the same time that they serve particular interests. For example, an inter-state trucking system may be in the national interest and also of disproportionate benefit to truckers; thus, when trucking lobbyists argue for inter-state highway funds, they are both universalizing their own interests and also arguing for a general interest.

In practice, private groups often receive a disproportionate advantage from producing public good (as when contractors are paid excessively for building roads or defense equipment).[22] This is especially likely in representative governments with largely passive citizenry who are aroused to protect their interests from the special-interest-supported representatives only in extreme cases. This skewed practice is, however, theoretically redeemable in each individual case, and this book focuses on the process by which such redemption may occur.

There remains, however, one further conceptual problem in this process, and it arises precisely from the dualistic nature of the internal structure of the rhetorical process. Whenever audiences accept a mis-universalized claim (a claim that overserves an interest group), there is a tendency to suggest that the audience has been duped by "mere persuasion" rather than addressed with rational argumentation. Of course, this distinction is always politically loaded (our interests are argued, theirs are falsely addressed). This practice of political labelling, however, does not invalidate the theoretical utility and accuracy of the distinction between the persuasive and argumentative elements of rhetoric. Persuasion includes all non-argumentative tools that might influence an audience to adopt the position advocated by a speaker—emotional arousal, delivery, figures of style (e.g., alliteration, rhythm, or antithesis). These persuasive devices function through the aestheticization of the association between beliefs, attitudes, or values. In contrast, argument uses such elements of discourse as the "claim," supported by compelling and related evidence (sometimes called "data" or "ground"), linked by a warranting general principle.[23] Arguments are constructed by the kind of relationship we generally think of as "logical inference" or "reasons," but they are not limited to the propositional logic of philosophers. Instead, they are better characterized as *enthymemes, which require the audience to participate in the process of linking general principles to particular instances.[24]

Separating association-based persuasion from enthymematically based argumentation is always difficult, because it depends in part on one's assumptions about what inferential grounds are being used by an audience and ultimately upon what one assumes to be the "general interest" as contrasted with merely partisan smokescreens. However, in order to understand the process of public rhetoric it is often essential to make those distinctions, because associational persuasion and propositional argumentation have different social impacts. The interplay between persuasion and argumentation reveals the lines of social force in social decision-making (i.e., meaning-making) processes. Simultaneously, it is the tension between the two possibilities that helps to put into relief the internal structure of rhetorical discourse. The social balance of power thus often hinges on the aptness of rhetorical structures for various audiences.

If this account of the functioning of representative government is correct, rhetoric—as the process of public argument and persuasion—exerts a force of its own on the underlying social processes that it articulates. That is, public discourse is an active, change-producing, transformative process, not merely a passive conveyer belt. Because rhetorical units affect each other, in part through the consequences of specific discursive configurations themselves, particular ways of talking (and hence, of understanding and acting) may come into social being. Specific kinds of forces are exerted by the rhetorical process per se (e.g., the production of material/ideational compromises) and by the character of certain kinds of rhetorical units (e.g., the potent but limited social functions of narratives). Other kinds of forces are exerted by the unique contents of the vocabulary at issue in any particular contest (e.g., "life" vs. "the fetus" in the abortion controversy). Charting the changes in the units of discourse that appear in a controversy across time and relating these changes to the general and specific forces of rhetoric can produce better explanations of the processes that operate to bring about the particular forms that social changes take.

At this point, this model is no more than a hypothesis, and one for which I have not even provided sustained and detailed theoretical argument. Unless it can be applied to real historical situations, and unless the mechanisms via which rhetoric has actually shaped and transformed particular contests over changing material conditions can be described, there may be only ideological reasons to prefer it over other theories, especially given the rather extensive theorizing and evidence compiled by Marxists describing underlying material forces as in sole control of particular, historical social changes. The following study of the abortion controversy, I believe, provides an analysis of one real case in which the rhetorical mechanisms are clear. Through detailed attention to the impact of rhetorical manipulations of the public vocabulary upon that vocabulary, it illustrates the role and potentialities of rhetoric in the processes of social change.

Method of Study

In order to study discursive processes in this way, a series of choices about the proper way to approach a controversy must be made. To begin with, a set of public discourse must be selected. Ideally, of course, every utterance by every person occurring in the public space would be included. Unfortunately, since most public speech is never recorded, it is too ephemeral to allow that kind of completeness. For pragmatic reasons, therefore, the core of this study is built around several large but limited sets of texts. The first four substantive chapters are based on the discourse contained in the complete set of popular, mass-circulation magazines with articles about abortion, as indexed by the *Reader's Guide to Periodical Literature* for the period 1960 to 1980. The popular magazines reach large audiences, they are preserved in a complete form, they provide a manageable but large quantity of discourse, and they are clearly public media which discuss important political issues. In order to assure that the core sample is reasonably representative, I have supplemented the magazine articles with pamphlets, speeches, and newspapers.

Other chapters employ these sets of texts indirectly and add other texts. Chapter 6 is based on an examination of the legal discourse of *Roe* v. *Wade* and related cases and of the U.S. Congressional debates about abortion. Chapter 7 is based on the prime-time television portrayals of abortion. Chapter 8 is based on the local media coverage of the Pensacola abortion clinic bombings.

These sets of discourse are an intentionally "public" collection, because I believe that laws and public policies relating to large-scale social change are most directly derived from the public discourse, not from private or *in-group rhetoric.[25] As a consequence, this book does not include or analyze most of the internal discourse of the Catholic church or fundamentalist sermons nor any of the academic or other *in-group feminist discourse on abortion. This choice tends to reproduce something of a disparity: some popular religious journals (e.g., *America*) more or less directly reproduce some of the internal discourse of the pro-Life groups, but, as Petchesky has noticed, "On the level of the public discourse—policy, law, media representations—the feminist voice on the abortion question was and remains barely audible."[26] Omitting this discourse seems to reproduce the blanket of silence over these feminisms and to rely on a crude distinction between public, or *out-group, rhetoric and *in-group rhetoric.[27] However, the separation between sub-cultures and the dominant public vocabulary is real, even if not neat and tidy. And since it is not yet clear how in-group rhetoric directly influences public policy and public vocabulary, the examination of academic, socialist, and radical feminist publications, as well as internal religious discourse (sermons or the *Catholic World*), will have to constitute another set of studies. Accounting for the changes in the discourse *reaching* the mass audience is quite a large enough task.

The second methodological issue is the choice of focus for a study that surveys literally hundreds of documents. This choice is again theory-driven. I believe that three "units of discourse" are central to the persuasiveness and impact of public discourse.

The first unit is a kind of "ultimate term"—special words or phrases that express the public values that provide the "constitutional" commitments of a community.[28] These words or phrases are called *ideographs, and in the United States they include Life, Liberty, and Property. Unless an act can be justified under such constitutive values, it may be allowed but it cannot be defended as a right nor can a public agency be forced to act on it. Thus, in the abortion controversy, for women to gain the political *right* to abortion required a revision of American ideographic structure. Moreover, because of the character of ideographs in the process of persuasion, particular ideographic justifications (Right to Choice) were favored over others (Reproductive Freedom).

The second basic unit of public rhetoric is narrative in form. Narratives or "stories" are powerful and important forms in almost all human collectives.[29] When they are repeated frequently, and begin to ground action and other beliefs, we call them *myths. Such social myths are not necessarily true or false. Generally, they tell important truths , but they leave out important ingredients and, hence, distort. But even though they do not tell the "whole story"—no human language can—they are extremely powerful rhetorical devices.[30] In the abortion controversy, narratives were the first discursive units to break the icy public silence—the refusal to articulate abortion. As the narratives gained mythic status, they began to generate concrete

social changes. Again, however, narrative units have certain persuasive functions, forms, and limitations, and these shaped the role
of the narratives in the public argument.

Finally, narratives are constructed of *characterizations—universalized depictions of important agents, acts, scenes, purposes, or
methods. The term *characterization* or *character-type* encompasses the
earlier term *stereotype* but includes the positive dimensions of these
mass naming processes. Thus, in the abortion controversy the characterization of the scene of illegal abortion as the "back alley" was a
simplification, but a useful rhetorical simplification for summing up
the problems presented by criminal abortion. The characterizations of
"women" and "motherhood" were also central to the abortion controversy and, consequently, the peculiar rhetorical nature of character-
types as a class had important impacts on the path of the controversy.

Given this description of how public argument works, I have
focused on the ideographs, narratives, and character-types used in
the controversy, mapping their appearance and relationships across
time. I have sought to answer two questions. First, what new myths,
ideographs, and character-types (or constellations thereof) have been
added to the public vocabulary as the controversy progressed? Second, how do these new terms and constellations result from the
negotiations among the competing terms offered for public use by
opposed groups?

To get at this second issue, I have had to employ an approach called
in its various manifestations rhetorical criticism, hermeneutics, semiotics, or discourse analysis. Routinely, these methods are employed to
present a critique of a text or to explicate the manner in which it does
its work. I have turned these techniques to a somewhat different
end—the production of a *diachronic explanation of the discursive
formation of social changes. This kind of descriptive history requires
the moment of critical analysis because the changes one piece of
discourse cause in other discourse can be understood only if we
dissect the way in which its meanings are constructed argumentatively and persuasively. Such accounts will always contain the politics of the analyst; their accuracy is therefore to be judged not by
adherence to method but by the cogency of the account they ultimately reconstruct.

Focusing in this way on these units of this important public discourse reveals significant patterns in the way public understandings
of abortion shifted between 1960 and 1985 in the United States. The
argument marched through a series of distinctive steps and stages. At
each stage, new units of discourse were proposed and contested,

moving the argument forward by creating new understandings. The process was an additive one; the new vocabulary that emerged at each stage did not disappear in later stages; it simply became a part of an ever-expanding account of abortion.

Ultimately this arduous and exciting public contest will be revealed as a negotiated transformation of women's own private discourses, which, perhaps paradoxically, enabled circumscribed but substantial changes in the experiences of many women.

NOTES

1. Kristin Luker, *Abortion and the Politics of Motherhood* (Berkeley: University of California Press, 1984); James C. Mohr, *Abortion in America: The Origins and Evolution of National Policy, 1800–1900* (New York: Oxford Union Press, 1978); Rosalind Pollack Petchesky, *Abortion and Women's Choice: The State, Sexuality, and Reproductive Freedom* (Boston: Northeastern University Press, 1984); Colin Francome, *Abortion Freedom* (London: George Allen and Unwin, 1984); Connie Paige, *The Right to Lifers* (New York: Summit Books, 1983); Henry David, *Abortion Research: International Experience* (Lexington, Mass.: Lexington Books, 1974); Linda Gordon, *Woman's Body, Woman's Right* (New York: Grossman, 1976); Lawrence Lader, *Abortion* (Indianapolis: Bobbs-Merrill, 1966); Lawrence Lader, *Abortion II: Making the Revolution* (Boston: Beacon Press, 1973); Roger Miller, *Abortion, Baseball and Weed: Economic Issues of Our Times* (New York: Harper and Row, 1973); Carl E. Schneider and Maris Vinovskis, eds., *The Law and Politics of Abortion* (Lexington, Mass.: Lexington Books, 1980); Patricia Steinhoff and Milton Diamond, *Abortion Politics: The Hawaii Experience* (Honolulu: Union Press of Hawaii, 1977); Kristin Luker, *Taking Chances: Abortion and the Decision Not to Contracept* (Berkeley: University of California Press, 1975); Nanette J. Davis, *From the Transformation of Abortion in America* (Westport, Conn.: Greenwood Press, 1985).

2. Intellectual historians tend to study "philosophers" rather than public argument. For example, they might attend to John Locke's notion of "liberty" rather than to that of Peter Wentworth and Queen Elizabeth. See Michael Calvin McGee, *Edmund Burke's Beautiful Lie: An Exploration of the Relationship between Rhetoric and Social Theory* (Ph.D. diss., University of Iowa, 1974). My work may resemble that suggested by Michel Foucault, but his efforts focus on static epistemes. I am interested in the process of changing of such discursive formations.

3. Platonic philosophy, psychological behaviorism, American quantitative empirical sociology, and classic Marxism are all traditions that have disparaged public discourse as an irrelevant or irredeemable process unworthy of attention. Contemporary culture studies have gradually challenged this presumption, so that in sizable academic constituencies studies of discourse on its own grounds are increasingly credible. However, this trend has been so

strongly influenced by English and comparative literature that artistic and entertainment perspectives and texts are privileged. That means content-oriented studies of public discourses (especially intentionally political ones) continue to be excluded from the academic canon. Even scholars who have attempted to shift this orientation frequently end up denigrating the impact of their object of study. Joseph Gusfield, for example, attempts to take public discourse as a serious sociological phenomenon but ends up reducing the discourse's impact to "status display." See *Symbolic Crusade: Status Politics and the American Temperance Movement*, 2nd ed. (1963; Urbana: University of Illinois Press, 1986).

4. "Social Forces" are the prime focus of materialist historians, socialist feminists, and sociologists. Attention to actors and events and to private discourse is central in mainstream American history. For a critique of this focus, see McGee, *Edmund Burke's Beautiful Lie*.

5. Luker, *Abortion*, p. 226.

6. Luker's omission of these factors is all the more disappointing, given her vivid statements about the "framework of understanding" that was necessary to transform women's actions and beliefs (*Abortion*, pp. 111, 120). The problem appears to arise from a mistaken concept of "persuasion." Luker employs a standard definition that presumes that persuasion only occurs when an audience is hostile, or at the least, a "tabula rasa." Few tabula rasa minds exist, and hostile audiences are rarely persuaded. Therefore, persuasion cannot occur. However, recent definitions of persuasion indicate clearly that audiences are persuaded primarily by appealing to pre-existent "cognitive schemata" (see, for example, Mary John Smith, *Persuasion and Human Action* [Belmont, Calif.: Wadsworth, 1982]). Thus the articulation of latent potentials among previous beliefs and values is a potent and primary type of persuasion, and it ties in easily with the social process formulation I am elucidating here.

7. Petchesky, *Abortion and Women's Choice*, p. 250. Petchesky appears to believe that any moral decision is merely an inappropriate ploy by men to control women. I disagree. Although sometimes moral statements serve such purposes, I believe morality is an essential social commodity. The task is to construct a feminized morality. Consequently, we must consider all moral claims against us seriously. The case is made more fully by Beverly Wildung Harrison in *Our Right to Choose: Toward a New Ethic of Abortion* (Boston: Beacon Press, 1983).

8. Harrison heprovides a historically grounded analysis, but it is not a diachronic account. Other philosophical and ethal discussions are available in Judith Jarvis Thompson, "A Definition of Abortion," and other essays in *The Problem of Abortion*, ed. Joel Feinberg (Belmont, Calif.: Wadsworth, 1973), pp. 121–39; Sidney and Daniel Callahan, eds., *Abortion: Understanding Differences* (New York: Plenum Press, 1984); Daniel Callahan, *Abortion: Law, Choice and Morality* (New York: Macmillan, 1970); Norman Gillespie, "Abortion and Human Rights," *Ethics* 84 (1974), 237–48; Joseph Margolis, "Abortion," *Ethics*

84 (1973), 41–61; John T. Noonan, Jr., *The Morality of Abortion: Legal and Historical Perspectives* (Cambridge: Harvard University Press, 1970); Robert Perkins, ed., *Abortion: Pro and Con* (Cambridge: Schenkman, 1974); Norman St. John-Steva, *The Right to Life* (New York: Holt, Rinehart and Winston, 1963); H. Tristram Engelhardt, Jr., "The Ontology of Abortion," *Ethics* 84 (1974), 217–34; Fred M. Frohock, *Abortion: A Case Study in Law and Morals* (Westport, Conn.: Greenwood Press, 1983). A combination position is indirectly presented through Linda Bird Francke's *The Ambivalence of Abortion* (New York: Dell, 1982).

9. An extremely useful preliminary work is provided by Betty Sarvis and Hyman Rodman, *The Abortion Controversy* (New York: Columbia University Press, 1974). See also Marilyn Falik, *Ideology and Abortion Policy Politics* (New York: Praeger, 1983). Barbara Plant provides a fine discourse study for the period before 1960, *Abortion as a Secondary Birth Control Measure: A Functional Approach* (M.A. thesis, University of Windsor, Ontario, 1971). Several other smaller categories of abortion studies are available—various accounts of the conditions or "facts" of legal and criminalized abortion, along with a small set of activist and academic histories. These include many issues of *Family Planning Perspectives* as well as Edward Manier, William Liu, and David Solomon, eds., *Abortion: New Directions for Policy Studies* (Notre Dame, Ind.: Notre Dame University Press, 1973); Harold Rosen, *Therapeutic Abortion* (New York: Julian Press, 1954); Alan F. Guttmacher, ed., *The Case for Legalized Abortion* (Berkeley: Diablo Press, 1967); Garret Hardin, *Stalking the Wild Taboo* (Los Altos, Calif.: William Kaufmann, 1973); James Reed, *From Private Vice to Public Virtue* (New York: Basic Books, 1978); Carl Reiterman, ed., *Abortion and the Unwanted Child* (New York: Springer, 1971); German Grisez, *Abortion: The Myths, the Realities, and the Arguments* (New York: Corpus Books, 1970); Andrew H. Merton, *Enemies of Choice: The Right to Life Movement and Its Threat to Abortion* (Boston: Beacon Press, 1981); Michael Gorman, *Abortion in the Early Church* (New York: Paulist Press, 1982).

10. Contemporary rhetorical criticism is summarized in part in Bernard L. Brock and Robert L. Scott, *Methods of Rhetorical Criticism*, 2nd ed., rev. (Detroit: Wayne State University Press, 1980); see also James R. Andrews, *The Practice of Rhetorical Criticism* (New York: Macmillan, 1983); Carroll C. Arnold, *Criticism of Oral Rhetoric* (Columbus, Ohio: Charles E. Merrill, 1974). A fine recent example of a full-length rhetorical analysis that focuses on the structure or units of rhetoric in important social discourse is provided by David Zarefsky, *President Johnson's War on Poverty: Rhetoric and History* (University, Ala.: University of Alabama Press, 1986). See also Ernest Bormann, *The Force of Fantasy: Restoring the American Dream* (Carbondale, Ill.: Southern Illinois University Press, 1985). See also recent issues of the *Quarterly Journal of Speech* and *Central States Speech Journal*.

11. For scholars with disparate politics who are converging on this view, see Richard Weaver, *Ideas Have Consequences* (Chicago: University of Chicago Press, 1948); Paula A. Treichler's bibliography, "Language, Feminism, Theory:

Entering Decade Three," in *Women and Language* 10: 1, 5–37, and her "What Definitions Do: Childbirth, Cultural Crisis, and the Challenge to Medical Discourse," in *Paradigm Dialogues II: Research Exemplars in Communication Studies*, ed. B. Dervin et al. (Beverly Hills: Sage, in press); Louis Althusser, *Lenin and Philosophy and Other Essays*, trans. Ben Brewster (London: NLB, 1971); Fredric Jameson, *The Political Unconscious: Narration as a Socially Symbolic Act* (Ithaca, N.Y.: Cornell University Press, 1981); Stuart Hall, "The Problem of Ideology—Marxism without Guarantees," and "On Postmodernism," interview, ed. Lawrence Grossberg, and Lawrence Grossberg, "History, Politics, and Postmodernism: Stuart Hall and Cultural Studies," all in *Journal of Communication Inquiry* 10 (Summer 1986); Stuart Hall, Dorothy Hobson, R. Lowe, and Paul Willis, *Culture, Media, Language: Working Papers in Cultural Studies, 1977–79* (London: Hutchinson, 1980); special issue, entitled "Ideology/ Power," of the *Canadian Journal of Political and Social Theory* 7 (Winter/Spring 1983); Michel Foucault, *The Order of Things: An Archaelogy of the Human Sciences* (New York: Vintage Books, 1973); Jean Baudrillard, *For a Critique of the Political Economy of the Sign* (St. Louis, Mo.: Telos Press, 1981); Raymond Williams, *Marxism and Literature* (1977; rpt. Oxford: Oxford Union Press, 1985); Jean-François Lyotard, *The Postmodern Condition: A Report on Knowledge*, trans. G. Bennington and B. Massumi (Minneapolis: University of Minnesota Press, 1984); Falik, *Ideology and Abortion Policy Politics*. I am not arguing complete independence of discourse from material factors; I believe discourse is a material factor itself and that it is tied into the social structure as a material practice. However, I do not believe that it is solely a material practice. I believe, to borrow Kenneth Burke's term, that discourse has "substance"— both ideational and material elements. Kenneth Burke, *Grammar of Motives* (Berkeley: University of California Press edition, 1969). I also recognize the difficulties implied in recent criticism of the role of critics in analysis. A reply is available in Celeste Michelle Condit, "The Rhetorical Limits of Polysemy," *Critical Studies in Mass Communication* 6, no. 2 (1989), 103–22.

12. See note 11. Scholars in American public address, organized in the Speech Communication Association, have long held this perspective; their work is best represented in the *Quarterly Journal of Speech*.

13. For example, Janice Radway, *Reading the Romance: Women, Patriarchy, and Popular Literature* (Chapel Hill: University of North Carolina Press, 1984); Ien Ang, *Watching "Dallas": Soap Opera and the Melodramatic Imagination*, trans. Della Couling (London: Methuen, 1985); John Fiske, *Television Culture* (London and New York: Methuen, 1987); David Morley, *Family Television* (London: Comedia, 1986); Dick Hebdige, *Subculture: The Meaning of Style* (London and New York: Methuen, 1979).

14. See, for example, Michael Calvin McGee, "The Rhetorical Process in Eighteenth-Century England," in *Rhetoric: A Tradition in Transition*, ed. Walter R. Fisher (East Lansing: Michigan State University Press, 1974), pp. 99–121.

15. This is a concrete enactment of the "duality of structure" discussed in Anthony Giddens, *Central Problems in Social Theory* (Berkeley: University of California Press, 1979); see also Celeste Michelle Condit, "Crafting Virtue:

The Rhetorical Foundations of Public Morality," *Quarterly Journal of Speech* 73 (February 1987), 79–97.

16. *Annals of America* (Chicago: Encyclopaedia Britannica, 1968).

17. Condit, "Crafting Virtue."

18. The history of skewing explains the need for Jürgen Habermas's correction of Anglo-American theories of "free speech" through his formulation of the "ideal speech situation." The theory provides a useful political guide, even though his arguments about a "legitimation crisis" are faulty because of his failure to account for the ability of rhetoric to re-vivify shared values. Compare *Communication and the Evolution of Society* (Boston: Beacon Press, 1979) to *Legitimation Crisis* (Boston: Beacon Press, 1975).

19. Habermas, *Communication*; Douglas Ehninger, "Argument as Method: Its Nature, Its Limits, and Its Uses," *Communication Monographs* 37 (June 1979), 101–10.

20. Giddens; Murray Edelman, *The Symbolic Uses of Politics* (Urbana: University of Illinois Press, 1964), *Politics as Symbolic Action* (Chicago: Markham, 1971), *Political Language* (New York: Academic Press, 1975).

21. On "good reasons" see Karl Wallace, "The Substance of Rhetoric: Good Reasons," *Quarterly Journal of Speech* 49 (October 1963), 239–49, and Walter Fisher, "Toward a Logic of Good Reasons," *Quarterly Journal of Speech* 64 (December 1978), 376–84.

22. Jesse Jackson, in Democratic presidential primary debates, nationally televised, 15 January 1984, 23 February 1984, and summer 1987. Jackson repeatedly insisted that groups that get disproportionate gains from programs "in the public interest" be required to give back something additional in return (e.g., that Chrysler, in return for federal financial assistance, should have been required to increase commitments to minorities or workers in general).

23. This formulation is borrowed from what is widely called the "Toulmin model of argumentation." This model separates arguments into three major parts—the claim (or the "point" or "policy" of an argument), the data or ground (the support for the claim—often "evidence"), and the warrant (the principle that links claim and ground). See Stephen E. Toulmin, *The Uses of Argument* (Cambridge: Cambridge University Press, 1958), and Stephen Toulmin, Richard Rieke, and Allan Janik, *An Introduction to Reasoning* (New York: Macmillan, 1979).

24. On the enthymeme, see Lloyd Bitzer, "Aristotle's Enthymeme Revisited," *Quarterly Journal of Speech* 45 (December 1959), 399–408, but also Thomas M. Conley, "The Enthymeme in Perspective," *Quarterly Journal of Speech* 70 (May 1984), 168–74. For a discussion of the relationship between propositional logics and reason, see Jesse Delia, "The Logic Fallacy, Cognitive Theory, and the Enthymeme: A Search for the Foundations of Reasoned Discourse," *Quarterly Journal of Speech* 56 (1970), pp. 140–48. Further discussion is contained in Douglas Ehninger, "Argument as Method: Its Nature, Its Limits, and Its Uses," *Communication Monographs* 37 (June 1979), 101–10; Mills and Hugh G. Petrie, "The Role of Logic in Rhetoric," *Quarterly Journal of Speech*

54 (October 1968), 260–67; Wayne Brockriede and Douglas Ehninger, "Toulmin on Argument: An Interpretation and Application," *Quarterly Journal of Speech* 46 (February 1960), 44–53; Jimmie D. Trent, "Toulmin Model of Argument: An Examination and Extension," *Quarterly Journal of Speech* 54 (October 1968), 252–59.

25. Chapter 6 should indicate the manner in which public discourse becomes the substrate of the discourse of law more fully, providing a defense of this position. See also Condit, "TV Articulates Abortion."

26. Petchesky, p. 131. I think Petchesky overdraws the case because liberal feminism is amply represented through *Ms.* magazine and many other sources. However, the current battle for hegemonic definition of "feminism" in the academy is working feverishly to "write out" liberal feminism from the "accepted" corpus. See, for example, H. Leslie Steeves, "Feminist Theories and Media Studies," *Critical Studies in Mass Communication* 4 (June 1987), 95–135.

27. The dynamics of the balance between in-group and public rhetoric are discussed in Herbert Simons, "Requirements, Problems, and Strategies: A Theory of Persuasion for Social Movements," *Quarterly Journal of Speech* 56 (1970), 1–11.

28. The original formulation of this is contained in McGee, "The 'Ideograph.'" My own revisions to the theory are developed in "The Universalizing Influence of Public Argumentation," *Communication Monographs* 54 (March 1987), 1–18. In keeping with the tradition established by American printed oratory of the colonial and post-Revolutionary period, I demarcate ideographs by capitalizing them.

29. A celebration of the importance of narrative forms is widespread in several contemporary academic disciplines. See Jameson; W. J. T. Mitchell, ed., *On Narrative* (Chicago: Chicago University Press, 1980); Lance W. Bennett and Martha S. Feldman, *Reconstructing Reality in the Courtroom* (New Brunswick, N.J.: Rutgers University Press, 1981); Seymour Chatman, *Story and Discourse: Narrative Structure in Fiction and Film* (Ithaca, N.Y.: Cornell University Press, 1978); esp. Hayden White, "The Value of Narrativity in the Representation of Reality," in Mitchell. In rhetorical criticism the debate about narrative is contained in Walter R. Fisher, *Human Communication as Narration: Toward a Philosophy of Reason, Value, and Action* (Columbia: University of South Carolina Press, 1987), and replies by Barbara Warnick, "The Narrative Paradigm: Another Story," *Quarterly Journal of Speech* 73 (May 1987), 172–81; John Louis Lucaites and Celeste Michelle Condit, "Reconstructing Narrative Theory: A Functional Perspective," and Michael Calvin McGee and John S. Nelson, "Narrative Reason in Public Argument," both in *Journal of Communication*, special issue on "Homo Narrans," 35 (Autumn 1985), 90–108.

30. A similar point has been reached with different vocabularies and intents by Alfred Korzybski, *Science and Sanity*, 4th ed. (1933; 4th printing, Lakeville, Conn.: The Institute of General Semantics, 1958); Ludwig Wittgenstein, *Philosophical Investigations*, trans. G. E. M. Anscombe (Oxford: Basil Blackwell, 1963); Jacques Derrida, *Of Grammatology*, trans. Gayatri

Chakravorty Spivak (1967; rpt. Baltimore: Johns Hopkins University Press, 1976); Umberto Eco, *A Theory of Semiotics* (Bloomington: Indiana University Press, 1979). See also Molefi Kete Asante, *The Afrocentric Idea* (Philadelphia: Temple University Press, 1987); Sandra Harding, *The Science Question in Feminism* (Ithaca, N.Y.: Cornell University Press, 1986).

CHAPTER TWO

The Story of Illegal Abortion
Rhetoric and Narrative
——— 1960–65 ———

Conventional wisdom has it that in 1973 the Supreme Court of the
United States suddenly, unilaterally, and completely legalized abortion, bringing about a state of affairs unprecedented in the nation's
history.[1] This is far from an accurate account. Until well after the Civil
War, most abortions had been legal in this nation.[2] Even between 1870
and 1950, as many as 30,000 abortions were done "legally" each year
in the nation's hospitals.[3] Many more "criminal" abortions were performed outside the hospitals.[4] By 1971, well before the high court's
decision in *Roe* v. *Wade*, the trickle of legal abortions had become a
torrent—as many as 600,000 *legal* abortions were being done in the
country each year.[5] The primary impact of the national, judicial decision in 1973 was the homogenization of accessibility to abortion
through the elimination of the crazy-quilt patterns of disparate state
laws.[6] That was an impact of great consequence for many women's
lives. It was not, however, a wholesale revolution in law or practice.

The revolutionary importance of the Court's decision rested instead in its character as a national symbolic act. The *Roe* v. *Wade* case
officially legitimated a new set of shared meanings, which had been
argued into place in the decade before the Court's decision. The
transformation of the public meanings associated with "abortion"
began with the public construction of a powerful "story of illegal
abortion," itself made possible by crucial events of the 1950s.

The Fifties

The major shift toward legalization of abortion began in the fifties,
when the physicians, who had been in legal control of abortion
decisions for the previous eighty years, began to feel discomfort with
the responsibilities and consequences of this power.[7] Doctors re-

ported widespread concern about both the legal ambiguities surrounding the procedure and the traumatic health consequences to their patients, who were apparently choosing to risk illegal abortions in large numbers.[8] In the fifties, the number of professional conferences, books, and discussions on the topic of abortion grew, and the doctors turned over control of abortion choices to hospital committees to protect themselves from the variety of conflicting forces that had made the power to control abortion problematic.[9] The committee system and the professional discourse, however, could address only the professional problems of the physicians, not the larger social problems that had generated their discomfort. Consequently, the professional solutions rapidly proved inadequate. In 1959 the American Law Institute (ALI) formulated a "model law" to broaden the permissions for abortion from "risk to mother's life" to committee-approved cases of rape, incest, fetal deformity, and threats to the pregnant woman's health.[10] Gradually, doctors and other reformers began to seek a broader audience in support of legal changes.[11]

There was, however, a second group very concerned with abortion law and practice—the hundreds of thousands of American women affected in a variety of ways by abortion policies. It is impossible to tell these women's stories fully. Their voices were largely absent from the professional and public realms, their cases too disparate to provide a single collective voice. Moreover, many of their concerns about childbearing and raising were not yet fully articulated, encapsulated in a "disease that had no name." Ultimately, however, the actions and passions of women in their private lives created the public controversy: women forced doctors into uncomfortable quandaries; women turned up in hospitals suffering from illegal abortions; women, unable yet to articulate a legitimate public voice, nonetheless gradually forced the full discussion of the long-quiescent issue of abortion.

The Sixties

As the sixties quietly dawned, therefore, the actions of women forced the professionals to hand off the "abortion problem" from the professional realm to the public arena. For the public to deal with the problem, however, required that the issue be *articulated in public, and that was no small matter. A near-century of silence had seen the buildup of a coating of taboos about sex and motherhood that had coded "abortion" as a subject that should not be articulated. In order to breach the silencing wall, a special discursive form was needed—a form that could weave a compelling understanding of the abortion problem without engaging the powerful value sets that surrounded it. The rhetorical form suited to that task was *narrative.

A series of "exposés," the most dramatic of which was carried in the *Saturday Evening Post* beginning in May of 1961, provided the first rhetorical volley by vividly portraying the horrors of the illegal abortion "racket." The articles brought the abortion problem to public notice by constructing a distinctive "tale of illegal abortion."[12] Instead of advocating change in the laws, the earliest of these magazine essays merely recounted, in lively and lurid detail, the variety of problems generated by the abortion "underworld." Sexual restraint and better legal enforcement were the primary remedies halfheartedly suggested for these horrors.

Although the exposés themselves did not advocate new laws, by raising the issue they breached a floodgate, prompting a torrent of increasingly strident articles, many by female reporters. This second stream of coverage narrowed the focus to the women involved in illegal abortion, gradually recasting the issue from a general problem of law enforcement to a problem *for women*, deriving from the law itself. Public advocates began increasingly to argue for reform of existing abortion laws along the lines of the American Law Institute's model. Rapidly, flowing from a reservoir of the experiences of real women, an argument was joined.

The "tale of illegal abortion," which formed the dominant support for this argument, was widely reproduced. Magazines, speakers, and newspapers began to describe the experiences of women who faced unwanted pregnancies or sought illegal abortions, elaborating upon the methods, purposes, scenes, and characters involved.[13] Statistics delineated the scale of the problem, but narratives conveyed the nature of the human suffering and its moral status. One fairly typical version of the tale was reported by Muriel Davidson.

> At exactly 2:09 A.M., July 6, 1963, Mary O., aged 25, arrived at the emergency entrance of Kings County Hospital in Brooklyn, accompanied by her husband. Dr. Harvey Cohen, obstetrical resident in charge of admission, saw at once that she was in shock. He helped her to a chair, got her quavery signature on an admittance form, and proceeded to take the history of her illness. The mother of four children, ranging in age from eight months to six years, Mary O. told him she believed she was about two months pregnant. She said that the day before she had slipped and fallen in the bathroom, and had begun to bleed profusely. Thirty hours later, at exactly 8:09 A.M., Mary O. was dead. . . . Mrs. O. had *not* fallen in her bathroom. Rather, someone attempting an amateur abortion had killed her by injecting a caustic solution into her womb.[14]

Mary's story was joined by the abortion stories of many other women, widely repeated. These narratives provided a direct and stout rhetorical bridge, translating the private experiences of individual women into an argument for social change. They did not, however, merely *represent* the "women's true stories": as change-bearing discourse the stories could not be simply *expressive;* they had to be *persuasive,* capable of instigating social change. Thus the public narrative was a *strategic* adaptation of women's experiences; the reporters shaped and selected the narratives in particular ways. To be persuasive to the dominant audience, the stories had to *use* rather than *confront* the beliefs and social conditions in the existing American repertoire. The abortion story did so by respecting the crucial values and *characterizations of the culture while redefining the act of abortion itself. To understand the intended and unintended social consequences of this rhetorical process requires a detailed examination of the story's persuasive structure—its heroines, their purposes, methods, and the scenes in which they were portrayed.

The Tale of Illegal Abortion

The women in these dramatic horror stories were painted sympathetically. Marguerite Clark, for example, referred to the "wan nervous girl [who] could only see one way out of her dilemma."[15] The description of Mary O., above, emphasized her motherhood and the support of her husband. Later, Sherri Finkbine, whose special case is analyzed below, was favorably portrayed as "a healthy and happily married Arizona woman, mother of four" and host of *Romper Room.*[16] To be broadly successful in challenging existing beliefs (at least in contemporary America, the locale on which we focus), rhetorical narratives must produce personal involvement and emotional arousal of a large audience. For a broad public to feel sorry for the agent and angry with the forces that bring her suffering, the character depicted must be "good," or, at the least, unable to control her own destiny.

The rhetorical quality of "goodness," however, is determined by pre-existing categories in the social vocabulary. Even when challenging existing attitudes and values, a rhetorical effort must rely on some of those values and attitudes. In the early sixties, "motherhood" was the definition of goodness for women. Ironically, this meant that rhetorical narratives defending the ability to postpone or forego motherhood relied heavily on positive images of mothers. The blissful marital status of women seeking abortion was therefore often mentioned.

In addition to displaying goodness, however, to be persuasive the characters in the social narrative had to be ordinary people—individuals with whom the public could identify. Identification not only strengthens emotional appeal but is also particularly necessary for attitude change. Audiences are more likely to act on a social issue if they perceive their *own* interests as threatened—if they see *themselves* or others like them as vulnerable to the problematic social situation. Furthermore, *social* action can be justified only when a large number of individuals are threatened. "Ordinariness" makes such numerical strength more plausible.

For persuasiveness and consistency, the purposes of these good, ordinary women in seeking an abortion had to be as culturally potent as possible. Rhetorical narratives cannot explore subtle cases but, to gain the assent of a broad spectrum, must emphasize the strongest possible examples, based on the most widely shared valuations. Hence, the women of these stories were emotionally ill (had threatened suicide), had been raped, or were young girls of fourteen or fifteen who had been seduced by older men (even their fathers) and deserted.[17] Even those cases that referred to socio-economic reasons for abortions portrayed the most drastic possible instances of destitution—women who were "unwilling and unable to face the future with another mouth to feed."[18] Combinations of purposes were even more compelling, as in the case of a "mother of five children who recently has been operated on for cancer" or the "psychotic woman unable to care for the children she already has."[19] In each case, the purpose cited avoided challenging the key values held by the public at the time, generally by portraying the woman as a helpless victim. She was making a choice not *against* motherhood but against situations which themselves violated the idealized image of motherhood.

In harmony with the desperate depictions of the women involved, the portrayals of the actual methods for completing illegal abortions were often literally sickening. In contrast to what were described tersely as "safe and simple" legal operations in which the doctor simply "scrapes the products of conception out of the uterus,"[20] the popular magazines graphically described the instruments of illegal abortions: "bizarre items doctors have found include turkey quills, knitting needles, hairpins, rattail combs, plastic bottles and even elastic bandages," as well as "the most favored 'instrument' of the amateur"—"a straightened out wire coat hanger inserted into a catheter" used for a "pack job."[21]

These catalogues of instruments were often accompanied by dismal descriptions of entire abortions. One story of a young woman who had had an engineering student abort her recounted that he bought an ordinary flashlight, removed the batteries and cut the bottom off with a can opener. He used the flashlight as a speculum . . . . through this 'speculum' he pushed a catheter into which he had threaded a wire. He then forced air through the contraption, which, unknown to him, had penetrated a blood vessel in the girl's womb. An air bubble entered the blood stream and in seconds reached her brain. Today this young woman is totally paralyzed.[22]

Other grisly methods—falling down stairs or injecting caustic soap solutions into the womb—also were frequently described, utilizing the most shocking details possible. One such story told of an abortionist who thought he did not have all the fetal matter out and ended up pulling out a woman's intestines.[23]

These descriptions of the methods used in illegal abortions added great impact to the negative response to such abortions sought by the *pro-reform authors. The mere description of blood and violence to human bodies tends to generate an immediate emotional and physiological repugnance—a negative response easily transferred to illegal abortion per se because these particular methods were unique to the illegal procedures.[24] Methods or "agencies" often provide a powerful rhetorical element for change because they may carry strong emotional force without threatening core values, *myths, or characterizations.

As Kenneth Burke has noted, the container and the thing contained must suit each other, and the advocates of reform generally provided a suitable scene for the grotesque agency they had described.[25] The "back alley" has become the common term for the illegal abortion scene, but detailed depictions of dirty kitchens (some even with photographs) or back car seats were also plentiful in this period.[26] In addition, the connotations of the "underworld" and racketeers were developed in stories of women meeting strangers on street corners or in front of sleazy hotels, to be blindfolded and driven to temporary, hidden destinations. Direct references to other "rackets" such as prostitution and gambling were also included.[27] Such loathsome scenes are often available for characterizing illegal activities. Consequently, the social activist usually has a fund of evil and repulsive elements upon which to draw when building transitional narratives. These rhetorical tactics "work" because the good agent is vividly depicted as in opposition to such evil and, hence, threatened by it. The tension between a good agent and an evil scene provides a powerful incentive to alter the scene.

The tale of illegal abortion, then, was emotionally compelling because of the basic structure it fit. It told the story of a good, ordinary person faced by social (not natural) circumstances that led her into evil scenes and self-destruction, magnified by gory details of the methods and scenes she was required to face. The story was socially effective because it spoke to the real experiences and needs of an increasingly powerful constituency (*wage-laboring women), and it was well designed to utilize the pre-existent values of a larger segment of the entire public audience.

The repetition and restatement of any such story bearing strong emotional force may create a *mythic commonplace. Social *myths are often deprecated as imprecise or false, but such an evaluation is itself a half-true distortion. Although inevitably partial, social myths also generally capture and preserve important truths and portray them with emotional intensity. Achieving these functions requires extensive public exposure under the right circumstances, so that a broad public hears and responds to the tale. In the abortion controversy, this mythicizing process was crystallized by the public portrayal of the abortion chosen by Sherri Finkbine in 1962.[28]

Sherri Finkbine's Story

Sherri, the public narrative emphasized, was the host of the children's television program *Romper Room* in Phoenix, Arizona. She had four children and seemed to exemplify the happy ideal of American womanhood. When she became pregnant for a fifth time, however, her discomfort led her to take tranquilizers. After her supply ran out, she borrowed some of her husband's. But this was 1962; her husband had been abroad; and his tranquilizers contained pure thalidomide. When Sherri later heard warnings about thalidomide, she anxiously consulted her doctor. He confirmed that she had indeed taken the dangerous substance; her child had a 50 percent chance of bearing the terrible thalidomide deformities—nonexistent arms, twisted legs, flaps of skin for hands and feet, or paralysis and a grossly deformed head. The doctor recommended an abortion, and the pictures of thalidomide babies convinced the Finkbines that he was correct.

The tragedy seemed on its way to a quiet conclusion after a hospital abortion was approved by committee, but Sherri made a crucial decision. She called the newspaper to tell her story as a warning to other women. Although her name was not contained in the original coverage, the publicity spread rapidly. The hospital was threatened with legal suits by Catholics and other religious persons who argued that abortion constituted the taking of a human life. Since Arizona law allowed abortion only for the protection of the mother's life, the hospital had some grounds for concern. Other abortions similar to

Sherri Finkbine's had been performed in hospitals on the grounds that problem pregnancies, by causing psychological de-stabilization, threatened the mother's health and life. All such abortions remained legally questionable, however.

The hospital therefore filed suit, hoping for a declaratory judgment in favor of the abortion, but the judiciary dodged the issue and refused to rule. Meanwhile, Sherri's name was revealed. Since her pregnancy was rapidly reaching a time when even legal abortion would carry health hazards and fearing that the publicity would keep all other American hospitals from providing her an abortion, she decided to seek an abortion abroad. When Japan proved to require too much red tape, she flew to Sweden to seek approval from a complex committee system there. The hospital abortion was granted. In Sweden, a deformed fetus was scraped from the womb of this "all-American" woman.

Sherri Finkbine's story was important to the mythicizing of the illegal abortion drama because it provided a near-perfect example of the abortion tale personified in a singular, real human being who spoke and wrote about her experiences. Sherri fit the description of the "good woman" demanded as the agent of a persuasive drama at this site in American history. She was a family woman who loved children and surrounded herself with them even in her work. She wanted to bear another child (and did so two years later). Her purpose in seeking an abortion had been brought about by accident, not intent; she was not seeking to avoid the responsibilities of sex or pregnancy but had been trapped by fate into taking an evil medication that destroyed the health of her child. Her abortion clearly did not attack the key social symbols of "family" or "motherhood." Finally, perhaps ironically, Sherri insisted that her act be a legal one. She refused the agency of illegal abortion and thus uniquely represented the possibility of a good/legal abortion. Sherri's story also earned sympathy because she seemed to be a pawn of the professionals—the courts and hospitals and churches, fighting over her pregnancy.

Sherri Finkbine's tragedy thus provided a perfect vehicle for challenging the status quo in the most narrow (and hence most persuasive) possible way, attacking only criminal abortion, not families, healthy fetuses, children, or mothering. Even given the tight way in which this narrative's persuasiveness was structured, however, the narrative would be effective only if the new social conditions that shaped the narrative were broadly distributed. A German measles epidemic that threatened the fetuses of many women expanded the "generality" of the problem in one way, but the larger set of conditions leading many parents to desire to control their childbearing gave it even larger substance. For millions of Americans, Sherri's "perfect story" mythicized the illegal abortion drama by providing a shared, real case exemplifying their experiences in their store of conventional knowledge. Not everyone shared the myth, however.

For those who have no positive contact with the conditions underlying a new social myth, no depiction of the agent will seem adequately good, because the pre-existent belief system will interpret the choices made as evil ones. Thus, *Catholics and others wrote passionately condemning Sherri Finkbine's choice, and still today the story of illegal abortion is frequently and vehemently refuted by those who do not share the life conditions and beliefs of wage-laboring women.[29] They respond that adoptions are preferable, that each life (deformed or otherwise) is a worthy miracle, that mothers ought never to deny motherhood, or that women who suffer from illegal abortion thereby get what they deserve.

The persuasiveness of social narratives thus depends upon the

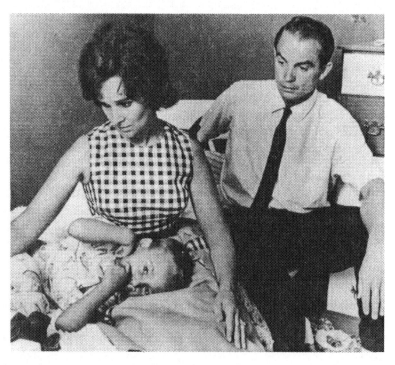

National newsmagazines portrayed Sherri Finkbine as a caring mother. Photo from the Associated Press

tale's structure, the pervasiveness of the conditions, and the relative social power of the affected groups. Those with the power—economic, positional, or political—to propagate their narratives will aid the success of the new belief system carried by the narrative. Hence, the Finkbine case was also important because Sherri was a middle-class woman. As a member of the middle class, attempting to adhere to its ideology, Sherri Finkbine forced middle America to look at itself and its abortion policies.

In the abortion controversy, therefore, rhetorical narratives provided a unique transitional device between old belief systems and new social conditions. Because they focus on the plight of worthy individual human beings and therefore use relatively de-politicized language with a lower agonistic charge, narratives can restructure parts of dominant belief sets to suggest new conditions without having to come in direct conflict with the politicized public vocabulary. Here discourse and material conditions are closely linked; individually generated personal narratives express the new conditions of the lives of a social group and thereby persuade more members of that group and of the public to adapt, as a collective, to those conditions. Thus through the rhetorical device of very carefully constructed narrative forms, new groups are able to circumvent the dominant vocabulary to allow "their case" to be heard.

Narrative Tensions—Old Beliefs vs. New Conditions

Such transitional narrative structures contain their own problems. As we have seen, the abortion narratives had to use images of motherhood to argue for a choice against specific instances of motherhood. Moreover, the narratives were limited to cases in which the purpose for the abortion was dramatic and, hence, most acceptable within the reigning ideology. The needs or desires of the majority of women who sought abortion were thereby masked, or at least not articulated, because of these persuasive conditions. These problems arose precisely because of the tension and contradictions between old beliefs and new conditions.

According to most prominent narrative theorists, this should not present a problem at all. Levi-Strauss's widely accepted theory indicates that myths "contain" and help express social contradictions in ways that allow dominant groups enhanced control. Fredric Jameson has extended this function of "contradiction-suppression" to narratives in general.[30] The discourse of the abortion controversy, however, suggests this is not true for sociopolitical narratives.[31] Instead,

as a sociopolitical tale is continually retold, the contradictions between new conditions and old beliefs may become more and more
evident, eventually forcing some modifications in beliefs or conditions.

The contradictions revealed by the retellings of the abortion narrative were, indeed, legion. The mythic images, deriving from direct
experiences with illegal abortions, were not yet either separated from
the previous ideology or well enough integrated into a complete new
belief system to be fully consistent.

The most blatant contradictions occurred in the depictions of the
agents involved—both the women having abortions and the men
(most frequently they were men) performing the abortions. The nar-
rators of the story of illegal abortion appeared unable to decide which
women most often sought illegal abortions. Some authors would
dramatically and vividly depict the victims of abortion as young,
unmarried women, while others might note, almost in conscious
refutation, that illegal abortion really affected married women more
frequently: "not the wanton teenager . . . not the naive girl in the big
city . . . but the young (between 21 and 25 years) married woman is
most likely to undergo an abortion," they warned.[32] Some charac-
terizers contradicted not only each other but themselves. A *pro-
reform article might describe two or three "typical cases" of young
victims, often having already declared that such cases were not typical
at all.[33] By their explicit attention to the issue, the advocates signalled
the importance of portraying a consistent and appropriate agent for
generating a rhetorically compelling story. However, because of the
place of the narrative in the social structure, they constructed contradictions instead of consistency.

These inconsistencies and contradictions arose in the first place not
because the story was "wrong" or "false" but because of an inherent
problem in change-seeking discourse: it must bridge old beliefs and
new social conditions, which are themselves inevitably inconsistent.
In the first place, the reigning public vocabulary rhetorically "preferred" abortions for unmarried women, because the "myth of motherhood" had become so idealized that bearing children outside of
sound marriages was viewed as seriously negative.[34] Simultaneously,
however, if abortion itself were to be a "good" act, it had to be
undertaken by "good" women; and given the terms of the dominant
vocabulary, only mothers fully qualified in that category. The inconsistencies in the reigning ideology thus generated rhetorical pulls in
two opposite directions.[35] These were reinforced by the fact that

abortion was apparently shifting from a practice of married women who had families in place to unmarried women who did not (at that time, in those conditions) wish to create new families.[36]

In the second place, the dominant ideology did not fit the existing social conditions, as is evidenced in the additional tensions that surfaced in depictions of the "purposes" of these ambiguously portrayed women. The mythic tale of illegal abortion addressed an audience that thought in terms of the "old" belief set, and responded best to stories that generated sympathy for the unfortunates who, through no fault of their own, were forced into an abortion. The entrenched public vocabulary held that only married women should have sex, and if sex in marriage resulted in pregnancy, then every wife would want to carry through that pregnancy to enact or re-enact the joys of motherhood.[37] Women were held generally responsible for their pregnancies; only youth, rape, or catastrophe could excuse them. For rhetorical effect, the pro-reform depictions were aligned with these catastrophic cases.

This persuasive structure of motives, however, contradicted the real and quite different motivating force that generated the uncountable thousands of illegal abortions—the desire to control one's family, life-style, and economic status through abortion.[38] The force of this discrepancy between the conditions generating the expressions and the limitations of the ideology within which they could be expressed was bound to be manifested.[39] Yet, because the women's liberation ideology had not been widely and fully articulated *in public*, there were no salient arguments readily available to express this need in the form of a demand, and no public advocates able to express the political needs of women. Therefore, until the later sixties, the reality remained only a footnote incongruously juxtaposed to the myth built by the arguers to express it.[40]

A second, striking contradiction existed in the reform advocates' descriptions of abortionists. On the one hand, abortionists were described as "hacks" and "incompetents." They were men who "lead disorganized lives—numerous divorces, alcoholism, drifting from job to job and place to place. Police sometimes find pornographic literature in their possession. Sometimes abortionists have sexual relations with their patients before aborting them."[41] And they were unrepentant: "One abortionist, while on trial, performed an abortion during a noon recess."[42] These general lists of negative characteristics were also assembled into composites of the "typical" abortionist. According to Muriel Davidson, "An example of the type of person who becomes an amateur abortionist is Hugh M. Pheaster, a surgical-tool salesman who was arrested in Santa Ana, California, last March on charges of bank robbery and auto theft."[43]

Contradicting these portraits, the reformers emphasized elsewhere that, in fact, "90% of all the illegal abortions are performed by physicians using sterile procedures."[44] Sympathetic character sketches described "a genial, graying family doctor who had served them [the community] for thirty years . . . founder of the Grove Public Library, former city councilman and the PTA's choice for Father of the Year in 1960."[45]

This contradiction in the depiction of the abortionists developed from the distinctive difference between the types of abortionists available to different classes. Upper-middle-class women were often able to get safe abortions from competent physicians. At the least, they could travel to Cuba, Mexico, and Puerto Rico for abortions that might not have been completely legal but may have been fairly routine. More frequently, perhaps, their close contact with their private physicians allowed them to get abortions locally as well. Poorer or younger women, with less cash to offer and less chance for close contact with physicians, turned to the abortionist quacks.[46]

This contradiction could not be explained in the dominant public vocabulary of the time, and the vocabulary of "discrimination," which resolved the inconsistency, did not become available until later in the decade. In the meantime, the emotional power of the narrative set up a problem of public meaning, and the tensions within the narratives exacerbated the uncertainty, thereby generating the energy for discursive change and the discursive conditions for that change.

Summation

In the early years of the contemporary American abortion controversy, rhetorical narratives played an initiatory and crucial role in communicating the social conditions facing a group of women. Since no collective can respond directly to changes in social conditions, public rhetoric in the form of narrative was essential. As Kristin Luker so clearly reports, we tend to explain our *personal* contacts with changed social conditions in terms of personal failures or through belief systems derived from previous conditions.[47] A rhetorical narrative, however, allows, first, a large audience to identify with a particular human being in a particular case and, second, the causes and effects in the case to be clearly specified as social ones, beyond the control of individuals.

Stories about individual women, because they were transferable into social myths, thus translated widely shared private experiences into a public concern by expressing those experiences through the dominant vocabulary, albeit with a new "point" to the story. Careful manipulations of language (i.e., "rhetoric") in opportune social conditions thus materialized a new set of discourses in the public realm.

Such myths, however, necessarily contained contradictions because they embodied competing social forces. "New" interests had to use the old *public vocabulary to express their demands, and that vocabulary was loaded against them. That tension was a creative one, crucial for moving public understandings forward toward new vocabulary and policies that would provide articulations consistent with the new social conditions faced by a wide variety of women.

Some of the limitations of the narratives nonetheless had long-term consequences, which arose from both the logical limitations of narrative as a form and the social limitations of narrative as a persuasive process. In general, there may not be a direct link between the emotion we feel for one suffering individual and the social policy advocated alongside the narrative. What policy is appropriate to alleviate the problems of illegal abortion? Reform? Repeal? Mandatory birth control? Abstinence crusades? More than individual narratives are needed to answer that question. In the opposite direction, narratives may restrict, inappropriately, the laws designed to alleviate the conditions that the stories express. Persuasive narratives always present the most extreme cases with the most noble purposes. The dominant ideology strictly limits which narratives can be perceived as persuasive, which purposes and agents perceived as pitiable. Hence, social narratives are not likely to describe fully the social conditions they bring to public thought and discussion. In the abortion case, the problem of thousands of mutilations and deaths from illegal abortions was not resolvable by legal changes that allowed abortions for the few rhetorically compelling cases of rape, fetal deformity, or maternal survival. However, the more limited legal changes formalized by the American Law Institute's "model code" were those most widely discussed, and passed, in the early period. The rhetorical conditions that would make abortion a matter of "socially good excuses" rather than a consequence of the wishes and desires of women (their "reproductive freedom") were therefore established in the first public telling of the women's narratives themselves.

Another long-term limitation of the "tale of illegal abortion" was its focus on the abortion problem as faced by the white middle class. Sherri Finkbine's story was only the most visible of the versions of the tale which defined the problem primarily in white and middle-class terms. Because the dominant audience was largely constituted of the middle and upper class, these cases were most likely to be persuasive in the public realm. This meant, however, that the often quite different problems of other groups of women were not articulated.

In contrast to recent claims that narrative thought can provide us with a complete "paradigm," the narratives in the abortion controversy provided incomplete discussions.[48] They did not fully communicate the beliefs, values, and conditions which generated them. They provided grounds and fuel to generate an argument but did not point us fully toward precise social claims. The rhetorical narratives about abortion activated and crystallized the potential for new frameworks of meaning and evaluation, but they constituted only a first move in the complex endeavor of communicating social change. Chapter 4 will describe the second stage of the argument, but first we must attend to the response—immediate opposition. They were rapidly answered in kind by a pro-Life heritage tale, the dynamics of which also shaped the path of the discursive change.

NOTES

1. The claim to the unique action of the Supreme Court is made, not surprisingly, in a wide variety of *pro-Life advocacy. It is, however, prevalent in *pro-Choice advocacy as well. See, for example, the pro-Life advocacy of John T. Noonan, "Right to Life: Raw Judicial Power," *National Review*, 2 March 1973, pp. 260–64, and John Willke, "A Matter of Life," public lecture at the University of Illinois, Urbana, 6 February 1987. For pro-Choice advocacy, see, for example, Faye Wattleton, "A Matter of Choice," public lecture, University of Illinois, Urbana, 4 February 1987; John Irving, mailing from National Abortion Rights Action League, Summer 1987. The "conventional wisdom" is also evident in the newsmagazines—for example, "America's Abortion Dilemma," *Newsweek*, 14 January 1985, p. 20.

2. In common law, abortion was clearly legal until *quickening. After that point, the exact legal status is unclear (whether it was legal for the women but not for an abortionist, or to what degree of severity that act was punished, has not fully been established). See, for example, James C. Mohr, *Abortion in America: The Origins and Evolution of National Policy, 1800–1900* (New York: Oxford Union Press, 1978).

3. These abortions were done on various grounds relating to the "life" of the mother. As the strictly physical indications for such abortions declined, the psychological indications increased (e.g., the threat of suicide). These abortions might have been challenged as not fitting the letter or spirit of the law, but they were not. Hence, until the sixties the consensus by doctors and others was that they were legal. Calculation of the number of abortions, even

those performed in hospitals and nominally legal, is difficult in this period. Many abortions may have been recorded as "dilation and curettage" rather than as abortion. However, Lawrence Lader describes the number of hospital abortions per year as declining from 30,000 to 8,000; Lawrence Lader, *Abortion* (Indianapolis: Bobbs-Merrill, 1966), p. 24; see also Nanette J. Davis, *From Crime to Choice: The Transformation of Abortion in America* (Westport, Conn.: Greenwood Press, 1985), chapter 4. On the shift in "indications" for abortion, see "Abortions on the Increase," *America,* 25 September 1965, p. 31.

4. Calculation of the number of illegal abortions is even more difficult than calculation of the number of legal abortions. Nonetheless, even the lowest data-based estimates leave us with significant numbers of illegal abortions. The ranges cited in the popular press were generally 200,000 to two million annually, based on studies extrapolating from a variety of small sample studies, including the Kinsey data. See, for example, Marguerite Clark, "Abortion Racket, What Should Be Done?" *Newsweek,* 15 August 1960, pp. 50–52. One of the sturdier estimates seems to me based on the calculation that there were 350,000 admissions to hospitals for "incomplete" abortions. Although this number may under-represent illegal abortions by failing to count some "incompletes" labeled as other procedures and illegal abortions that did not result in medical problems, it provides a minimum marker indicating with reasonable certainty a significant number of illegal abortions in this period. See F. Von Moschzisker, ed., "Abortion Comes Out of the Shadows," *Life,* 27 February 1970, pp. 20–29. This figure is further substantiated by the noticeable drop in maternal mortality after New York legalized abortion. There, maternal mortality (which had been falling steadily earlier), dropped as much as 50 percent, changing from a yearly improvement rate of .02 deaths fewer per 1,000 live births to .03 fewer deaths per 1,000 live births per year. Given a simultaneous large-scale decrease in the number of live births (also attributable to legalized abortion), this led to a considerable decline in actual mortality. See "Abortion: Rhetoric and Reality," *Christian Century,* 21 July 1971, and *Vital Statistics of the United States* (Washington, D.C.: U.S. Dept. of Health, Education, and Welfare, Public Health Service), for 1965 through 1972.

5. See Lawrence Lader, *Abortion II: Making the Revolution* (Boston: Beacon Press, 1973), pp. 166–67; Center for Disease Control in Atlanta, "Abortion Surveillance: Annual Survey," reported in Stanley Henshaw et al., "Abortion in the United States, 1978–1979," *Family Planning Perspectives* 13 (January/February 1981), p. 7; Edward Weinstock et al., "Legal Abortions in the United States since the 1973 Supreme Court Decisions," *Family Planning Perspectives* 1 (January/February 1975), pp. 23–45.

6. Because abortion was available only in some states, some women who wanted legal abortions had to travel to other states. In addition, the lack of medical coverage made abortion expensive and, hence, not available to all women. Although legalization by the Court did not eliminate these variations (access problems still present formidable barriers to rural and poor women), it did improve the homogeneity. This entire claim runs contrary to Judith Blake's argument that the Supreme Court "outran" public opinion. Blake,

however, conflates "public opinion" with popular opinion polls, a move I argued to be fallacious (see chapter 1). More specifically, I suggest that the Court moved in the *same direction* as public opinion and was constrained from "enacting" popular opinion precisely because of the character of legal principle (see chapters 6 and 8). Compare Judith Blake, "The Abortion Decisions: Judicial Review and Public Opinion," in *Abortion: New Directions for Policy Studies*, ed. Edward Manier, William Liu, and David Solomon (Notre Dame, Ind.: University of Notre Dame Press, 1977), pp. 51–81, to Eric M. Ulsaner and Ronald E. Weber, "Public Support for Pro-Choice Abortion Policies in the Nation and States: Changes and Stability after the *Roe* and *Doe* Decisions," in *The Law and Politics of Abortion*, ed. Carl E. Schneider and Maris A. Vinovskis (Lexington, Mass.: D. C. Heath, 1980), pp. 206–23. I deal with the poll data in detail in a later chapter.

7. The current emphasis on the role of the doctors in controlling abortion law in the United States since the 1800s is over-stated. Although the physicians clearly have been major players, a variety of other factors have been involved as well. The fact that the physicians have been influential is well documented by Mohr for the early period and for the fifties by Davis and by Kristin Luker, *Abortion and the Politics of Motherhood* (Berkeley: University of California Press, 1984). See chapter 6, notes 14, 15.

8. The range of forces impinging on doctors has yet to be fully elaborated. Petchesky argues that the numbers of illegal abortions had increased because women's improved economic position encouraged them to delay or control childbearing independently of male support. This may have resulted in greater demand for legal abortions, which doctors were unable to cope with given the rigid ideological prescription against abortions for such reasons. Another factor was the change in the presumption of "motherhood" for all women at all times. In addition, the decreasing "covering" grounds for legal abortions may have been a component, further enhanced by the fact that doctors were less used to "loosing" young patients in this era. See Rosalind Pollack Petchesky, *Abortion and Women's Choice: The State, Sexuality, and Reproductive Freedom* (Boston, Mass.: Longman/Northeastern University Press, 1984), and Celeste Condit Railsback, "The Contemporary American Abortion Controversy: A Case Study in Public Argumentation" (Ph.D. diss., University of Iowa, 1982), chapter 3. The reports of the doctors' *feelings* about these forces are quite clear, both in testimony of activists and in polls. See Bernard N. Nathanson with Richard N. Ostling, *Aborting America* (Garden City, N.Y.: Doubleday, 1979); Anthony J. Mandy, "Reflections of a Gynecologist," in *Therapeutic Abortion*, ed. Harold Rosen (New York: Julian Press, 1954); Herbert L. Packer and Ralph J. Campbell, "Therapeutic Abortion: A Problem in Law and Medicine," in *The Case for Legalized Abortion Now*, ed. Alan F. Guttmacher (Berkeley, Calif.: Diablo Press, 1967), p. 150. The fact that the doctors were primarily concerned about controlling their own problems rather than about the freedom of women to make choices is poignantly suggested by the about-face of Nathanson. Nathanson was an active worker for reform laws, but

when women gained full control through abortion on request, he switched to the "pro-Life" position.

9. See Betty Sarvis and Hyman Rodman, *The Abortion Controversy* (New York: Columbia University Press, 1974).

10. The abortion section was approved as part of the draft in May 1959, but the code was not approved as a whole until 1962. See Anthony Lewis, "Legal Abortions Proposed in Code," *New York Times;* 22 May 1959, p. 15, and Anthony Lewis, "Model Penal Code is Approved by the American Law Institute," *New York Times*, 25 May 1962, p. 1.

11. Doctors appear to have been major players in changing state laws, but their relative prominence varies by state. Compare Luker's account of California's legal process to Patricia G. Steinhoff and Milton Diamond, *Abortion Politics: The Hawaii Experience* (Honolulu: Union Press of Hawaii, 1977), or Segar C. Jain and Laurel F. Gooch, *Georgia Abortion Act 1968* (Chapel Hill: University of North Carolina Press, 1972), and by the same authors and press, *California Abortion Act 1967* (1969) and *North Carolina Abortion Law 1967* (1969). According to descriptions in the popular magazines of the time, physicians tended to be pro-reform rather than pro-Choice.

12. John Bartlow Martin, "Abortion," *Saturday Evening Post*, 20 May 1961, pp. 19–21; see also Marguerite Clark, "Abortion Racket, What Should Be Done?" *Newsweek*, 15 August 1960, pp. 50–52. These early articles reflected the "dominant ideology" quite fully; they argued against abortion to "avoid the responsibility of motherhood" and against "abortion on demand." The "shroud of silence" that had engulfed abortion practices was explicitly recognized by those who broke it—e.g., Walter Goodman, "Abortion and Sterilization: The Search for Answers," *Redbook*, October 1965, p. 70; *America*, 25 March 1961, p. 811.

13. These five elements form the five options for *character-types. I have derived the units from Kenneth Burke's pentad. See *A Grammar of Motives* (1945; Berkeley: University of California Press, 1969).

14. Muriel Davidson, "The Deadly Favor," *Ladies Home Journal*, November 1963, p. 53.

15. Marguerite Clark, "Abortion Racket, What Should Be Done?" *Newsweek*, 15 August 1960, pp. 50–52.

16. "Abortion and the Law," *Time*, 3 August 1962, p. 30.

17. For example, Clark; James Ridgeway, "One Million Abortions," *New Republic*, 9 February 1963, pp. 14–17; "Why Did You Do It? France's Biggest Postwar Mass Abortion Trial," *Newsweek*, 10 June 1963, p. 54.

18. Clark, p. 51; Alan F. Guttmacher, "Law That Doctors Often Break," *Reader's Digest*, January 1960, pp. 51–54.

19. Ibid.

20. Martin; "Abortion Facts Reported," p. 86; Faye Marley, "Legal Abortion Safer," *Science News Letter*, 2 March 1963, p. 134.

21. Davidson, pp. 53–54.

22. Ibid.

23. Martin, p. 21.

24. Theodor Adorno notes the basic moral substantiveness of such physio-emotional responses. *Negative Dialectics* (New York: Seabury Press, 1979), pp. 351, 365.

25. Burke, p. 3.

26. Martin, pp. 19–20; Walter Goodman, "Abortion and Sterilization: The Search for the Answers," *Redbook,* October 1965, pp. 70–71; Jack Starr, "Growing Tragedy of Illegal Abortion," *Look,* 19 October 1962, pp. 52–53.

27. Martin, pp. 19–20; Lader, *Abortion,* pp. 65–66.

28. Material on Sherri Finkbine is obtained from the *Arizona Republic* and other newspapers published throughout the nation in July and August of 1962, along with a wide variety of material provided in magazine accounts in the period and rhetorical narratives in books by advocates later. I am concerned here not with what "really happened" in the Finkbine case but with how it was portrayed in the public press.

29. Kristin Luker establishes the link of activists and their beliefs to their life conditions. *Abortion and the Politics of Motherhood* (Berkeley: University of California Press, 1984). There must be a large, fairly well-organized constituency to get a "voice" heard. This does not mean that such an argument will "win" the legal and cultural battles. "Winning" requires the ability to convince the uninvolved, the ambivalent, or the politically powerful.

30. Claude Levi-Strauss, "The Structural Study of Myth," in *Myth: A Symposium,* ed. Thomas A. Sebeok (Bloomington: Indiana University Press, 1958), pp. 81–106, and Fredric Jameson, *The Political Unconscious: Narrative as a Socially Symbolic Act* (Ithaca, N.Y.: Cornell University Press, 1981), pp. 79–88.

31. See John Louis Lucaites and Celeste Michelle Condit, "Reconstructing Narrative Theory: A Functional Perspective," *Journal of Communication* 36, no. 4 (Autumn 1986), 90–108, in which we argue that, since not all discourse functions to entertain, error frequently occurs when literary models are extended to other discourse forms.

32. "Abortion Racket: What Should Be Done?" *Newsweek,* 15 August 1960, pp. 50–52; Clark, p. 51; "Abortion: Precept and Practice," *Time,* 13 July 1962, p. 52.

33. Ibid.; Goodman, pp. 70–71.

34. The ideological tension and the potential for contradiction in the "cult of motherhood" is suggested in Petchesky, chapters 1 and 2, esp. p. 75. She notes that the myth prescribed motherhood as a high ideal for women's lives and that it prescribed a limited number of children, so that they would get an ideal upbringing. The growth of the argument that unwanted pregnancies produced "unwanted children" and that this was seriously undesirable was an outgrowth of this ideological tension. I discuss this issue in chapter 9.

35. The reformers seemed to recognize that they were dealing with an ideology that was inconsistent. They routinely cited the "hypocrisy" and inconsistency of the existing legal situation. Alan F. Guttmacher was one of the most active physicians seeking reform. See, for example, "Law That

Doctors Often Break," *Reader's Digest,* January 1960, pp. 51–54; "Abortion, Legal and Illegal," *Time,* 25 December 1964.

36. See Petchesky and "Abortions on the Increase," *America,* 25 September 1965, p. 31.

37. To document the full and precise characteristics of the public vocabulary would require a full-length work. The discourse, however, gives many indications of the prevalent beliefs and assumptions. For example, Richard P. Vaughan suggested of any woman who aborted that "the immature side of her nature rebels against the prospect of being a mother," but at another level she craves "the experience of fulfillment and creativity that accompanies motherhood," in "Psychotherapeutic Abortion: Bill under Consideration in California," *America,* 16 October 1965, pp. 436–38. See also "Abortion by Consent?" *Christian Century,* 1 February 1967, p. 132, which seems to view abortion as only a temporary whim. The dramatic "fetus talking to its mother" articles draw on these stereotypes as well. "Slaughter of the Innocent," trans. L. F. Chrobot, *America,* 2 June 1962, p. 39. In addition, the contrast between articles about women who desperately want children but miscarry and the women who desperately want abortions speaks to the tensions here.

38. See Walter Goodman, "Abortion and Sterilization: The Search for the Answers," *Redbook,* October 1965, pp. 70–71; "Abortion Sought Abroad," *Science News Letter,* 24 July 1965, p. 63; Harold Rosen, "Abortion: Questions and Answers," *Today's Health,* April 1965, pp. 24–25; "Abortion: Legal and Illegal," *Time,* 25 December 1964, p. 53; James Ridgeway, "One Million Abortions," *New Republic,* 9 February 1963, pp. 14–17; Alan Guttmacher, ed., *The Case for Legalized Abortion Now* (Berkeley, Calif.: Diablo Press, 1967), pp. 52–53.

39. To the extent that the force derived from an adequately powerful "constituency," it would get a voice, but that voice was bound to manifest the contradictions because of the requirement to "be persuasive"—that is, to address the public on their terms, not the group's own.

40. This is, of course, a reflexive relationship; the abortion conditions helped to establish the narratives and then used the ideology once it was developed. There was no smooth and simple time-line because different groups received or communicated the ideology or parts of it at different times. Even in later periods, the full belief set (including the narrative) had to be continually articulated.

41. Martin, p. 52.

42. Ibid.

43. Davidson, p. 55.

44. Estimates in the popular magazines ranged from "many" to 75 to 90 percent. "Abortion Facts Reported," *Science News Letter,* 24 July 1965; André E. Hellegers, "Law and the Common Good," *Commonweal,* 30 June 1967, pp. 418ff; Ridgeway, p. 14. See also Paul H. Gebhard, Wardell B. Pomeroy, Clyde E. Martin, and Cornelia V. Christenson, *Pregnancy, Birth and Abortion* (New York: Harper Brothers, 1958), chapter 8.

45. "Doc Henrie's Farewell," *Newsweek,* 30 July 1962, pp. 22ff.

46. The facts of availability are difficult to document, but the public dis-

course held these distinctions to be true, and they are persuasive, given the economic structure. In specific, anecdotes of the "foreign options" are routinely mentioned, but I have been unable to locate any estimates of the numbers of these abortions. See Gebhard et al.; Goodman, p. 71; Lader, *Abortion*, pp. 56–57; Davidson, p. 54; Linda Bird Francke, *The Ambivalence of Abortion* (New York: Dell, 1982); Kristin Luker, "Abortion and the Meaning of Life: Autobiographical Statement," in *Abortion: Understanding Differences*, ed. Sidney Callahan and Daniel Callahan (New York: Plenum Press, 1984), p. 26.

47. Describing the "conversions" of understandings of pro-Choice activists, Luker notes, "These people, who later became so active in changing abortion laws, had considerable personal experience with illegal abortion in one way or another and had seen or suffered the experiences of the illegality of abortion, yet none of them was directly 'radicalized' by the experience itself . . . . *they did not question the legitimacy of the laws*," p. 107.

48. Walter Fisher, "Narration as a Human Communication Paradigm: The Case of Public Moral Argument," *Communication Monographs* 51 (1984), 1–22.

CHAPTER THREE

The Pro-Life Heritage Tale
Rhetoric and History
———— 1965-85 ————

As the sixties matured, the vivid story of illegal abortion garnered support for change in abortion policies. Popular coverage of the issue in the national media grew, various bills were considered in state legislatures, organizations formed across the nation, and in 1965 the American Medical Association's Committee on Human Reproduction voted to support the ALI's reform "model code."[1] The dramatic reform narrative had begun to chip away at what seemed to be the American heritage—a largely inarticulate sense that abortion was "wrong."

When such cultural *presumptions are attacked, supporters of the status quo re-tell the "story of our past" in order to re-invigorate the *heritage, giving it enough force to combat the new tales. This is precisely what the pro-Life rhetors hurried to do. The move to restore a heritage is, however, a risky one. In transferring the heritage from the realm of background feelings into explicit statement, all of the related assumptions and grounds upon which the heritage has rested once again come into public view. Serious gaps, power moves, contradictions, or other weaknesses will be exposed either in the direct content of the story or in the rhetorical tactics through which the narrative is constructed. Such weaknesses may reveal the heritage as illegitimate, giving opponents further grounds for demanding reconstruction. The pro-Life heritage tale was widely persuasive, but its argument contained gaps serious enough to leave it stalemated against the reform narrative that had forced its retelling.

A Pro-Life Human History

History offers resistance to change in two forms.[2] First, the material encrustations it leaves—habits, institutions, distributions, and materiel—offer a concrete, physical recalcitrance that makes real work necessary to re-form them. In addition, however, verbal reconstructions of the past—*hegemonic histories—place the weight of a unified humanity against "new" actions by identifying who "we" are and thus, what it is that we *should* do. Since we "are" what we have always "done," we violate our true selves if we act in ways that are different. In order to carry such authority, however, "heritage tales" must be constituted by only one collective, and this collective must have operated with a near unanimous voice.

Faced by the challenge to old meanings, habits, and actions, the pro-Life rhetors sought to construct such a preservationist narrative. As the massive anthropological collections of George Devereux have established, however, and as was evident in the pro-Life rhetors' own histories, there have been a wide variety of human collectives, holding a variety of positions on abortion.[3] Therefore, in order to unify this cacophony into a unified chorus, skilled rhetorical effort had to be brought to bear.

The chief means by which this unification was accomplished was the narration, by many advocates, of a selective and coherent account portraying a specific strand of white, Western, Christian history as the authoritative and legitimate American heritage. The pro-Life advocates described how, throughout the Western tradition, abortion had been written and spoken against by important institutional and moral authorities. Although disagreements had occurred in the past, they indicated that there had been a clear path of "moral improvement" through history—prohibitions against abortion had become more and more restrictive through time, as humankind became increasingly aware of the fact that abortion represented the killing of a human being.

In order to explore the rhetorical structure and consequences of this heritage tale, I will focus on the most widely cited version of it—the historical account produced by John Noonan.[4] Although Noonan's history of the past was not the earliest one, it reflected most versions of the tale, it was quoted repeatedly in public speeches across the nation by prominent activists like John Willke and Basil Uddo, and it was also referred to frequently in the written pro-Life histories.[5]

In order to portray the diverse voices of history as bearing a single authority opposed to abortion, Noonan carefully framed his arguments with a title that was to be frequently quoted—"An Almost Absolute Value in History." As we shall see, since Noonan could not truthfully claim that opposition to abortion had always been an "absolute value" or gain the same rhetorical force from the claim that it was "a widely held value," he used the near-oxymoron "almost absolute."

In addition, he used the ambiguous term *value* (as opposed to *practice, law, religious precept,* or even *belief*). Finally, he omitted a subject, refusing to identify just what had been an almost absolute value. His title set up and balanced the rhetorical force and the plausibility of the history he would recount.

Having established an authoritative tone, Noonan described the practices of different groups or eras and indicated how each era or group fit into the general historical frame. Thus, he indicated that if the Greco-Romans had allowed abortion it was merely because they were products of a "culture generally distinguished by its indifference to fetal and early life" (p. 7). Their error was soon corrected when "the Christians proposed a rule which was certain, comprehensive, and absolute" (p. 7). Similarly, if certain historical writers had not agreed that abortion was the taking of a human life, then, Noonan's *framing suggested, at least they agreed that it was a sin against marriage or a failure of love (pp. 22–23). Even when components of the narrative itself appeared to indicate that there was less agreement than the overarching frame of the title would claim, Noonan reassured the reader that at least there was a "development" toward such an absolute valuation (pp. 36, 38, 46).

This framing process required the use of multiple themes, related but ambiguous. No simple singular theme—"abortion has always been treated as murder" or "abortion has always been outlawed"—was true. No broader theme—e.g., "abortion was always problematic"—would have adequate rhetorical force. If no single theme could successfully capture all of the events of the human past and simultaneously indicate narrowly and forcefully that abortion should be outlawed and treated as murder, then the rhetor could employ multiple themes to create a frame that at least gave the general impression of universal condemnation.

For example, in discussing early Christian attitudes toward abortion, Noonan described the opposition to abortion as based upon its identity with murder (he cited Augustine, p. 16, and St. John Chrysostom, p. 17). When he came to Gratian, however, he had to admit that this influential figure believed that "abortion was homicide only when the fetus was formed" (p. 20). Consequently, Noonan had to shift grounds. He was, however, well prepared for the swerve. Rather than defining abortion as sin because it was murder, he had framed the intervening section by saying abortion was a transgression of the Christian commandment to "love" and a violation of marriage and the sexual function. He could therefore, regardless of Gratian's technical disagreement on timing, continue to frame the history as bearing "an almost absolute value" by concluding that "all the writers agree that abortion was a violation of the love owed to one's neighbor" (p. 18).

This is a stunning rhetorical move. The issue of murder was, of course, the issue of universal concern; public law might well forbid murder, but it would find itself in profound difficulty if it punished our many failures to make grave sacrifices for love of other human beings. Murder, the motive of public concern, did not provide "an almost absolute" definition of abortion in the human past. Consequently, to gain the accurate and unified force of a heritage he used the theme of "love," but to gain the force of proscription he simply cited "murder" in as many paragraphs as possible and then ended the chapter with a discussion of abortion as the taking of human life, thereby implying that fetal life had been the "absolute value" of interest all along.

By shifting back and forth between these themes—murder vs. love and sacrifice—pro-Lifers like Noonan framed the "history of abortion" in such a way as to gain both the technical grounds for saying abortion has always (within the tradition that counts) been opposed (on grounds of love) and also the stronger connotations that gave the reader a sense that abortion had always been equated with the heinous crime of murder.

The use of multiple themes under a guiding ambiguous frame, such as "an almost absolute value," thereby created the sense of a compelling, unified, authoritative history.[6] At this point, it might be tempting to disregard this history as one which seduces with shifting themes rather than proving with solid grounds. This rejection would be premature, for all heritages are built through the process of framing and very few can be built without such shifts. After all, Noonan's history proves (at least to my satisfaction) that an identifiable Western heritage has found abortion to be a failure of love for others and that many found it to be a crime close to homicide. The key questions in tracing social consequences become: even if the "themes" are not univocal, might not the "frame" as a whole be legitimate, and is it not persuasive for the American audience?

One test will move us toward answers to both these questions. Given egalitarian American ideology, as well as some of the most sophisticated social theory our species has developed, a "legitimate" set of frames would be one derived from widely based political and moral authorities who represent the experiences and interests of all members of the community.[7] In contrast, illegitimate frames—those likely to be subject to effective argumentative challenge—feature the "teachings" of only one partisan group in the community (thereby getting us to act in their interest by passing off "their heritage" as "ours").

To determine whether frames are grounded in wide or narrow interests, one need only look at a simple rhetorical tactic—the particular "differentiations" made by the rhetor. The most important of such separation devices is the polarization of persons and parties into two opposed streams—the good and the evil. The rhetor will indicate that the "good" and "wise" have all sided together in history to support her or his heritage-tale; the evil or foolish have been opposed. An examination of the groups which show up as the "heroes" or the "villains" gives an empirically verifiable and concrete list of whose heritage is being promoted.

Often the separation of "good" and "bad" takes place through the device of "scapegoating." Noonan did not have to resort to that extreme in order to establish a dominant, credible "heritage." Instead, he used the theme of "development" to show how earlier components of our heritage were incorporated, but "surpassed" by later elements. For example, by implying a sense of "moral progress" Noonan was able to dismiss the troubling fact that the Greco-Roman world did not perceive abortion as murder. He simply indicated that

> it was in this culture generally distinguished by its indifference to fetal and early life that the Christian teaching developed; it was in opposition and conflict with the values reflected in popular behavior that the Christian word was enunciated. Where some wise men had raised voices in defense of early life so that the question was in the air and yet not authoritatively decided, where even the wise presented hesitant and divided counsel, where other authorities defended abortion, the Christians proposed a rule which was certain, comprehensive, and absolute. (P. 7)

Noonan accomplished a double purpose here. Without completely denigrating the Greco-Roman heritage, he denied legitimacy to the example of permissiveness toward abortions granted by the Greco-Roman world *and* he replaced the authority of that world in favor of the *Catholics. Noonan thereby simultaneously dismissed competing interpretations of abortion *and* increased the hegemonic influence of the Catholic heritage. Only the Catholic tradition (and its offspring, Christianity in general), which transcended the previous tradition in goodness and knowledge, would count as a "true history" by which we should know and evaluate ourselves. Other events and practices that had occurred in human history were not applicable because they were divided and because even in such cultures, the "wise" spoke up on the "right" side.

In almost all of Noonan's differentiations between good and bad streams of human history, the Catholics are on the good side and almost all others—non-Christians, early Western thinkers, many non-Catholic Christians—are to be disregarded. Where "wise" or credible individuals had disagreed with Noonan's "heritage," however, the clean alignment of good and evil was imperiled. He handled these cases by careful labeling. Thus, wise Aristotle, who argued that the fetus undergoes a progressive development toward a rational soul and advocated eugenic abortion, was gently treated. Noonan said that Aristotle's proposal evinced "remarkable caution" *for his day* and that if we combined some of what Aristotle said with other of his political and biological prescriptions, this "might have permitted only contraception" (p. 5). Aristotle, therefore, moved the tradition in the right direction.

The last alternative the pro-Life historians used to distinguish and eliminate "outsiders" from the heritage was simple omission. Noonan did not mention the practices of the Chinese, the Africans, the Polynesians, or even the Saxons or Goths. Simply by speaking of only one set of authorities, Noonan constructed an authoritative historical heritage and brought it to bear against abortion. Mere *presence or social "volume" thus constitutes a crucial rhetorical element.

By paying attention to the rhetorical tactic of differentiation, therefore, we can quite easily and factually locate the underlying interest groups served by Noonan's "heritage." His was not only a "Western" history but also predominantly a Catholic heritage. Quite simply and visibly the authorities and witnesses he cited favorably were overwhelmingly Catholic (not to mention white, male, and often celibate). Others were dismissed as naive, evil, or at least cautious for an "early" period. At best, this tradition could be stretched to being a "Christian" one, but that Christianity clearly leaned on a narrow set of doctrines and was fundamentally influenced by a vision of Catholicism as the historical center-post of Western Christianity.[8] All other tributaries to the American heritage—the Saxon and Norman pagans, the ancient Greek and Roman polytheists, the Africans and native Americans, and many more—were simply "written out" of this tale.

This history was not, therefore, a universal history of all of the American people and the nation's past. Although Catholicism is certainly one major current in the American heritage, it is not the only one. The claim of Noonan's heritage to present an authoritative argument on the grounds of the shared past of all Americans was, therefore, unjustified. I will soon note the consequences of this weakness in the development of the public argument.

A second question remains. In spite of its argumentative weaknesses, would this be a convincing history for the American public? Given that the broad outline of the narrative is so similar to our typical secondary school account of "Western Civilization"—it begins with the Greeks, progresses to the Romans, then to the Catholic church, and then to the Protestants—the question is urgent. To answer it, one must assess the role of Catholicism in America.

America has been strongly and, in general, legitimately influenced by Catholicism. That influence has arisen from the role of the Catholic church in Western history, from the active involvement in the nation of the nearly one quarter of the population who are Catholics, and from the advantages of a large, hierarchical, tax-exempt institution in America. Because of this diverse ideological and material power base, a Catholic-based heritage tale might be widely persuasive in America today. The test is its ability, by its persuasive form and contents, to tap into the broader Protestant presumptions. This we can discover by examining another set of the uses of "history" by pro-Life historians.

The Lessons of History

The Protestant pro-Life historians generally did not recite the Catholic heritage tale at much length. Instead, Protestant pro-Life advocates worked to place *Roe v. Wade* within a strand of "evil" in history—one of a series of trials that Americans had always been able to overcome. Like the construction of a positive "heritage," this device functioned by collecting a set of historical events and framing them under themes that could be identified with the issue in question. Because the meaning of history arises from the intertwining of theme and event, and because the dimension of evil is a powerful magnifier, this was a forceful technique.[9]

The pro-Life historians applied this tactic by building analogies between slavery, the holocaust, and abortion. In the comparison of abortion and slavery, President Reagan was likened to a modern-day Lincoln freeing the "unborn slaves." The introduction to *Abortion and the Conscience of the Nation*, the book that contains Reagan's pro-Life essay, noted cleverly, but none-too-bashfully, "Surely all must agree that Mr. Reagan's testament is an historic document, instantly memorable if only because it evokes the moral passion of Abraham Lincoln against Slavery."[10]

To establish a history in which *Dred Scott* and *Roe* v. *Wade* were thematically linked and historically plotted, Reagan recounted key "events" of American history, portraying them as the enactment of principles. His story was clearly aimed at establishing that Americans had always believed in and acted in accordance with the principle of "the sanctity of life." In part, Reagan's history of America ran as follows:

> America was founded by men and women who shared a vision of the value of each and every individual. . . . We fought a terrible war to guarantee that one category of mankind—black people in America— could not be denied the inalienable rights with which their Creator endowed them. The great champion of the sanctity of all human life in that day, Abraham Lincoln, gave us his assessment of the Declaration's [of Independence] purpose. . . . As a nation today, we have *not* rejected the sanctity of human life. (Pp. 27–28)

And earlier Reagan had noted that "this is not the first time our country has been divided by a Supreme Court decision that denied the value of certain human lives. The *Dred Scott* decision of 1857 was not overturned in a day, or a year, or even a decade" (p. 19).

It is important to recognize that the relationship of theme to event derives less from historically accurate accounting than from a plausible, rhetorically constructed sense of the *meaning* of America's heritage. Professional historians have suggested, for example, that Lincoln's prime concern was with the sanctity of the *Union* and that he was quite willing to sacrifice many human lives for that.[11] Further, proponents of slavery did not usually argue that slaves were not human beings and might be killed at will (even if the laws ultimately permitted that indirectly). Thus, Reagan's theme was not accurately and logically linked with the event.

Nonetheless, Reagan's linkage was largely convincing because it was *plausible*. It provided a nominally appropriate chronological account featuring identifiable similarities (Supreme Court decisions were made) and a theme true of both events (they concern issues of human life). Given that our popular heritage had rewritten Lincoln's goal as a concern with the humanity of blacks and the inhumanity of slavery, the equating of abortion with slavery and *Roe* v. *Wade* with *Dred Scott* was believable. Consequently, the two events appeared as a single line of "villainy" to be overcome by Americans. As a result of this linkage, abortion was not only "written out" of the American heritage, it elicited the same kind of passionate hatred stirred by a long-past Civil War. The effect is even more vivid in the comparison of abortion to the holocaust.

The comparison of abortion clinics to "Nazi ovens" was a commonplace of the pro-Life rhetoric between 1960 and 1985. Its uses included both simple allusions and detailed examinations. In all cases, the fundamental link was made through the theme of "the sanctity of human life." Since the Nazis did not value human life, they killed innocent humans. The abortionist was similarly accused of failing to value the "sanctity" of human life and therefore killing innocent humans. In the fullest illustrations, the advocates examined the purported underlying causes. For example, Surgeon General Everett Koop recounted how "medicine under dictatorship" began with a simple Hegelian bent toward utility, gradually shifted toward the unethical experimental use of "marginally useful" humans, and then extended to the killing of more and more groups.[12] Koop compared this "utilitarianism" to the underlying "quality-of-life ethic" that he believed dominated the "abortion mentality."

Once again, the analogy was established by the fact that both events could be "constructed" to fit similar themes or to work for similar purposes. Historically, the Nazis had not necessarily been viewed as killing Jews for the sake of "efficiency" or "utility" (but rather for "purity"), but the popular cultural belief in the efficiency of fascism made the "utility" link seem plausible. This analogy was compelling because the American audience most powerfully dreaded another Nazi era. Moreover, the key discursive links were made directly through the acts of destruction. Nazis conducted mass executions, and abortions could be metaphorically identified as mass executions—both supposedly "executed" for purposes of "convenience" or "utility." The full force of the horrors of the Third Reich were thus brought down against abortion.

At this point, we can assess how the Protestant "negative" heritage was entangled with Noonan's "positive" heritage. The non-Catholic works touted, explicitly and precisely, a Christian set of values as the guardian of the "sanctity" of life and opposed non-Christian values (such as efficiency, lack of "sanctity"). The end terms of both the Protestant and Catholic "heritage tales" were, in other words, the same (i.e., "life"). Most of the means terms were the same as well, and these terms were allied against the same enemies. These shared values, and many shared events, made it easy for Noonan's Catholic heritage tale to "cross over" into the larger controversy to become a public account. In fact, this apparently occurred on a fairly broad scale. Even though feminist scholarly accounts overwhelmingly discounted this heritage, even many pro-Choice activists were caught up in and retold parts of Noonan's tale.[13]

Although Noonan's history harbored fundamental weaknesses as an argument about our national heritage, his Catholic-based heritage tale and the "negative" heritages of other pro-Life rhetors gained some public credence because the values they promoted were shared by many Americans and the historical linkages they suggested were plausible and emotionally potent ones. These convincing historical narratives provided a forceful response to the "tale of illegal abortion," thereby helping to check the move toward social change. As a result, the particular interests of the Catholics were served, but only because those interests meshed fairly well with the values embraced in the broader social history.

Re-Forming History

The public success of the pro-Life heritage tale does not, however, tell us about the full range of social effects of the historical narrative. While the pro-Life history was likely to be broadly persuasive, its logical ambiguities or partisan elements were glaring enough to allow opposing partisans to *feel justified* in their attacks upon it. In the eyes of an astute opposition, the evident partisanship of the tale destroyed its legitimacy. Unless a history identifies "us" accurately, it loses its authority to limit our actions. Audiences are restrained by the link between their identity and their past actions only to the extent that they feel a history presents a true and essential shared identity. The pro-Life tale lost its ability to control the opposition activists because it was unable to claim a universal "we"; the reform partisans easily saw themselves as excluded or marginalized in this history. Even though the reformers adopted fragments of the tale, the history's partisanship precluded it from carrying sufficient *authority* to restrain the reformers' arguments or actions. They responded by firing away at the weaknesses in the heritage tale in two ways.

The first attack on the heritage tale was the widely repeated, vehement argument that the Catholics should "not impose [their] morality on others."[14] Various pro-reform authors argued that the Catholic church was the primary supporter of criminalization of abortion and that their support was grounded in religious dogma. In the United States of America, they noted, religious freedom was guaranteed, and so the Catholic effort was unconstitutional. It is impossible to tell how much of this argument was generated simply by the vivid presence of the Catholics as a special-interest religious denomination. In the early stages of the controversy the Catholics were undeniably the most visible anti-abortion group. Catholic journals produced almost all of the pro-Life advocacy in the popular magazines. In some states Catholic representatives—including nuns, priests, bishops, and doctors—provided much of the legislative testimony against abortion reform laws. Pro-Life rallies featured religious signs and slogans, and the buses of Catholic schools were used to transport school children and others to rallies and to legislative chambers. In addition, religious vocabulary constantly crept into the discourse. Pro-Life advocates regularly referred to the "sanctity" or "sacredness" of fetal life and inadvertently included other religious language, ranging from "rest his soul" to public prayers to answering "Amens."

Catholics have charged that their mere presence has been the cause of the "imposing morality" issue and that this constitutes bigotry, or the denial of their rights to participate in the governing process.[15] It seems equally likely, however, that the "don't-impose-your-morality" argument was a response to the attempt of the Catholics to rewrite American history as a Catholic heritage. Such a reaction to an opposition's hegemonic persuasion cannot be easily labelled "bigotry."

In any case, the argument against "imposing morality" had important force throughout the controversy. It was crucial for the self-motivation of the reformers, because it allowed them to feel reassured that they were fighting against special interests, not against the genuine, universal value of "life" that those special interests professed.[16] Moreover, the argument had discursive consequences for the content of the new public vocabulary: by featuring "imposition" and "force" as negative values, the pro-reform advocates set up the discursive conditions that would make the opposite value—"choice"—attractive in later stages of the controversy.

The most direct and intense effort of the reform advocates in response to the heritage tale, however, was a different one. They attacked the concept that there had been *any* unified heritage in the human past. Reformers emphasized the multitude of human abortion practices in various societies and denied the unifying themes postulated by the dominant group's "history." The sheer variety of human events provided a wide set of positions, laws, and practices from the human past that included a broader range of groups than those described by Noonan.[17] Moreover, they did not need to be highly skilled rhetors: they did not have to construct a complex frame; they had only to juxtapose the simple statement that "there is no universal historical theme" to create the sense of variety at which they strove.

Thus in an early and influential article presenting a "Historical Background," Lester Kinsolving began with a theme indicating that the pro-Life heritage arose from a limited partisan "dogma" that was itself inconsistent. He argued that the pro-Life position "is rather a current teaching, and that it has been specifically denied by no fewer than three of the Roman church's most prominent saints and by two of its popes."[18] Kinsolving's narrative ran in part like this:

> Both Albertus Magnus and his pupil St. Thomas Aquinas held that each soul is directly created by God and is infused into the embryo not at the point of conception but when the embryo is sufficiently formed to receive it. In the fourth century St. Gregory of Nyssa maintained that the soul was infused into the body at the moment of conception, but in the 12th century St. Anselm disagreed with this contention. Previously, Tertullian and Apollinaris had introduced traducianism. . . . In 1588 Pope Sixtus V, in his bull Effraenatum, reversed his predecessor by defining all abortions as homicide. Within three years, however, this declaration was reversed. . . . Not only have saints and popes disagreed with the concept of life as beginning at conception, but many non-Christians as well.

Kinsolving's procedure was simply the reverse of Noonan's. Where Noonan focused on the broadest possible value, Kinsolving recounted the past discussions of the narrow issue of "when life begins." Where Noonan carefully distinguished among motives and practices and laws, Kinsolving simply listed the different positions and actions. Since the genre of discourse we call "history" leads the audience to expect that the story will be as coherent as possible, the lack of framing and inter-relating leads the audience to read "juxtaposition" as "unmotivated differences." This denies history a theme and, hence, its authority.

Kinsolving and Lawrence Lader, an important journalist activist, also applied personalization to deny history any authority.[19] Noonan always spoke of institutional groups vested with power and authority—for example, the "decision by Roman congregations, teaching by popes, affirmation by pope and general council" (p. 46)—or he referred to "causists" and "canonical authority." In contrast, the reform rhetors spoke of personalities: Basil, as an individual, or Sixtus, harboring a personal crusade, had written and made decisions. Thus, Lader described Sixtus V as having "set out vehemently to cleanse the Renaissance Church, even making adultery in Rome a hanging offense" (p. 79), and he labeled Basil an "extremist" (p. 77).

Labeling the participants in history negatively and personalizing their motives challenged or destroyed the mystique of an absolute, certain, and guiding history. Instead, the audience members simply were introduced to individuals working on their own non-generalizable and questionable behalf. On a broader scale, the motives of history could be challenged as a whole. Lader argued that our most recent past had been guided only by "Christian philosophy" (p. 75)— a religious and therefore illegitimate motive for public American conduct. He also asserted an even less appealing motive, claiming that a callous concern for raw human power to supply capitalist industry was the motive for banning abortion (pp. 81, 83). The sanctity of "life" was merely the protection of an adequate number of "lives" for creating wealth. Finally, he claimed that the opposition's goal was simply part of the "long struggle to suppress [sexual] sin by legislation" (p. 90).

By investigating human purposes, the challengers painted a non-universal, questionably motivated image of the history of the hegemonic past one hundred years and thereby denied its legitimacy. Instead, they focused on a broader history in which "most societies before the Catholic Church included abortion in their basic framework of government and morality" (Lader, p. 75). They described the "history" of abortion practices as widely variable and individually influenced.

Instead of providing a comforting heritage to replace the pro-Life tale, this Pro-reform history offered an "anti-history." As such it was unstable. Its only common theme was diversity and individual motivation, which were not persuasive grounds for motivating individuals to *collective* action. It did, however, preserve room for the reform activists to continue their own argument and, eventually, for feminist academics to produce a countering history.[20]

Summary

Early in the abortion controversy the pro-Life rhetors rallied to the challenge constituted through the story of illegal abortion by reconstructing a heritage tale in which abortion was always abhorred. This partisan tale skillfully conflated opposition to abortion on grounds of love and sacrifice with opposition to abortion on grounds of murder, covertly promoting the Catholic/Christian heritage as the sole heritage of America. In spite of such imbalances the heritage tale had some substantial success because it was close enough to the center of dominant American discursive traditions to be absorbed into the larger "American tale" told by non-Catholic Christian rhetors such as Reagan and Koop. Since this heritage was publicly plausible, it provided a successful and forceful justification for pro-Life activists. It helped to select and motivate to activism those who were likely to become involved in the pro-Life argument—the religious and "traditional" Americans.[21]

This mutually reinforcing spiral of predisposed actors and pro-Life rhetoric was not, however, the sole effect of the historical narratives. The heritage they constructed contained enough evidence of their partisanship to be easily dismantled by those with different partisan identities. The reformers were successful, to their own satisfaction, in destroying the rhetorical force of this heritage for their own potential membership. Even though their members absorbed some fragments of the tale and even though they could not immediately provide a counter-heritage that would be forcefully persuasive for the public, they could effectively loose themselves from the authority of a dominant heritage they perceived as partial and non-inclusive.

The sum of these two forces—(1) a pro-Life heritage effective for pro-Lifers and some portion of the broad public, yet (2) partisan enough to de-legitimize it for potential reform activists and their allies—combined to insure that the argument would continue and escalate. Moreover, the heritage tale had consolidated disparate traditions only by appealing to an underlying, shared constitutive base of values. These values provided the grounds by which the narrative stalemate would be moved to a different level of argument.

NOTES

1. For discussions of these early activities see Lawrence Lader, *Abortion* (Indianapolis: Bobbs-Merrill, 1966), esp. p. 145, and Lawrence Lader, *Abortion II: Making the Revolution* (Boston: Beacon Press, 1973). Lader has a decided pro-reform slant, but as an activist/writer of the period he provides much useful information. See also Betty Sarvis and Hyman Rodman, *The Abortion Controversy* (New York: Columbia University Press, 1974), in which they provide a list of the dates and types of bills passed in state legislatures. See also Kristin Luker, *Abortion and the Politics of Motherhood* (Berkeley: University of California Press, 1984), chapter 5.

2. Because histories suggest that things "be done as they always have been done," they exert a profoundly conservative force upon public discourse. Nonetheless, the historical is probably pragmatically necessary, in some form, for human collectivities. Histories can be painted as more or less univocal and demanding or multiplicitous and enabling.

3. George Devereux, "A Typological Study of Abortion in 350 Primitive, Ancient and Pre-Industrial Societies," in *Therapeutic Abortion*, ed. Harold Rosen (New York: Julian Press, 1954), pp. 97–152, and idem., *A Study of Abortion in Primitive Societies*, rev. ed. (1955; New York: International Universities Press, 1976).

4. John T. Noonan, Jr., "An Almost Absolute Value in History," in *The Morality of Abortion*, ed. John T. Noonan, Jr. (Cambridge: Harvard University Press, 1970). Noonan weaves portions of this history into his other works: *Contraception* (Cambridge: Harvard University Press, 1966) and *A Private Choice: Abortion in America in the Seventies* (New York: Free Press, 1979).

5. Noonan himself has presented this history in public lectures around the nation—e.g., University of Iowa Law School, 7 February 1982; Basile Uddo, public lectures at Tulane University and Loyola University, February 1985 and 21 March 1985; John Willke, public speech, University of Illinois, Urbana, 4 February 1986. Harrison also notes its "widespread use in scholarly literature." Beverly Wildung Harrison, *Our Right to Choose: Toward a New Ethic of Abortion* (Boston: Beacon Press, 1983), p. 290, note 9. She also notes strong similarities in the other major historical works. See, for example, John Connery, *Abortion: The Development of the Roman Catholic Perspective* (Chicago: Loyola University Press, 1977); Roger John Huser, *The Crime of Abortion in Canon Law* (Washington, D.C.: Catholic University of America Press, 1980).

6. Harrison provides historical grounds, in addition to these discursive ones, for dismissing Noonan's history. They are predicated both on historical criteria and on recognition of feminist claims against the dominant historical practice.

7. The work of Jürgen Habermas prescribing the "ideal speech situation" seems to me to reflect a pragmatic critique pointing to the way in which American aspirations toward the maxim "all persons are created equal" might be operationalized. Both of these sources provide foundations for this test of legitimacy. See Jürgen Habermas, *Communication and the Evolution of Society*, trans. Thomas McCarthy (Boston: Beacon Press, 1976).

8. Harrison emphasizes that this was also an extremely limited and partial rendition of the Catholic heritage itself, with its own anti-feminine bias at root. She argues that abortion was only rarely discussed in the tradition, and when it was proscribed, it was prohibited on grounds that non-procreative sex was itself murder, rather than as a specific response to fetal life.

9. The description of history as combining theme and event is common to historians at several points in the political spectrum. Compare Savoie Lottinville, *The Rhetoric of History* (Norman: University of Oklahoma Press, 1976), esp. pp. 4, 43, 51, and Hayden White, "The Value of Narrativity in the Representation of Reality," in *On Narrative*, ed. W. J. T. Mitchell (Chicago: University of Chicago Press, 1980). A middle perspective is presented by Paul Ricoeur, *The Reality of the Historical Past* (Milwaukee: Marquette University Press, 1984).

10. Ronald Reagan, *Abortion and the Conscience of the Nation* (Nashville: Thomas Nelson, 1984), pp. 9–10.

11. For a discussion of the competing interpretations of Lincoln's motivations, see D. E. Fehrenbacher, *The Changing Image of Lincoln in American Historiography* (Oxford: Clarendon Press, 1968), esp. p. 22.

12. Reagan.

13. See chapter 2, note 1. In depicting legal abortion many media charts

and even scholarly charts tend to begin with 1973 (see, e.g., issues of *Family Planning Perspectives*). Feminists also accepted *Roe* v. *Wade* as a lone event that marked a radical break from previous American practices and values. They began their charts and graphs of "legal abortion" in 1973 or referred to that as the time when "abortion was made legal."

14. For example, Jack Starr, *Look*, 11 July 1967, pp. 67–69, or idem., *Look*, 19 October 1965, pp. 158ff.

15. Catholic responses were strong—e.g., *America*, 25 February 1967, p. 273, or Richard John Neuhaus, "The Dangerous Assumption," *Commonweal*, 30 June 1967, p. 409.

16. These replies normally charged that Catholics were inconsistent in their defense of life—e.g., Lester Kinsolving, "What about Therapeutic Abortion?" *Christian Century*, 13 May 1964, pp. 632–35.

17. Devereux.

18. Kinsolving.

19. Lader, *Abortion*.

20. These histories are still incomplete, but see Harrison, Luker, and Rosalind Pollack Petchesky, *Abortion and Woman's Choice: The State, Sexuality, and Reproductive Freedom* (Boston: Longman/Northeastern University Press, 1984).

21. For an examination of the social class and conditions of the activists, see Luker.

CHAPTER FOUR

Life, Equality, and Choice
Rhetoric and Values
—— 1965-72 ——

The story of illegal abortion and the tale of American heritage, both narrated in the early part of the contemporary abortion controversy, were emotionally compelling. They generated concern and disagreement about the practice of abortion in the nation. The narratives, however, provided an incomplete rhetoric. Since America's public vocabulary is largely constituted through *myths, it can be powerfully stirred by stories, but the national life cannot be "re-Constituted" solely through a change in narratives.[1] In order to present a demand for social action in legal or constitutional terms, narratives must be fitted to the broad network of *constitutive public values called "ideographs." If the political right of women to "control their own bodies" was to be recognized, giving them "equality" with men, then the key terms of the nation's Constitution would have to be re-deployed. Between 1965 and 1972 a contest over this value framework was played out, centering on three different ideographs—Life, Equality, and Choice.

The Defense against Change

Throughout the abortion controversy, the major constitutive value grounding the anti-abortion position was Life.[2] Although the term itself was constant, an examination of the development of its usages indicates that, in order to enhance its persuasiveness, it was applied in an increasingly precise sense as the controversy developed.

In the early sixties the argument about Life had been presented as though it were an undisputed statement of fact. The pro-Life advocates apparently assumed that the public shared the belief that a fetus was a human being and that aborting it was murder, for they usually made the claim without producing any support for it. They also assumed that preservation of life was of such preeminence that it automatically preempted conflicting values and interests. Hence, when faced with the emotionally powerful tale of illegal abortion, the pro-Life rhetors responded that the alternatives to illegal abortion were adoption, charity, and chastity. Rather than repudiating the existing value sets, such suggestions produced alternative solutions consistent with the existing *ideology.

These advocates were soon shocked to find that such statements and beliefs were inadequate to preserve and protect the values and practices that had previously reigned. By the late sixties, many states were enacting *reforms* in abortion laws. In 1967 Colorado, North Carolina, and California all modified their statutes more or less after the limited reforms suggested in the American Law Institute's Model Code. In the same year the Clergy Consultation Service was formed— a major event with both practical and symbolic effects. This group overcame harassment and fear of prosecution to develop a nationwide network of abortion counseling and referral services. The agency did more than provide relatively safe abortions to a few thousand women; it also had a significant impact in modifying the symbolic morality of abortion. When clergy of several denominations became actively involved in finding safe abortions for women, it became tremendously more difficult to frame abortion as an immoral act.

Although the pro-reform group suffered some failures in this period (in 1969 a major reform bill was defeated in New York), most of their efforts brought continuing success. In 1969 the California Supreme Court overturned that state's previous, restrictive law on grounds that it was unconstitutionally vague, and Washington D.C.'s law was overturned by Judge Gesell on even more comprehensive grounds. Additionally, Kansas, Delaware, Arkansas, New Mexico, and Oregon were added to the reform state roster.[3]

In response to these reforms, the pro-Life forces hurried to expand their argument. The character of their response was dictated by the nature of the losses they were experiencing. At this point, central values of "motherhood" and "family" were *not* being directly attacked, weakened, or replaced. The *ALI model and most of the laws being enacted did not recognize the reproductive freedom of women; the laws allowed abortion only by approval of a committee and only for reasons that did not challenge the myth of idealized *motherhood— rape, incest, fetal deformity, health of the pregnant woman. Consequently, the pro-Life rhetors did not need to respond by defending the value of procreation and the sanctity of motherhood—the reasons they had historically advanced against abortion throughout Western history.[4] Instead, they sought a continued ban on *all* abortions, by emphasizing that the humanity and Right to Life of the fetus was paramount in all cases.[5] From the late sixties onward, the major rhetorical effort of the pro-Life movement was therefore expended in constructing and amplifying the verbal linkages between the terms *fetus* and *Life*.

The concrete term *fetus* and the abstract value of Life were woven together primarily through a frequent recitation of the claim that the authority of "science" had discovered that the fetus was a human being from the time of conception. "Science," "biology," and "genetics" were repeatedly quoted, as when Brendon Brown claimed that "according to the new science of molecular biology, this [zygote] is a human being with all the gene structure of the fully grown."[6]

The references to the authority of science were supported by widespread use of graphic material proofs—pictures of aborted fetuses, often sickeningly mangled. The consensus seems to be that in Michigan a major change in public opinion was eventually brought about by these visual materials, which portrayed the fetus not as a "blob of tissue" but, in the later stages of gestation, as a "baby."[7] Thousands of picture packets were distributed, and television ads as well as billboards focused on the human-like features of the physical appearance of the fetus. Most Americans had had no idea what a fetus looked like at any stage of development. Once they saw the late-stage fetus, it was more plausible to characterize the fetus as a human person and much more difficult to dismiss the relevance of Life (the image of the fetus is more fully discussed in the next chapter). Thus, visual display and supporting scientific argument worked together to characterize the fetus as a human being.

The authenticity of the defense of Life by these groups has been challenged by feminist scholars and pro-Choice activists. They argue that, historically, Western civilization, including Christian theology, has enunciated little explicit concern with protecting fetal life. Additionally, they point out that many powerful supporters of the pro-Life vocabulary do not consistently support the Right to Life in issues such as the death penalty. Hence, the feminists suggest, the pro-Life movement's defense of the term is ungenuine.[8]

This attack is imprecise and inadequate because it reflects an incomplete understanding of this abstract but important term. Life is indeed an important constituting value for this nation. Moreover, the term *Life* is *genuinely* defended by the pro-Life movement. However, there is a fissure between the liberal formulation of the rhetoric of the *Right* to Life and the conservative pro-natalism which is the underlying motive for defending *Life*.

In defending the sanctity of life, pro-Life rhetors are centrally motivated by pro-natalism. In the past, this support of *maximal human reproduction was accomplished by the strict linkage of women's sexuality to procreation. In the sixties that link no longer worked: although motherhood was still a strong positive value in the culture, non-procreative sexuality was no longer as strongly negative for women. Therefore, the advocates of maximal procreation had to defend an increase in the number of *lives* more directly.[9] They did so initially by promoting the "sanctity of human *life*." However, the dominant public vocabulary at the time made the religious, conservative focus on sacredness and sheer quantity of life suspect or even illegitimate and therefore not adequately persuasive. The pro-Life rhetors consequently modified their favored terms to adapt to the process of public persuasion. "Sanctity of human *life*," rooted in a conservative concern for pro-natalism, was translated into the liberal individual discourse of a basic human right—the Right to Life.

In spite of the adoption of the liberal formulation, the pro-Life movement's basic pro-natalist purpose for promoting the rhetoric has been clearly articulated, especially by the most conservative of the pro-Life politicians. On national television, for example, Republican presidential hopeful Pat Robertson replied to a question about the abortion issue with the following rationale:

> We've got a true genetic problem in these United States of a magnitude beyond what we can conceive of—Pete mentioned it—the fact that by the year 2020 we're going to be running out of workers. There won't be enough to support the retirees. And, as a matter of fact, by the year 2000 we will have aborted 40 million children in this country. Their work product by the year 2020 will amount to 1.4 trillion dollars; the taxes from them would amount to 350 billion; and they could insure the fiscal stability of the social security system, which is going to be near bankrupt by the year 2015. We've got to do something about it. And of course I personally favor a paramount human life amendment, but I've said something else: as president I would guarantee a veto of any appropriations measure which included one dime of funding for planned parenthood.[10]

As Robertson's statement—and similar arguments advanced by others—makes clear, the constitutive value Life, as used by the pro-Life movement, most fundamentally prefers the conservative cause of "pro-natalism," not the liberal-individual concern with "rights." The promotion of Life by these rhetors is therefore genuine, even if the concern with individual Rights to Life is not.

This complex relationship between the argument, the rhetors, and the persuasive moves they adopted had a similarly complex impact on the public process of social change. At the persuasive level, it greatly augmented the attractiveness of the pro-Life argument for the general public. Simultaneously, it exacerbated the tensions between the pro-Life and pro-Choice advocates. The pro-Choice advocates were frustrated by the feeling that the pro-Life movement was lying and "duping" the public in order to profit themselves at the costs of women. At the same time, the rhetoric gave the pro-Life movement grounds for even greater self-righteousness. Focusing on the fetus allowed them to sidestep the possibility that, in asking women to sacrifice themselves for reproduction, they were asking women, directly and unfairly, to serve the society more than men did.

At the argumentative level, this liberal framing of the issue moved the contest away from the explicit competition of interests between the underlying power groups involved—*wage-laboring women vs. Christian capitalist males. Instead, the public argument became focused on the contest of rights between women and fetuses. In the long term, this new focus had a major impact because it demanded a different set of refuting arguments from the pro-Choice movement (an argument against fetal rights, which was not widely addressed for many years). In the short term, the new focus on the rights of the individual demanded and generated a new type of argument by the pro-reform opposition.

Equality

The pro-Life argument rested the case against abortion on the constitutional Right to Life of an individual fetus. The movement to this ideographic level of argument necessitated a response from the reform group on an equally fundamental level. They could have denied the linkage of fetus and Life. As a rule, however, this was not their primary reply. Instead, to counter the weight of these claims and to resolve the contradictions generated within their own narrative, they developed their own ideographic argument.

In this period the right of all citizens to Equality, frequently articulated as opposition to "discrimination," formed the anchor for the claim to a right to abortion. The appropriateness of Equality arose from the unique way in which it "explained" the contradictions in the tale of illegal abortion. Although the question of whether civil rights really were advancing in the sixties is controversial, it is obvious that Equality was becoming more salient at this time. Many people, whether they approved of desegregation or busing or other concrete changes, still held that people should be treated "equally."[11] This public emphasis on Equality had a stunning impact on the abortion issue. As "discrimination" became a salient negative form of the ideograph, the inconsistencies in the tale of illegal abortion were instantly explained.

Did the story of illegal abortion contradict itself, indicating that sometimes women received safe illegal abortions and other times they did not? Socioeconomic disparity—an unjustified "discrimination"— explained why: different classes of women received different kinds of abortions. Were abortionists depicted sometimes as congenial family doctors, other times as dangerous "mechanics"? Again, socioeconomic disparity—unjustifiable "discrimination"—explained why. Reform advocates argued that the existing laws discriminated against the poor, who were often racial minorities. Because abortion was illegal, poor women were forced to risk their lives in dangerous abortions, while rich women could circumvent the law to get safe abortions anyway. A legal system that caused one group of women to risk their lives because they lacked money violated the belief in Justice.[12] Thus, Equality provided a socially viable warrant for the elimination of existing abortion laws on grounds of existing public commitments (to Justice). This grounding in constitutive values had previously been lacking.

The claim to Equality had another important basis. In the sixties various feminist groups were active in the abortion movement. Their argument—that women should have a right to control their own bodies—was not widely reported in the public press.[13] By employing the term *Equality* as central to the meanings surrounding abortion, the reform rhetors created a way for the feminist discourse to be introduced (i.e., newly understood) in the public vocabulary. Equality could be described as balancing the Property rights of the individual woman over her own body and the universal Justice served by society's interest in the fetus, or the "just rights" due to an "unborn child." Gradually, from this point, portions of the feminist discourse, although rarely identified as such, began to be articulated in the public space.

The shift from a narratively based argument (a story) to an ideographic argument based on Equality had one other radical consequence: it turned the *desire* for an end to illegal abortions into a constitutional *demand* for the repeal of all abortion laws. A change of policy goals was necessarily tied to a change in argument. *ALI-type reform laws had been reasonable when the justification for changes in abortion law relied primarily on poignant stories of pregnant women who had been raped, were mentally unstable, or were in poor health. When the primary justification changed from these narrative-based arguments to the constitutional value of Equality, mere reform of laws to permit abortions in "hard cases" was logically inadequate. Such reform would not eliminate discrimination. The resultant demand for virtually complete repeal of abortion laws represented the major feature of the argumentation in the closing years of the decade, and it brought about temporary success in the legislatures. At the turn of the decade Alaska, Hawaii, and New York adopted virtual repeal laws. Soon over 200,000 abortions were performed in New York in a single year, as women came from all over the country to seek "safe and legal" abortions.[14]

The Challenge to Equality, 1971–72

As the sixties neared their end, legal abortion was apparently a new social practice gaining increasing support and instantiation in the laws and funding mechanisms of the society. The appearance of momentum or inevitable progress was misleading, however. The contest had only begun. As the argument entered the seventies, the shift from the ideologically minor argument for reform laws to the major demand for Equality and repeal laws brought vigor to the anti-abortion reaction.

A massive campaign to revoke the still-young "repeal" bill passed both the house and senate in New York. Only a veto from Governor Nelson Rockefeller stalled a return to criminal abortion. The reactionary trend also included the massive defeats of referenda on proposed repeal laws in Michigan and North Dakota; Connecticut responded to judicial censure of its restrictive abortion statute by rewording and reinstituting another restrictive statute; and the Pennsylvania legislature rejected reform or repeal.[15]

Even the courts participated in this counter-tide. In 1971 the Supreme Court overturned the Gesell ruling—the decision from the federal court in Washington, D.C., that had held most restrictive abortion statutes to be unconstitutionally vague. The High Court concluded that a physician would know reasonably well when a woman's life or health was endangered by pregnancy, and therefore the statutes were not vague.[16]

Several reasons account for this apparently radical and rapid change in public mood. First, the anti-abortion forces had become well financed and organized, and their support had begun to extend beyond the Catholic church to include other powerful religious groups.[17] Additionally, pro-reform forces seemed to have been quiescent—either because they were focusing their efforts on the courts or because they were content with the previous successes that allowed most middle-class women to travel to New York for a legal abortion.[18] All of these "causes" were reflected in and summed up by the nature of the discourse at the time, and its limitations.

The regulative term Equality had served to promote abortion from an emotional regret lacking any legitimate stake in the legal realm to a contest of "rights." That upped the ante. Concomitantly, however, because the argument was based merely on a *regulative ideograph, it could negotiate only between existing power interests, representing the new interests only indirectly. This limitation became visible in the dominant group's responses to the rhetoric of discrimination.

One of the most frequent responses to the claim that abortion laws should be eliminated because they "discriminated" was to deny the force of the regulator, Equality. Pro-Life advocates indicated that if the laws "discriminated" they did so not by any *legal* feature, and hence legal Justice was preserved. That is, they suggested that the *law* did not allow rich women abortions. If some groups were able to violate the law because of their resources, that was no concern of the law itself. In one instance of such a response, Mary Fisk answered the discrimination issue in a letter to *America*, asking, "When do we base our moral judgments on the economic convenience of an issue?"[19] R. M. Byrn similarly argued that we cannot "make the vices and evasions of some of the rich the norm for our public policy."[20] Essentially, the fact that discrimination in abortion arose from Property rights granted by the law made the law impotent in attempts to redress the discrimination. Indeed, any other premise would have invalidated a great many laws, perhaps even the basis of the legal structure, as a balance of Justice and Property itself.

Some advocates took this claim even further by reversing the term. They argued that the law favored the poor: it kept them from being "immoral." Too bad the rich could not be similarly controlled, they lamented. Rep. Henry Hyde, for example, in applying this claim to his proposed ban on funding, said that "it is the unborn children of the middle class and the rich who are discriminated against by this legislation because we have no way to limit their abortions."[21]

Thus, those who had access to Property, if it were legally attained, were accepted as being outside the control of law and morality. In other words, the *dominant elites could not be restrained by the reigning ideology, for it was, at base, their voice. These responses reveal the weakness of a regulative term such as *discrimination* as an argumentative ground of a new coalition of interests. Because a regulative term mediates between end terms, any end term has more force than does any mediator. The end terms, of course, serve entrenched interests.

The same fact was revealed in another refuting argument used by Pro-Life rhetors. Advocates often responded to the appeal for allowing abortion in "hard cases" with analyses denying the legitimacy of the various justifications offered by the ALI-type laws for abortions— rape, deformity, and economics.[22] Pro-Life persuaders argued that in a rape case two wrongs did not make a right. The evil of a rape could only be compounded by the taking of an innocent fetal life. They insisted that deformity was not an adequate cause for the sentence of death and that monetary concerns also were inadequate to justify murder by abortion. Each of these arguments, variegated as they might seem, depended on the original ideograph Life. The fetus was equivalent to a full human person. Its *substantive* "rights" could not be traded for a *regulative* norm. In the end, given the Constitution of the United States and its current interpretation, the force of Equality was inadequate to overcome either the Property rights of the state or the claimed just rights of the fetus (as a full human being).

The Right to Choice

Equality thus gained a hearing for abortion *as a right*, but the regulative term was ultimately unable to defend that right against the rights of instantiated groups. Moreover, the uses to which the constitutive value were put were fundamentally indirect in their articulation of women's needs or desires. After all, women did not desire simply to be equal with each other. If that were the case, then Hyde's reversal would have been fully adequate as a response to the discrimination issue: an *effective* abortion ban would have been "non-discriminatory." Instead, the tale of illegal abortion demanded more fundamentally grounded values; Equality and Freedom were to be combined in a new demand for a Right to Choice.

Even in the earliest stages of the controversy, for some activists the rights, freedoms, or choices of women were at issue. Although these voices did not become the most audible ones until the seventies, a public rhetoric gradually developed which framed the controversy as a "woman's Choice." Recent feminist scholarship has been highly wary of the term *Choice*, on the ground that it can be interpreted as a liberal rhetoric permitting only political rights, not recognizing economic realities.[23] Such a version of Choice would fail to recognize that most women do not have the economic freedom to make *real* choices, and so the larger concept of Reproductive Freedom is suggested for the feminist demand. While I have no reason to prefer or oppose either label, I suggest that this argument fundamentally misunderstands both the character of ideographs and public discourse, and the development of the term *Choice*.

On the first count, in a liberal political system any constitutive value can be interpreted in a liberal manner as a political, not economic, right. Reproductive Freedom can be interpreted like our "freedom to travel"—allowed, but not supported. The term *choice* is no more open to such processes of interpretation than any other. It is precisely the effort to control the meanings of ideographs that form long-term power struggles. Various battles in the courts and Congress have played a major role in shaping these meanings (see chapter 6). However, these negotiations do not deny the potency of the novel ability to gain articulation of women's interests in the public realm that occurred with the rise of Choice.[24]

On the second count the term *Choice*, as a contestant for ideographic representation of women's needs in the polity, is particularly fascinating because it was so concretely indigenous to women's experiences. "Choice" was a direct articulation of material demands faced by women in two ways. In the first place, it arose rather directly from the early discourse by and about women on abortion. In the early narratives about illegal abortion, the stories told that women faced these horrific conditions precisely because they felt that they had "no choice." Throughout the controversy the term was frequently employed by real women, expressing their own personal needs. The demand for *Freedom* to Choose was a key component of the development of liberation for these women. The ordinary women who employed this language were expressing—simultaneously discovering and elaborating—those things which were fundamentally necessary for them to experience equality with men and freedom as human agents (whatever contemporary academic feminists think of those goals).[25] The promotion of "choice" to ideographic status thus represents a uniquely direct and powerful expression by women of their own political needs in a particular time and place (for evidence, see chapter 9). Those needs of these women had evolved from real and pressing changes in the public vocabulary describing women's *biological choices* and in the range of their *occupational choices* which had developed following World War II.

Biological Choice: The Birth Control Pill

The idea that the birth control pill increased women's biological control of their fertility and thereby increased their "choices" seems obvious enough. The claim, however, has become ideologically controversial. The uniqueness of the pill has been denied by many feminists who do not like the fact that (1) the pill is controlled by the male medical establishment, (2) it entails risks to women who use it, and (3) it threatens to turn a complex social change into a merely technical matter.[26] If we strip away such ideologically based objections, however, the arguments advanced to deny the *importance* of the pill seem misdirected.

A primary objection to the pill's importance in providing "new choices" is that reasonably reliable birth control alternatives (the diaphragm and condom) were available long before the pill. The pill's detractors suggest that the need for contraceptives (to allow the continuance of careers) generated the technology, rather than the technology generating the desire for Freedom.

Perhaps, however, the rhetorical features of the birth control pill, rather than its technical merits, are the causal agents. Two different rhetorical features indicate the real significance of the birth control pill. First, the pill is more effective than the condom and diaphragm. While, indeed, the earlier methods were "highly effective," the pill *claimed* to offer more. Any reasonably effective birth control device allows one to reduce the number of children one will bear and usually to space them out. Nonetheless, such measures do not promise to allow one nearly certain choice over when one would have the exact number of children one wanted. The birth control pill, with its marketed effectiveness rate of 99 percent plus, produced the image of complete control (via publicly acceptable means). No longer were one's children to be spaced according to when birth control measures failed. Instead, fertility could be turned on and off at will. Although in practice the birth control pill did not deliver that level of effectiveness, the *promise* of that kind of control was enough to revolutionize the expectations regarding female fertility.[27]

Of even greater importance, however, was the manner in which the pill must be used. The birth control pill shifts the locus of control completely to the woman. The condom and withdrawal are clearly male-controlled contraception. Even the use of a diaphragm requires varying degrees of male cooperation, and, as Andrea Dworkin and Catherine Mackinnon have revealed, male control of the sex act is not confined to those instances we have classically defined as rape.[28] Only if a woman wore a diaphragm at all times would she be protected from impregnation against her will, and that option was not medically viable. Abortion, of course, might have offered the sense of complete control at an historically earlier point, but abortion was not initially *publicly* acceptable for a variety of substantial reasons. It was perceived not as a preventative but as an after-the-fact treatment. It also entailed immediate and dramatic physical risk to women.[29] Therefore, abortion did not, initially, provide a clean and forceful model of biological choice. By separating contraception and sex in time, the birth control pill provided a round-the-clock preventative. Individual women thus wrested virtually complete control of procreation, not only from biology but, perhaps more importantly, from individual men. In a crucial way, therefore, the pill made the social demand for control or "choice" *appear* as a biological and physical possibility. Only when the dominant public vocabulary recognized that women had biological choices could they persuasively demand social Choice.

Occupational Choices: Working Women

In addition to wresting procreative choices from biology and from individual men, the rise of women's Choice proceeded from changes in the social images of women's occupational choices. The Gallup polls extending back before World War II indicate that the application of political Equality to women in concrete ways has a long history in America. The claim that women should receive equal pay for equal work was supported by 78 percent of the people as early as 1942 and by 87 percent in 1954.[30] Other ideals of equality also grew between the forties and the eighties. In 1949 the number of people who said they would vote for a qualified woman as president (52 percent) nearly equalled those who would not , while the same year 54 percent approved of a specific woman becoming a minister.[31]

Although Americans may, long ago, have begun to apply Equality in a way that included women, the percentages of Americans supporting such Equality certainly increased steadily across time. In 1937, for example, only 34 percent of those polled claimed they would vote for a qualified female for president. In 1945 the position remained a minority one, but a plurality agreed to a woman on the Supreme Court and in other "responsible" government posts. By 1955, 52 percent indicated they would vote for a woman for president, and by 1967 this had increased to 54 percent. By 1971, 66 percent indicated they could support a woman as president. Overall, the trend changed slowly between 1937 and 1967. Between 1967 and 1971, as the previous attitudes were consolidated, the trend accelerated more rapidly.[32]

The general inclusion of women in the constitutive value Equality was thus virtually completed by the early seventies. Change on this ideographic level was accompanied by one important change in the concrete images or *character-types of women—the declining importance of women's role as "mothers" and an increasing importance in their role as waged workers. In 1936 only 18 percent of those polled thought that it was acceptable for a married woman to work if her husband could support her. Gradually that opinion changed, so that by 1976 a substantial majority—68 percent—approved of such married women working.[33] This trend matched a steady increase in the number of women, including married women, working, which reached a high in 1977, when three-quarters of all married women had worked.[34]

Complementing this change was an altered perception of the ideal family size. Even before the "baby boom" period after World War II, 34 percent of the populace had wanted a family of four or more children. That figure grew to 49 percent in 1945.[35] A slight reduction occurred after that, but the largest reduction did not happen until the period from 1968 to 1971. In 1968, 41 percent of the respondents still wanted four or more children. By 1971 that percentage plummeted to 19 percent. Those who thought two children ideal reached 49 percent by 1978.[36]

The period between 1940 and 1980 therefore brought major changes in the expectations about women's social roles as "mothers." Because of smaller families and other changes in household duties, the job of mothering was not to be a full-time, lifetime occupation for most women. Because of an increasing willingness to allow married women to work and an increasing acceptance of women as potential workers, even in areas such as high government posts, women could use this "other time" as waged workers. Changes in public attitudes thus brought women to the seventies ready for and expectant of new occupational *choices*.

These conditions crystallized the issue of abortion and produced the constitutive rhetoric of Right to Choice. Abortion represented the final and most complete control over childbearing and the consequent availability of "choices" other than mothering, but because it was employed after pregnancy, it was socially more complex than other means of control. That complexity made it the best grounds for defenders of the status quo, and they therefore made it the issue that carried the central public argument about maternity choices.

The rhetoric of denouncing outside control of a woman's fertility was sounded in many different keys. Some advocates of Choice asserted forcefully that women had literally been an "oppressed" group and that "compulsory motherhood is a form of slavery."[37] Gloria Steinem argued that "women's bodies are society's most basic means of production. We produce the workers and the soldiers of the patriarchy."[38] Other attacks were less assertive, noting simply that "there are women who after two children are begging 'please let me live a life now.'"[39] Contrary to rightist and anti-feminist propaganda the arguments did not usually condemn pregnancy and motherhood. By implication, however, they did challenge its preeminence in the hierarchy of values. Motherhood was no longer assumed to be more important than any other concern or activity of women, and thus it became reasonable to suggest that "some women can't afford to raise another child, some don't want to bear a child out of wedlock and some don't want to interrupt their careers."[40] It became possible, further, to note that pregnancy was not all bliss, that it entailed "great physical and emotional stress."[41] This re-designation of motherhood as one among many choices may have appeared to "lower" the status of motherhood, but only for those who viewed the other choices negatively.

Indirectly, then, the demand for Choice presented major challenges to the dominant ideology and interests. It suggested that women be treated as free agents, capable of making "choices" about their fertility, their work lives, and their families. These choices came, primarily, from the men who had held the choices and the exclusive rights to jobs. Consequently, by publicly articulating the material demands of women as a claim for rights, the Right to Choice suggested a profound reconstitution of the American people and their rights and powers. Women were no longer to be subject to biological predispositions or male whim; they were to be free agents with their own Liberties. The demand was a radical one, and the competition of interests set in motion a major ideological retaliation that did not blossom until the eighties.

Summary

During the late sixties and early seventies the argument about abortion began to involve the fundamental value commitments of the society. The pro-Life advocates broadened and strengthened their demand for Life, narrowing it to an individualist focus on the Right to Life of the fetus. The pro-reform movement, which had expressed the story of women's trials by illegal abortion, became a "pro-Choice" movement, after the demand for Equality (among women) evolved into a demand for a Right to Choice (taken from men), directly articulating the experience of many women who, with greater biological, social, and personal freedoms, had begun to see room in their lives for "choices" in addition to motherhood.

At this point, the fundamental logical and argumentative grounds of the controversy were established. The controversy would move in two directions. One path would be the legal adjudication of the competing claims to rights (chapter 6). The other path was the crucial development of a discourse much less abstract than ideographs in the popular arena. In the broad popular realm concrete *images would be the most potent factors in determining the ultimate public vocabulary adopted for the practice of abortion. In this contest, the images indigenous to a rhetoric of Choice were far overmatched by the depictions of the fetus as a human being, ever more vividly developed over the next two decades.

NOTES

1. I am in no way trying to deny the importance of narrative forms in human societies. This importance has been widely and richly documented (see chapter 1, note 32). I nonetheless maintain that human beings are complex enough to be simultaneously wrapped in stories and also controlled and influenced profoundly by other discursive forms, including ideographs, maxims (or "principles"), and characterizations. Consequently, to take narrative as the entire paradigm for human communication is to make a reductionist error. I would therefore wish to add dimensions to Walter Fisher's account of public moral argument, *Human Communication as Narration: Toward a Philosophy of Reason, Value, and Action* (Columbia: University of South Carolina Press, 1987).

2. I agree with John Lucaites that it is useful to set ideographs off with < >. In technical writing addressed primarily to others in my field I use these markings. However, because my audience here includes those from other fields who find such technical precision aesthetically displeasing, I have chosen instead to denote ideographs by capitalizing them. This follows the tradition of the printed oratory of the American colonial and post-Revolutionary period. See John Louis Lucaites, "Flexibility and Consistency in Eighteenth-Century Anglo-Whiggism: A Case Study of the Rhetorical Dimensions of Legitimacy" (Ph.D. diss., University of Iowa, 1984), p. 48, note 71.

3. All of these events are covered in the popular press of the period. A quick summary is available in Lawrence Lader, *Abortion* (Indianapolis: Bobbs-Merrill, 1966), p. 145, and idem., *Abortion II: Making the Revolution* (Boston: Beacon Press, 1973), pp. 109–15. A list of the legislation can be found in Betty Sarvis and Hyman Rodman, *The Abortion Controversy* (New York: Columbia University Press, 1974).

4. Beverly Wildung Harrison emphasizes this as the primary reason employed against abortion in the Catholic church through history. See *Our Right to Choose* (Boston: Beacon Press, 1983). It was also visible in the struggle in the eighteenth and nineteenth centuries, both in a direct form and in nativist fears about the balance of procreation in ethnic groups; see James C. Mohr, *Abortion in America* (New York: Oxford Union Press, 1978).

5. I believe the feminist account, which attributes the entire contemporary controversy to desires for continued male control of procreation, is unable to account for this obstinacy. With the ALI-style laws men had found a way to maintain their control of abortion, while still allowing some "exceptions." I believe that at this point one has to take seriously the more universal concern with Life claimed by the Catholic church and others. In other words, we cannot simply dismiss the concern with the fetus as inauthentic. I argue below, however, that this concern with the fetus comes not from a standard individualist defense of rights but from a theocratic desire to increase the number of lives.

6. Brendon F. Brown, "Criminal Abortion," *Vital Speeches*, 1 July 1970, pp. 549–53; Harold B. Kuhn, "Now Generation Churchmen and the Unborn," *Christianity Today*, 29 January 1971, p. 38; Virgil C. Blum, "Public Policy Making: Why the Churches Strike Out," *America*, 6 March 1971, pp. 224–28; Rev. James Fisher, letter to the editor, *National Review*, 9 February 1971, p. 116.

7. Russel Kirk, "The Sudden Death of Feticide," *National Review*, 22 December 1972, p. 1407; "Twisted Logic: Propositions to Legalize Abortion," *Christianity Today*, 22 December 1972, pp. 24–25. The arguments of these conservatives are supported by the silence of the pro-Choice advocates on this loss. Especially note Lader's studied avoidance of the issue.

8. See Harrison and, by implication, Rosalind Pollack Petchesky, *Abortion and Women's Choice* (Boston: Northeastern University Press, 1984). Note also the attacks on the Catholics as being "inconsistent" in their defense of Life: Jean A. Miller, letter to the editor, *Commonweal*, 14 April 1972, pp. 131, 151; "Anti-Abortion Campaign," *Time*, 29 March 1971, p. 73. Most pro-Choice advocates indicate their denial of the authenticity of this argument by employing the "don't impose your morality on me" maxim and by omitting refutation of the argument.

9. Pro-Life rhetors continually inveigh against the "quality of life" ethic. They do not, to my knowledge, admit to holding the opposing "quantity of life" ethic, but it is an apt term. They base their argument on the quantitative biblical injunction to "go forth and multiply"; the rigorous proscriptions against birth control and non-procreative sexuality further communicate this ethic. These values are grounded in sectarian interests in propagation of one's own clan (in part, as opposed to others). In addition, the link to capitalism's need for ever-increasing numbers of producers and consumers to preserve and increase capitalist profits (cited by Lader, chapter 2) should not be discounted. The opposition between capitalism and feminism in their current configurations thus has an even more material base than has previously been recognized by feminist scholars (although it has been recognized by some feminist activists; see, e.g., Steinem, below).

10. My transcription from videotape of *The Firing Line*, broadcast 28 October 1987. See a similar argument advanced by John Willke, "A Matter of Life," public lecture at the University of Illinois, Urbana, 6 February 1987 (interestingly, Willke advances the argument, directing it to "those who might be interested," but attempts to distance himself from it, apparently sensing its problematic contents). It is ironic that the argument forced the pro-natalists (who are intrinsically theocratic) to adopt a liberal individualist ethic, while the Court system fell back upon the statist standard of "compelling state interest" to restrain the women from their individualism (see chapter 6).

11. Various Gallup polls indicate the salience of the term and the increasing openness toward Equality. A shift in attitudes relating to the desirability of black neighbors to whites, for example, can be traced in the period. From 1958 to 1963, the primary position changes on Equality occurred in the South. From 1963 to 1965, there were also changes of as much as 10 percent in the North. George H. Gallup, *Public Opinion: 1935–1971* (New York: Random House, 1972), pp. 1572–73, 1824, 1941. See also Milton Rokeach, "Change and Stability in American Value Systems, 1968–71," *Public Opinion Quarterly* 38, no. 2 (Summer 1973), 222–38.

12. Because of its role in the Anglo-American tradition, Equality was discursively suited to regulate this type of conflict. In Anglo-American history, Equality has generally, although not always or necessarily, served as a *regulative ideograph, balancing among other more *substantive ideographs. See Michael Calvin McGee, "An Essay on the Flip Side of Privacy," *Argument in Transition: Proceedings of the Third Summer Conference on Argumentation*, ed. David Zarefsky, Malcolm O. Sillars, and Jack Rhodes (Annandale, Va.: Speech Communication Association, 1983), pp. 105–15. While the Right to Life was explicitly mentioned in the Constitution's "Bill of Rights" (Fifth Amendment), Equality was not recognized as a basic human right until the Fourteenth Amendment passed in 1868. Even then, it guaranteed only "equal protection of the laws," not substantive Equality. Therefore, in the Constitution, and in the broad American tradition, Equality was a means to protect other substantive rights (specifically Life, Liberty, and Property). Equality or identity of interests and treatments has not generally been seen as an important end in itself. Indeed, in a discourse community that values "individuals," such identity is often vigorously denounced. However, Equality has been necessary to balance two other end values—Justice and Property rights. Absolute Justice would require exact identity of treatment—an absolute generalizability of all rights. The concept of unique, non-generalizable Property rights, however, inherently conflicts with such a concept. Equality of opportunity, or of political right, is cited to regulate the resulting disputes. The regulative term *Equality* was peculiarly appropriate as a mediator in the early abortion conflict because of its extraordinary salience and its fit with the contradictions in the tale of illegal abortion. Kenneth L. Karst, "Why Equality Matters," *Georgia Law Review* 17, no. 2 (Winter 1983), 245–89.

13. An example of the non-serious attention given to the feminist argument is available in John Bartlow Martin, *Saturday Evening Post*, 20 May 1961, pp. 19–21ff. Martin includes, in the same sentence, the statement that "no one

has proposed to repeal the abortion laws outright" and that feminists "assert the right of a woman to decide whether to continue a pregnancy." The poor coverage of the feminists represents a distinct ideological bias of the press in contrast to their frequent citation of reform physicians and anti-abortion church officials.

14. Lader, *Abortion II*, pp. 166–67.

15. See note 7 and Lawrence Lader, "Guide to Abortion Laws in the United States," *Redbook*, June 1971, pp. 51–58.

16. "Supreme Court and Abortion," *America*, 1 May 1971, p. 433; "Abortion Battle," *Newsweek*, 3 May 1971, p. 115.

17. There was still overwhelming Catholic participation, but there had been a conscious attempt to de-Catholicize the movement. See Fred C. Shapiro, "Right to Life Has a Message for New York State Legislators," *New York Times Magazine*, 20 August 1972, pp. 10–11. An interview with a Right-to-Life official set 1970 as the date of secularization (p. 34). By the eighties the support of the fundamentalist religions had clearly established the movement as religious, but non-denominational.

18. Lader, *Abortion II*, pp. 194–200. Jimmye Kimmey, executive director of the Association for the Study of Abortion, made this claim, cited in Lawrence Massett, "Abortion Legislation: A Fundamental Challenge," *Science News*, 17 January 1979, pp. 75; "Veto for Abortion, Maryland," *Newsweek*, 8 June 1979, pp. 51–52. Another way to describe the reversion is as a normal stage in a social change process in which two sides are roughly balanced. The side that organizes first enjoys a temporary advantage, but once the opposition responds, territory may be traded repeatedly.

19. Letter to the editor, *America*, 21 February 1976, p. 141.

20. R. M. Byrn, "Confronting Objections to an Anti-Abortion Amendment," *America*, 19 June 1976, p. 529.

21. Hyde was addressing the funding issue specifically. See "New Limits on Abortion," *Time*, 19 December 1977, p. 12.

22. "Abortion and the Law," *America*, 25 March 1961, p. 811; Robert M. Byrn, "The Future of America," *America*, 9 December 1967, p. 712; "Desperate Dilemma of Abortion," *Time*, 13 October 1967, pp. 32–33; Andre E. Hellegers, "Law and the Common Good," *Commonweal*, 30 June 1967, pp. 418ff.

23. For example, Petchesky, Harrison.

24. This conflict concretely exemplifies the tension between feminism and socialism. See Michelle Barrett, *Women's Oppression Today: Problems in Marxist Feminist Analysis* (1980; rpt. London: Verson, 1985).

25. It has been suggested to me that the term *reproductive freedom* was more original and central to the "women's movement." In part, this depends on who we define as constituting that movement. My focus here is on the voices in the public controversy. The term *reproductive freedom* was developed by activist and academic feminists, working largely outside the public arena, who, on greater theoretical reflection, noted two things. First, that the Right to Choose abortion was intimately tied in with other procreative rights. "Reproductive freedom" encompassed these other rights and did so in a way

less likely to make the more controversial issue of abortion the rhetorical focus of women's agenda. Second, that the women who first articulated the demand for abortion tended to be middle class and, hence, economically self-sufficient. The fact that these women were the first articulators of abortion rights (because of their greater access to the mechanisms of articulation in the social system) has tended to frame the issue as one of political rights rather than economics. These women had less need for the economic support so crucial to other women and therefore tended not to articulate this component of women's needs. We should be careful to separate, however, the stories and lives of "ordinary" women from the theoretical reflections of academics and the more intensely developed discourse worlds of activists. Active feminists will have a different "recollection" of what the path of the abortion controversy was like, because their recollections are shaped by discourse arenas other than the public space.

26. For example, James Reed, *From Private Vice to Public Virtue* (New York: Basic Books, 1978), pp. 99–100, 110, 120, and Linda Gordon, *Woman's Body, Women's Right* (New York: Grossman, 1976), pp. 39–45; Petchesky, p. 171.

27. Susan M. Scrimshaw, "Women and the Pill: From Panacea to Catalyst," *Family Planning Perspectives* 13, no. 6 (November/December 1981), 254–62.

28. Catharine A. MacKinnon, *Feminism Unmodified: Disclosures on Life and Law* (Cambridge, Mass.: Harvard University Press, 1987); Andrea Dworkin, *Right-Wing Women* (New York: Coward-McCann, 1983).

29. No definitive arguments can be made about the relative safety of abortion before the period of hygienic surgery. However, claims that abortion has always been safe seem to fly in the face of the apparent morbidity of illegal abortion in the mid-twentieth century. I believe that the claim that safe abortion techniques have always been available is relatively true if we consider the higher morbidity associated with childbearing in earlier periods, but not true in comparison to current medical standards. See Harrison, chapter 6.

30. Gallup, pp. 322, 1240. The claim for "equal pay for equal work" can be viewed either as a regulative ideal or as a substantive one. It does not promise the substance of pay or a job, but only that if those things are given, then equal pay should be provided. In a reasonably full-employment economy, that would mean a substantive payoff. The debate over "comparable worth" suggests that the term "for equal work" is in need of clarification for that substantive ideal to be achieved.

31. Gallup, pp. 861–62, 837.

32. Gallup, pp. 67, 548, 1315, 2189, 2319.

33. Gallup, p. 39; George H. Gallup, *Public Opinion 1972–1977* (Wilmington, Del.: Scholarly Resources, 1978), p. 702.

34. Rosalind Pollack Petchesky, "Antiabortion, Antifeminism, and the Rise of the New Right," *Feminist Studies* 7 (Summer 1981), 233–34.

35. Gallup, *1935–1971*, pp. 43, 524.

36. Gallup, *1935–1971*, pp. 2168–69; Gallup, *1978*, p. 268.

37. James W. Prescott and Douglas Wallace, "Abortion and the Right to Life," *Humanist*, July-August 1978, p. 24; Ellen Willis, "Abortion Backlash:

Women Lose," *Rolling Stone*, 3 November 1977, p. 65.

38. Gloria Steinem, "Update: Abortion Alert," *Ms.*, November 1977, p. 118.

39. Norma Rosen, "Between Guilt and Gratification: Abortion Doctors Reveal Their Feelings," *New York Times Magazine*, 17 April 1977, p. 71; Steinem, "Update," p. 188.

40. "They Made the Choice," *Newsweek*, 5 June 1978, p. 40.

41. Linda Birde Francke, quoted by Elaine Fein, "The Facts About Abortion," *Harper's Bazaar*, May 1980, p. 76; Willis, p. 66.

CHAPTER FIVE

Constructing Visions
of the Fetus and Freedom
Rhetoric and Image

The pictures—a baby-like fetus, a smiling fetus, a fetus that sucks its thumb. Butchered fetuses—bloody mounds of human tissue, hacked arms, mangled legs, crushed skulls. Without these compelling and brutal photographs the American abortion controversy probably would not continue. But the photographs have been widely disseminated throughout the country—passed through church pews, tucked under windshield wipers, flashed on screens in public meetings. Moreover, the photographs and films have gained such public presence precisely because the fetus has an important substantiality that can be photographed. The meaning constructed from those pictures and that substance was not, however, a simple matter of natural fact. The complex rhetorical tactics that generated a meaningful image of the fetus also generated complex social impacts.

The Power of the Pro-Life Images

The first task is to establish that these fetal pictures *are* persuasive. For some readers this may seem rather obvious—a "merely academic" argument—but scholars and activists alike have argued that these pictures are not convincing. Kristen Luker provides the most important dismissal of their impact, claiming that "our interviews show that with rare exceptions these presentations, including the slide shows, were persuasive only to people who had sought them out because they were already troubled or concerned about abortion."[1] There are several responses to this claim, based as it is on an overly simplistic model of public persuasion.

Consider first that Luker did a relatively small number of inter-

79

views (212). The fact that there *were* rare exceptions, even within this small sample, is important. Advertisers have learned that their ability to persuade only a small percentage of their audience can make them millions of dollars. Similarly, political contests are often won and lost over a percentage point or two. In mass persuasion, "rare" success in bringing about absolute change of opinion is the norm, but it is frequently sufficient.

More important, perhaps, Luker's interviews were of activists, the group most likely to be unaffected by such persuasion. Pro-choice advocates have a well-developed ideology to protect themselves from the force of these images. According to Luker's definition, pro-Life activists cannot be persuaded because they are "already 'primed'" for the message. The far more numerous uncommitted persons whom Luker did not interview are more likely to be swayed by potent images. Moreover, even the dismissal of the claim that pro-Life activists were persuaded is inappropriate. Although such persuasion does not change pro-Life advocates and supporters from a completely hostile to a supportive position, it does justify, integrate, and activate their beliefs. The images intensify commitment, motivate the believers to work for the cause, and give them reason to believe that they can persuade others. When pro-Life rhetors talk about why they believe as they do, the role of the photographs and films becomes quite clear. Without these pictures, pro-Life advocates would have only an abstract argument about the importance of chromosomes in determining human life or a religious argument about the "soul," and neither of those options could sustain the righteous fire of the public movement.

My own experience in attending many public presentations of these images confirms that the pictures *do* move some uncommitted members of audiences. Certainly, there is a fairly wide range of responses from viewers. Some young people just moan, "Oh, gross," and turn away from the images, shutting them out. Others question their authenticity. A few actively deconstruct the images, building a cognitive defense against them.

A substantial group of people, however, sit quietly, visibly stunned by what they have seen. In lobbies and coffeehouses they speak in subdued voices about what these images must mean. The impact muffles the certainty of those with pro-Choice leanings and increases the uncertainty of those who are ambivalent, making them even more concerned about the inadequacy of unilateral "pro-Choice" or "pro-Life" positions.

Images in Public Persuasion

Frequently, such pictures and the responses to them are dismissed as an unfair irrational duping, inappropriate to responsible public argument. However, that critique misinterprets the role of visual images in public argument. Images may either replace narratives or summarize narratives visually (the pro-Life images did the former, the pro-Choice images, the latter). Like narratives, visual images provide concrete enactments of abstract values and thereby allow a different kind of understanding of the meaning and impact of an ideographic claim about public life. They help "envision" the material impacts of abstract policy commitments. Images therefore provide a useful form of grounding for the acceptance of an argument. They, like any other form of argument, however, are subject to analysis of the accuracy of the claims they make.

Visual forms of persuasion present special problems of analysis. Visual images seduce our attention and demand our assent in a peculiar and gripping fashion. Many audiences are leery of verbal constructions, which only "represent" reality, but because we humans tend to trust our own senses, we take what we *see* to be true. Therefore, our trust in what we see gives visual images particular rhetorical potency.

More "sophisticated" audiences, of course, have learned that pictures regularly lie, that cameras and motion pictures systematically distort the material world in transferring it to the photograph or film. This allows a small space for the rhetorical. There is, however, a larger, more thoroughly concealed space for rhetoric in the presentation of images. It is in the translation of visual images into verbal meanings that the rhetoric of images operates most powerfully.

Because visual images are inexplicit (one picture is potentially a thousand *different* words), an image can function in an argument only if its meaning is actively focused. This focusing is accomplished through the classic means of "figures of speech"—rhetorical tropes (e.g., *metaphor, *synecdoche, and *hyperbole). As the ancient Greek rhetoricians recognized, the operation of these rhetorical tropes has a powerful poetic dimension that makes it difficult for audiences to decode carefully the arguments they are receiving.[2] The speed, aesthetic appeal, and audience participation necessary to the production and understanding of tropes grant skilled speakers a special power to enchant audiences into accepting a rhetor's visual argument uncritically. Because arguments based on images are completely dependent on tropes, they are open to the dual possibility of persuasive potency and argumentative inaccuracy.

Pro-Life rhetors made extensive figurative use of photographs to construct an image of "the fetus" that would authorize the legal protection of fetuses as human babies. In the early period of the controversy advocates brought pickled fetuses in jars to legislative hearings. In the middle period packets of photographs presented the image. In the later period the photographs were more widely disseminated in mass media and on billboards and joined by films, such as *The Silent Scream* and *Eclipse of Reason*, as well as by thousands of lapel pins sporting tiny feet.

The impact of these images has been twofold. On the one hand, the pictures were widely persuasive in the popular realm. They account, I believe, for the public fervor of the pro-Life activists, for the timidity of liberal Congressional representatives, and for the rarity of pro-Choice arguments directed at denying the Right to Life of a fetus. On the other hand, they were also argumentatively imprecise; they did not fully prove the claims of the pro-Life advocates. Consequently, the legal system, attuned to deductive argument, rejected their claims at the same time that the public force grew. This bifurcated impact of the pro-Life images can be established and explained by examining the operation of the basic tropes that translated these visual images into public arguments.

Metonymy

The persuasiveness of the pro-Life pictures, films, and pins arose first from a metonymic reduction. Metonymy is the figure of speech in which a technical, precise, or denotative name for some class of things is replaced by a different name that stresses a quality, attribute, or connotative image (e.g., instead of the "territory of the United States" one might refer to the "land under the striped flag of freedom"). In metonymic translations of visual images into verbal statements there is, of course, no precise name for the complex chaos of the visual image. Therefore, the process is necessarily one of reduction—the creation of a simple label or name for a whole entity from *visible* attributes or associations. In the abortion case the wide variety of beings that constitute developing unborn human life-forms—the blastocyst, embryo, fetus, viable baby—were reduced to a single entity through the creation of a single vision of the "unborn baby."

An examination of the available public images indicates that a unified image of the fetus as an "unborn baby" was constructed for public understanding primarily by widespread dissemination of pictures of a fetus in the third or late second trimester. In the pictures the fetus was largely independent of its placenta and umbilical cord. The photographs featured no blood or placental tissue to turn stomachs queasy, and they focused on head and feet, for reasons which will become more clear. This image of the fetus was projected through a relatively sparse collection of photographs (perhaps a half dozen or so were repeatedly reused). A beautiful picture of a nineteen-week fetus was the most widely disseminated version.[3] When pictures of younger fetuses appeared, they were either prominently labeled "baby," surrounded by older fetuses and by babies, or accompanied by text that attributed baby-like features to them (e.g., thumb-sucking, heartbeat, brain activity).

The metonymic reduction of the wide variety of developing human forms into a single entity—"the fetus as an unborn baby"—was a crucial rhetorical move. Instead of producing a clear, static image, multiple images of blastocyst/embryo/fetus at different stages would have emphasized development as a process. The pro-Life rhetors, however, wanted the American public to respond to the fetus as if it were one single distinct entity—a human baby; therefore, they worked to generate a *single* image of the fetus.

Even if developing humans at all stages were reduced to a single rhetorical image, the meaning conveyed by that image would not have been sufficient to support the pro-Life persuasive claim unless it was also metaphorically interpreted as *essentially* identical with a full human being. This layer of meaning was added metaphorically.

Metaphor

The metaphor is the most basic of tropes because it is founded on the most basic of logics. It defines an identity: "A is B" (or "see A as B"). Pictures and films, at the most fundamental level, make a metaphoric assertion: "This *is* me at my graduation," we say, proudly displaying a group of lines and squiggles. Because we automatically metaphorize in interpreting pictures, it is easy to make larger metaphoric leaps in the employment of pictures in arguments. The pro-Life images that functioned by means of such metaphors included "The fetus IS a human" and its corollary, "Abortion IS murder." However, these metaphors, drawn from the pictures of the nineteen-week-old fetus and of the body parts of aborted fetuses, did not function through a simple artless presentation. The pro-Life rhetors employed the rhetorical tactics of *selection, *continuity, and *commentary to focus their meaning.

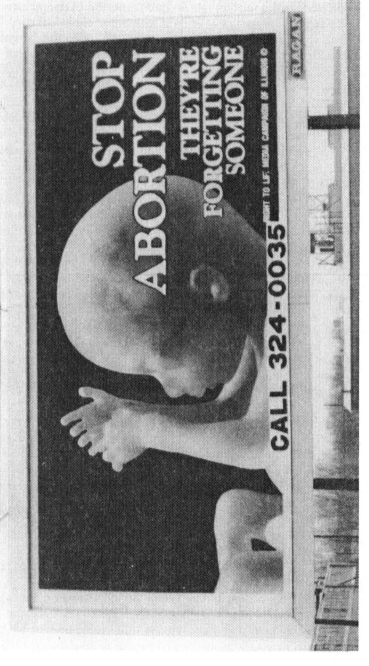

Billboards gave substantial presence to carefully selected images of the fetus. Photo by Bruce Railsback

Careful *selection* made potent the most important visual trope for the pro-Life argument—that the fetus IS a human being. In order to defend the single image of the fetus as equivalent to "a human being," later-term fetuses were most prevalent. A two-week-old fetus does not *look* like a human being and so could not be used as the center of a *visual* argument. The visual metaphor can reveal only visual qualities, not intellect, chromosome content, creativity, or "potential" of any kind. If we were to show naive viewers pictures of two-week-old fetuses and similarly aged fetal monkeys, they would not know the difference. The visual argument, therefore, is utterly dependent on a highly rhetorical *selection. Not only was a *single* image of "the fetus" generated, but that image was carefully selected to maximize the similarities between "fetus" and "human being."

These selections were so crucial to the visual rhetoric that without them, the pro-Life visual argument could not have been made; nonetheless, the principle of selection does not provide a complete account. Context was also crucial for the visual rhetoric of abortion, and *continuity was one of its most important elements.[4] In the relatively rare instances where two-week fetuses were presented, for example, they were generally preceded by a series of later-term fetuses. Pro-Life rhetors consciously specified that slide shows should start with a baby and work backward in development to establish the continuity of the life forms. Only in this way could the indistinguishable embryo be "seen" as a human.

The response to the image of the fetus also depended on a cultural context. Americans, like many other human groups, have learned to be relatively flexible readers of images. Even our children's dolls—the "Cabbage Patch Kids," for example—have taught us to read "humanity" or "personality" into a broad range of images. In a culture where even the bright look in a dog's eye can be interpreted as "*personality*," it is not surprising that the public was able to read fetal pictures as human beings. Our code for what is visually human is very broad.

Skillful selection and contextualization were vital influences on the creation of this rhetorical image of "the fetus," but the most important influence was simply that of verbal commentary. Without verbal commentary, pictures DO NOT ARGUE propositions. An image may suggest "this looks like x," but the assertion of identity, that "this IS x," must be verbally supplied. In terms of argument theory, a picture provides the substance for a ground, but the precise ground must be made verbally explicit and a claim must be supplied for the rhetor to control the process of inference. It is not surprising, therefore, that a great variety of commentary surrounded the presentation of the image of the fetus. One popular picture's label indicated that "when they tell you that abortion is a matter just between a woman and her doctor they're forgetting someone." Another said "living 14-week unborn child in the womb," another "intra-uterine battered child," another "suction abortion—done on this baby at 10 weeks."[5] The image was almost always explicitly labeled as a "baby." This repeated naming was crucial, gradually or swiftly strengthening the public association of "fetus" with "baby."

Such captions were the most routine: it is not a subtle rhetorical art that labels a fetal picture a "baby." More skillful rhetors used an even greater tool—"identification"[6]—to encourage audiences to see the fetus not only as "human" but as the same as one's self. One caption, for example, informed its viewer that "this is what your feet looked like when you were only 10 weeks old. Perfectly formed? Yes! You even had fingerprints then." Another caption on a fourth-month fetus read, "Your face took on facial expressions similar to, yet distinct from those of your parents and of your grandparents . . . . You squirmed or fluttered about . . . you grew and grew until you became half as tall as you would be at birth." Personification here worked most effectively. The fetus was not only a person; it was *you*.

The meaning of even the least human-looking pictures was controlled through artful labeling. A greatly magnified cluster of cells at week one was named the "ball of life"; a two-week-old, in a picture that resembled the surface of the moon, was labeled "the new individual 'nesting' in the soft lining of the womb"; and an eleven-week fetus in an alien-looking placenta was compared to an "astronaut." Thus, once the image had been established, in the right context, with continuity and powerful commentary, even a visually dissimilar image could become part of the image of "the fetus as unborn baby."

The most stunning example of the force of commentary, however, came in the film version, *The Silent Scream*. This highly controversial film—attacked and defended on national television—claimed to include a real-time "sound picture" of the abortion of a twelve-week-old fetus. Pro-Choice advocates made many criticisms of the accuracy of the film, but the most important group of comments all centered on the fact that, although the pro-Life movement touted the images of the film as most convincing, the commentary of the film really made the argument.

Most basically, the ultrasound image is so vague that without commentary many viewers would not have had the faintest idea what they were watching (as has been the case in my classes where I have shown students just the ultrasound image, without the sound or prior commentary). It is often very hard to see the fetus in this image. Moreover, even when the wispy "clouds on a radar screen" can be visualized as a fetus, the fetus does not appear as dramatically human. The resolution of the image is simply too poor to make a forceful argument in itself.

The commentary, however, artfully tells the viewer what to see. Before the abortion begins, the narrator, Dr. Bernard Nathanson, instructs the audience in the proper emotional reaction to the film. He recounts the story of an attending physician and assistant who, after seeing the ultrasound, refused to perform abortions again. The audience is thereby provided credible models who suggest the film is convincing and that they too should be shocked at the death they will soon see. Having been helped to feel, the auditors are next helped to see. Nathanson holds up a series of model dolls to help them visualize what the fetus looks like. He holds one of these against the ultrasound screen and traces the outline of the fetus in comparison so that viewers can "see" the fetus. As the abortion begins, Nathanson repeatedly tells the audience what the fetus is "doing." He uses terms that assume feeling and intelligence in the fetus—saying, for example, that the "child definitely feels its sanctuary is being invaded" or that "it senses mortal danger." As the abortion is performed, we—the audience—may have flashes in which we can actually see the shape of the fetus, primarily through context and continuity—that is, the three-dimensional movement allows us greater perception. But we cannot tell what is really happening; we only know that there is a lot more movement once the abortion begins (allegedly, the film is changed from slow time to real time). Nathanson, however, continually instructs us in what is happening and points out the abortion instruments on the screen. In the end, we are even given a demonstration of the use of forceps to "crush the skull,"since the ultrasound does not depict that element of this abortion.

Simply stated, if *The Silent Scream* had really been silent, it would have had no rhetorical impact. The majority of audiences could not have interpreted the film on their own, let alone read it as the violent murder of a small human baby. Once the commentary is provided, however, we almost unavoidably experience the full emotional impact of what we have "seen."

Visual images work metaphorically, but the production of those metaphors is dependent on the verbal rhetoric which explicitly classifies components of the image. "Clouds" on an ultrasound become a "fetus," and we suffer with the fetus as we are told that what we watch is a human death struggle. Less extremely, we see pictures of a nineteen-week fetus and are told that this means that "a fetus is a human person from conception." Our eyes indeed do not lie, but they also do not construct precise claim-bearing meanings without the words that provide interpretations.

Synecdoche

Through metonymy the pro-Life images produced a singular "fetus" and through metaphor persuaded Americans to see this fetus as a human baby. The third visual trope that constructed rhetorical images—the synecdoche—strengthened this connection, ironically by using even more incomplete visual information. Synecdoches encourage us to substitute the image of the part of an item for the whole of another, concluding that PART A = A = B. The more the rhetoric of a visual image must use partial similarities to claim "identity," the more will synecdoche be a useful device.

One of the most popular images of the pro-Life movement was that of the feet of a ten-week-old fetus, held gently between two adult fingers. The image appeared thousands of times in slide programs, on posters at rallies, and most recently on lapel pins. This image functioned to charm audiences even more fully than did the picture of the nineteen-week fetus. Many viewers responded to pictures of the fetal feet with loving "oohs" and "aahs." How could feet captivate and mean so much?

This image was most persuasive because of its synecdochic structure. An accurate, full picture of a young fetus includes features not associated with adult human beings—the placenta and the umbilical

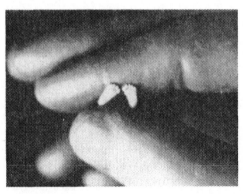

Photo and caption from Willke, *Abortion Questions & Answers*, Hayes Publishing Co., Cincinnati, Ohio. Used with permission.

This is what your feet looked like when you were only 10 weeks old. Perfectly formed? Yes! You even had fingerprints then.

cord and, in a six-week fetus, even a "tail." With these and its un-
gainly face and head, off-balance and poorly formed, a young fetus
looks like a wretched creature, bloody and undernourished. Such
"negatives" and "variances" weigh heavily against the "A is B" formulation. Fetal feet, however, are very close to baby feet in shape. The
identity of the part is crucial. Our visual logic "recognizes" such feet
as "small human feet" and we synecdochically expand the unseen
picture to see a full "small human." Thus, the synecdoche tightened
the identity between fetus and adult by eliminating all those components that reveal the differences between the two, focusing on one
single, stunning similarity.

The same synecdochic technique was evident in the less frequently
used picture of the face of a fetus with one eye partially open. It
functioned most powerfully, as well, in the images of butchered
fetuses. These pictures featured the recognizable arms and legs of
fetuses amid a pile of blood and tissue. Audiences could, synecdochically, reconstruct from this visual evidence the death-through-
dismemberment of a human being.

Finally, synecdoche was also employed more subtly in the most
widely disseminated pro-Life pictures. The image of the nineteen-
week old fetus mass-distributed in national magazines did *not* reveal
the non-human features of the fetus. The picture was cropped to cut
off the lower portion of the fetus, its umbilical cord, placenta, and its
distorted torso. Notably, this image, not other more complete pictures, was chosen for mass distribution in the early period, when the
meaning of the fetus was first being established. Thus, the pro-Life
image of the fetus relied heavily on the constructive capabilities of the
synecdoche to erase differences and feature similarities, tightening
the claim that "the fetus is a human person."

Other Tropes and Their Logic

The images featured by the pro-Life activists also functioned rhetorically by means of other tropes. Abortion was compared to euthanasia,
infanticide, and the end of the entire human race. Similarly, pictures
of slaves and of wagons of slaughtered Jewish prisoners from con-
centration camps were paired with photographs of slaughtered
fetuses. The comparisons were striking, relying on metonymic association: "a society that does not care for one form of human life does
not care for others." Replace "Jews" with "pre-born babies" and audiences could "see" the holocaust being replayed, even to the gaunt
limbs and deformity of the human shape entailed by death. In con-

trast, the metonymy which compared fetuses to slaves in cages failed as a visual rhetorical image. The placenta is hardly a cage, and the slaves chained together generally lived, at least a while. Although "emancipation" and "freedom" of the slaves made a good verbal comparison, the *visual* elements were not strong enough to make the metonymy-by-image effective.

The pro-Life rhetoric also employed the trope "hyperbole"—overstatement—to great force. The images of fetuses, sometimes in "real" dimensions—only one-half inch, two inches, or even five inches long—were magnified on slides to hundreds of times their real size, giving the fetus an enormous "presence" that granted it greater "substance" than it actually has. Very immature fetuses were, in this manner, visually equated with babies by being magnified to the size and substantiality of babies.

Many visual tropes thus delicately constructed the meanings of the pro-Life images. Ultimately, each of the tropes that translated a visual image into a verbal claim functioned on a tropic logic, whose roots are very similar to all other logics, resting on substitution, association, and amplification. We are left, then, with a very logical question—a complex mathematics in non-numerical form: what is the substance of the visual argument presented by the "image of the fetus" and what is the remainder?

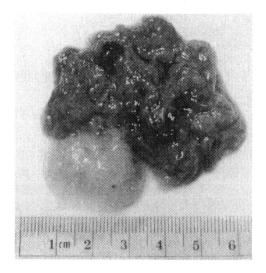

In contrast to the image of the nineteen-week fetus used by pro-Life rhetors, this photo shows the products of conception at eight menstrual weeks' gestation (weight 16 grams). The drawing of the embryo indicates its approximate appearance and size. Photo © 1989 by Warren Martin Hern

As I indicated at the outset, I believe that the pictures argue forcefully for the substance and value of the fetus. The piles of tissue, the legs and arms, state directly to me that this creature has substance and is *like* me. It engages my empathy. The awesome photograph of the twenty-four-week-old fetus tells me that this is a creature that should be preserved. The troubling film of an eight-week-old fetus responding repeatedly to the prick of a pin tells me that there is life there. The proof of the substance of the fetus and its similarity to myself is strong. It should be included in any final evaluation of abortion (see Appendix A).

The analysis of tropes also suggests that the pro-Life rhetoric works hard to obscure the differences between me and these developing, incomplete human forms. And this factor must also be included in any final evaluation of abortion. Ultimately, if I sift out the particular rhetorical tactics of the pro-Life rhetors—their overstatement via metonymies, metaphors, and synecdoches—and look at *all* the pictures of fetuses, in all their completeness, I recognize that there are major *differences* as well as *similarities*. I know, therefore, that a fetus has substantial value and that a fetus is not, at all stages, substantially the same as me. This creature shares my identity far more at twenty-four weeks than at eight or two. And so, at least on the basis of the visual evidence which constitutes the mainstay of this pro-Life persuasion, I realize that humanity is indeed something a fetus grows into only gradually.

I conclude, therefore, that the pro-Life pictures bring us a weighty set of grounds and that those grounds substantiate the claim that fetuses are important and valuable and ought to be protected whenever it is possible to do so without treading on greater values. However, I also conclude that the pro-Life rhetoric attempts to construct a singular image that *identifies* this value for all blastocysts/embryos/fetuses with that of a full human baby. On the pro-Lifers' own grounds that is a false construction; by their own criterion (appearance), stages matter. Hence, abortion should be *viewed* as a different matter at four weeks than at twenty-four (for other criticism see Appendix A, "A Right to Life?"). The pro-Life image of the fetus thus offered the American public powerful persuasion, argumentative substance, and overstatement.

The dualistic limitations and substance of the pro-Life rhetoric of image are perhaps most powerfully summed up in their most technically advanced film, *The Eclipse of Reason*. The film uses laproscopy to allow its audiences to view various parts of a second-trimester fetus in utero. It later shows chunks of bloody fetal tissue—this same fetus—being ripped from between the legs of a woman. The impact of these images is substantial, but the film ultimately cannot knit those two images fully into one vivid picture of the killing of a human-like being. It is a profound visual metaphor when the substantiality of the woman's body and the fetal dependence on her for survival separate the synecdochic images of the human-like creature growing inside her from the mounds of tissue, dead, outside.

Images of Freedom

The pro-Life rhetors' considerable persuasive success in constructing the image of the fetus as a complete human being, who should be protected by a law banning abortions, was not matched by the three major images used by the pro-Choice rhetors, largely because the pro-Choice images merely summarized arguments, rather than grounding them. The pro-Choice images recalled or made vivid the narrative of illegal abortion but generally did not add any additional argumentative grounds of their own. Their persuasive force rested on their ability to speak the narrative of illegal abortion in abbreviated form where the longer narrative could not be told (for example, on posters).

A coat hanger, often dripping blood, may have been the image most universally employed by pro-Choice advocates. This *summarizing image represented the horrid means and consequences of the illegal abortions that occur when legal abortion is banned. The image had limited persuasive impacts, primarily because the hanger—even with its drops of blood—was not, of itself, a tremendously moving

The coat hanger provided the most frequently used visual image in the pro-Choice movement.

visual depiction. Although the sketches of blood might have carried some repulsive force, even that was far weaker than the photographic images of bloody mangled fetuses.

The persuasive impact of the hanger image rested elsewhere. It reminded the audience of what it already knew, repeating the argument rather than adding to it. For the coat hanger to move an audience against abortion, the audience must have already been told the complex narrative of illegal abortion. The summarizing image therefore worked for a narrow audience of the already committed.

A second pro-Choice image that attempted to use the force of visual representation pictured a dead woman, sprawled naked, face down on the floor in a stark room, her legs spread open on a pool of blood. Occasionally distributed, the picture appeared in *Ms.* magazine and on a few pamphlets; I have never seen a slide projection of it at a public lecture. Although the picture could generate strong emotional repulsion—perhaps stronger than the pictures of massacred fetuses—it shared the weaknesses of the coat-hanger image. The rhetorical point of the picture depended on an extensive narrative indicating why the woman was there, the victim of a back-alley abortion. If the audience did not come with a complete understanding of the story of illegal abortion, the ragged emotional force of the image may not have functioned to the intended end. As a narrative depiction, it lacked the strong metaphorical character that would have allowed the woman in the picture to be concisely characterized. Moreover, because of the complexity of the relationship between the picture and its grounds, the repulsiveness of the picture could be easily redirected against the woman herself. Audience members could define their repugnance at the picture as being the fault of the woman, rather than of the laws. She could be placed as one who "deserved" what she got, whereas no one could blame the fetus. This second pro-Choice image again provided no new argument of its own, and it was likely to carry persuasive force only for those who were already convinced of the basic soundness of the argument.

The last popular image of the pro-Choice movement worked differently and may have carried some force for non-activists. It was a symbolic characterization—the presentation of the Statue of Liberty. A pro-Choice pamphlet read, "There are no pictures in this pamphlet, because you can't take a picture of liberty." Although there was no "picture" of Liberty, the Statue of Liberty filled in as a potent symbol and was displayed on a large quantity of pro-Choice literature. The statue—as a woman, a symbol of the downtrodden, and a symbol of Freedom, Liberty, and home—embodied the ideal American representation of Choice or Reproductive Freedom. The symbol did not carry the force of the "seeing is believing" variety, as would a pictorial image, but it replaced that veracity with the force garnered from a powerful cultural icon. Through this association, the pro-Choice movement gained its strongest visual image. The image may even have added some indirect argumentative grounds. By associating the pro-Choice cause with a widely celebrated icon, it suggested that women, too, should enjoy the Liberty to which most audience members believe themselves to be committed. Further, the symbol required little explanation; hence, its simple association of Freedom of Choice with American values probably carried some weight, even if that weight was more diffuse than the immediate sensory force of the pro-Life image.

Conclusions

In the contemporary American abortion controversy the pro-Life images were more powerfully persuasive than the pro-Choice images. That persuasive power derived ultimately from the real material substance of unborn human beings as well as from the rhetors' skill with tropes. Persuasive force and argumentative probity must be distinguished from each other because they each had a different impact on the development of the public meanings of "abortion." The persuasive force of the image of the fetus, towering over the meager pro-Choice images, would powerfully influence the popular consciousness, eventually establishing elements of the pro-Life vocabulary deeply within popular culture and within the lives of polarized subcultures (see chapters 7 and 8). Ultimately, for some, it would justify the move to violence. In the meantime, however, the legal field would be vitally important, and legal tribunals were most influenced by the argumentative dimensions of the discourse. In the arguments before the Supreme Court, the argumentative weaknesses of the major pro-Life persuasive grounds would be determinative for American law.

NOTES

1. Kristin Luker, *Abortion and the Politics of Motherhood* (Berkeley: University of California Press, 1984), p. 150.

2. See Jacqueline de Romilly, *Magic and Rhetoric in Ancient Greece* (Cambridge: Harvard University Press, 1975), and, for example, Aristotle's *Rhetoric* and *Poetics*. The inter-relationships he draws between these two forms of

discourse are often interesting. See also Cicero's *De Oratore* or Quintilian's *Institutes*. This tropal theory of images is also found in Denise M. Bostdorff, "Making Light of James Watt: A Burkean Approach to the Form and Attitude of Political Cartoons," *Quarterly Journal of Speech* 73, no. 1 (February 1987), 43–59; however, I formulated this version of the approach independently in two versions of an earlier paper: "The Image of the Fetus: Lessons in the Rhetoric of Visual Text," presented at the Central States Speech Association conference, April 1986, and at the Speech Communication Association Seminar on Televised Text and Rhetorical Analysis, Denver, November 7, 1985.

3. The version of the image I have included is a black-and-white photograph of a billboard bearing the picture (taken by Loren Bruce Railsback). Another version of the image was published in a full-page advertisement in *Time*, 16 January 1984, p. 56.

4. Martha Solomon, "Redemptive Rhetoric: The Continuity Motif in the Rhetoric of Right to Life," *Central States Speech Journal* 31 (1980), 52–62.

5. Pamphlets include *Life or Death* (Hayes Publishing Company, 6304 Hamilton Ave., Cincinnati, Ohio 45224); Gary Bergel, *When You Were Formed in Secret* (1984; Intercessors for America, P.O. Box 1289, Elyria, Ohio 44036); John Lippis, *The Challenge to Be "Pro-Life"* (1982; National Right to Life Educational Trust Fund, 419 7th Street N.W., Suite 402, Washington, D.C. 20004); "Abortion: Attitudes for Action," *The Last Days* 7, no. 5 (Last Days Ministries, P.O. Box 40, Lindale, Texas); *Life Cycle*, special school ed. (1984; National Right to Life Educational Trust Fund); and other materials from Hayes Publishing Company.

6. Kenneth Burke, "Identification," in *A Rhetoric of Motives* (1950; rpt. Berkeley: University of California Press, 1969), pp. 19–29.

CHAPTER SIX

Enacting "Choice"
Public Rhetoric and the Law
—————— 1973-85 ——————

By 1973 a new public vocabulary articulating women's interests in waged-labor, childbearing, and abortion had developed through public argumentation. New values, narratives, and images had been given presence before the American populace. Simultaneously, opponents of this new vocabulary had elaborated and amplified a set of competing terms in order to preserve traditional values and power arrangements.

Once such competing vocabularies are developed, advocates frequently move the discussion into the domain of the law in order to place the coercive power of the state behind their vocabularies and, hence, their interests. State legislatures across the nation had haphazardly begun the formal process of adjudicating between the vocabularies of Choice and Life to produce a legitimated set of terms by which public action would be guided. Whenever competing fundamental interests extend to constitutional values, however, they almost inevitably come before the nation's highest judicial authority.

In the early seventies the cases of *Roe* v. *Wade* and *Doe* v. *Bolton* brought the abortion issue before the Supreme Court of the United States of America.[1] The Court's decision then embroiled the national Congress directly in the public negotiation process. In these two legal arenas, the public meaning of Choice was dramatically reshaped and the character of fetal Life restricted.

Decoding Judicial Rhetoric

The public import of the Supreme Court's decisions in the landmark abortion cases has generally been poorly understood. Like many other important decisions, they have been approached primarily through the artificially narrow lens of legal scholarship. In contrast, my focus is neither some legalistic standard that *Roe* either meets or fails[2] nor the sufficiency of the decision in terms of its effects.[3] Instead, I seek to describe the way in which the Supreme Court, as one locus of public discussion, processed the public vocabulary with which it was confronted. On these grounds the *Roe* decision appears as a reasonable and predictable product of four factors: (1) the balance of the public arguments, (2) the need for integration with the existing legal structure, (3) the comparative legal skills of the competing lawyers, (4) the political views of womanhood held by the justices.

In order to explore the process of constructing abortion law, we need to understand the law, not as an isolated and privileged professional field, but as an interface between the state and the public. Because the law must be able to control the public behavior of government officials and private individuals, legal discourse occurs, necessarily, in a public space. However, the legal debate is conducted largely by specialists in a specialized vocabulary. Moreover, legal discourse carries a kind of direct, *performative power open to very few other genres of public address.[4] It marshals the coercive power of the state behind certain vocabularies instead of others. The law, for example, takes the private Property (tax money) of citizens for the service of Public Defense, and it demands "affirmative action" and prohibits "discrimination," both in the service of Equal Opportunity.

The public arena of the law therefore combines the intersection of the general public and the state specialist, the public vocabulary and technical legal discourse, the universal value and the partisan interest. The character of this relationship is complex. The legal vocabulary itself is limited, being most extensively elaborated in procedural areas (e.g., "justiciability," "stare decisis," "strict scrutiny"). It relies on the propositions and key terms contained in the Constitution, in statutes, and in prior decisions. It is also accountable to the *ideographs enshrined in the nation's constituting documents (most frequently, Liberty, Property, and Life). Legal discourse, however, translates these constituting values into more manageable sub-categories that more closely specify the character of the rights to be protected (religion is protected under the "establishment clause" and the "free exercise clause," while abortion comes to be protected by "privacy," a sub-component of the broader class of Liberty). This elaborate set of procedural terms, sub-categories, and propositions helps to make legal discourse proceed in the semi-deductive manner associated with what Fisher calls "the rational world paradigm." Appellate legal communication thereby reduces its formal, explicit dependence on the narrative form that is so central to the rest of public address.[5] Conse-

quently, it is able to operate with proportionately less explicit attention to the social *myths central to most political communication. It is
this narrow, deductive, technically framed component of legal practice that legal scholars privilege.

The law, however, cannot escape the *characterizations and images
of mass public communication. Because the law must make its abstract principles control concrete agents and actions, it must articulate
bridges between ideographs and the characterizations that represent
those concrete entities. As a consequence, narratives become impli-
cated in legal decisions through the back door; the choice of characterization favors the myths constituted through a particular set of
*character-types. To understand how the Court processed the public
vocabulary about abortion therefore requires an accounting of the
interaction between the legal and ideographic principles and the more
popularly based characterizations.

Roe v. Wade

In the case of *Roe* v. *Wade* a poor and unmarried pregnant woman
challenged a Texas law that proscribed all abortions except those
undertaken to save a pregnant woman's life.[6] Roe's skillful attorneys,
led by Sarah Weddington, argued in December of 1971 and in the re-
argument of October 1972 that such state laws violated the fundamental liberties of women—especially their right to privacy. With substantially less skill two assistant attorneys general argued the case for
Texas. Robert Flowers and Jay Floyd directed most of their arguments
to procedural matters, insisting that the case was speculative and
moot, and therefore not justiciable. In addition, they argued that the
state legislature was the appropriate locus for such decision-making
and that the state had a valid constitutional purpose in the law—the
protection of the life of the fetus.

On 22 January 1973 the Court decided that the Texas law, and
reform laws such as the Georgia law that had been challenged in the
companion case, were unconstitutional. The decision, authored by
Justice Harry A. Blackmun, carefully outlined the constitutional
boundaries for state abortion laws. It specified that states could not
limit abortions performed in the first trimester of pregnancy, except to
require that they be performed by licensed health providers. It permitted regulation of abortion in the second trimester only to protect
the health of the pregnant woman. The Court ruled that the state
could outlaw abortion in the last trimester, except in cases where the
life and health of the pregnant woman would be threatened. The

companion decision, *Doe* v. *Bolton*, defined "health" very broadly. The seven justices arrived at this position through four crucial rhetorical moves.

Justiciability: Procedure and Practice

In shifting the public discourse into the legal arena, the first and most pivotal argument was about the power of the Court to decide the issue at all. Previously, pregnancy and abortion generally had been presumed to be matters that were not justiciable because pregnancies were always completed before the cases could finish the lengthy appeals process. Somewhere in the middle of court actions, such women complainants lost their standing, because the case became "moot." The Court noted that "the usual rule in federal cases is that an actual controversy must exist at stages of appellate or certiorari review" (p. 125). The Court, however, allowed the case to come to trial for two absolutely inter-dependent reasons, one legalistic and the other related to the public discourse.

The legal component of the ruling arose from the fact that the majority of the justices had come to recognize a class of disputes that modified the requirement for a case to present an "actual controversy." They found that, like some other special kinds of cases, pregnancy "truly could be 'capable of repetition, yet evading review'" (p. 125). Therefore, the issue was not exactly "moot." As a class action, it presented a type of ongoing actual controversy to the Court.

The decision to classify the case in this manner was influenced by the majority's larger sense of the issue's fundamental importance. The dissenting judges, who explicitly argued that the case did not involve fundamental issues, easily described minor technical reasons for refusing to hear the case.[7] The oral argument reveals, however, that the other justices accepted the claim the female attorneys forcefully put before them—that Roe and the class she represented had at least a plausible claim to a fundamental constitutional right and that this made it incumbent upon the Court to *consider* the issue.[8] Sarah Weddington argued for the appellants that

> a pregnancy to a woman is perhaps one of the most determinative aspects of her life. It disrupts her body. It disrupts her education. It disrupts her employment. And it often disrupts her entire family life. And we feel that, because of the impact on the woman, this certainly— in as far as there are any rights which are fundamental—is a matter which is of such fundamental and basic concern to the woman involved

that she should be allowed to make the choice as to whether to continue or to terminate her pregnancy.[9]

In this form the claim—drawn from the briefs, directly repeating the prior public discourse of the pro-Choice movement, and amplified through its presentation by a female attorney—was persuasive to the majority, even though it was not yet framed in legal terms.[10] The very fact that women had successfully voiced a compelling argument in the public realm made it difficult (although not impossible) for the justices to deny a "hearing" in the courtroom as well. This did not guarantee that the women would win their case, but the public voice encouraged the justices to allow the next step to be taken—a legal framing of the issue.

The procedural matter of accepting the case had breathtaking consequences: it allowed women to bring pregnancy (perhaps our single most important issue as women) into the judicial process in a definitive way. Clearly, fetuses could not bring such cases, and adults had been routinely denied the right to bring such cases for fetuses who were not eventually born.[11] Thus, by merely hearing the case, the Court granted women a crucial form of social power and standing that the fetuses could not have. The material reality that a pregnant woman could plead before a court of law, while a fetus could not, became a legal reality in America as well. This basic fact may well have been the single most important factor in the outcome of the case. In admitting this women's issue to legal review, the Court conceded that it would alter some indeterminate part of its vocabulary to deal with the unique concerns of this now-publicly vocal group.

History and Precedent

Once the Court had agreed to hear the women's complaint, the second issue it faced was to explain why it had not done so previously (in other words, to explain why prior precedent and legal vocabulary were not sufficient here). This is a serious and continuing rhetorical dilemma for the Supreme Court on those important occasions when it is forced to act in new arenas. In this case, as in others, the Court could quite accurately have found itself to have been derelict, or it could have described the evolution of birth control technology and women's careerism as creating a new substantive right. Neither of these alternatives fit within the bounds of permissible judicial reasongiving because they imply that the Court is not dealing infallibly with timeless truths.[12] That implication would challenge the ethos of the Court. In order to manage this public relations problem, Blackmun created a historical narrative showing that the constitutional principle at stake had always existed but that the constitutionality of previous laws had been dependent on a set of blocking conditions that no longer pertained. Empirical conditions having changed, the law might legitimately return to its root principles.

Blackmun's history strove toward objectivity by disregarding the historical narratives of both pro-Choice and pro-Life public advocates (pro-Life rhetors had focused on religious authorities; pro-Choice advocates had recounted human practices). Instead, Blackmun, a lawyer with long-standing connections with the medical research establishment, turned to the codified legal and medical history.

Blackmun focused not on the religious attitudes toward or actual practices of abortion but rather on the laws surrounding it. This history began with the Hippocratic Oath, proceeded to the English Common Law, to Statute Law, and then to more recent American legal precedent. The choice was appropriate to, and perhaps required of, a legal decision, and it just as clearly shaped the outcome. With two crucial exceptions, this legal history was one that had allowed abortion.

Blackmun disposed of the oldest exception, the Hippocratic Oath, by noting that it was the opinion of a small, somewhat eccentric religious group (the Pythagoreans), not an endorsed code drawing from a wide public consensus. Because it belonged to a "particular interest group," the discourse lacked objectivity and, therefore, legitimacy. The oath may have been symbolically potent, but it was not legally important or binding.

While symbolically difficult, that dispensation was relatively easy compared to the task of dismissing the second exception—the most recent one hundred years of American statute law. As Texas's lawyer suggested in oral argument, this last hundred years could be seen as a "culmination" of moral and even legal history.[13] In some senses this might have been the *expected* legal interpretation: the use of a vast body of recent precedent would seem fairly crucial to a judgment of law. These were, however, only state statutes, not necessarily binding on the national, Constitutional Court. The Court held, moreover, that the primary reason for the enactment of these state statutes had been the protection of the life and health of pregnant women from the early and unsafe surgical techniques for abortion. Since abortion was now reasonably safe, especially early in pregnancy, the state no longer had any compelling interest for maintaining these rights-abridging laws.

The rhetorical wedge provided by this historical accounting has come under sustained attack on two counts. On the one hand, it deviates from a standard judicial style because it features historical narrative. Such attacks ignore the rhetorical fact that in constitutional controversies the Court must address simultaneously an attentive public and a technical legal doctrine. To employ narrative to address the public (protecting the Court's ethos) does not make it impossible also to carefully and legitimately deal with the legal issues. A more serious attack on the "medicalization" of abortion that ensued from this approach is the claim that such emphasis on physicians and health detracts from the central issue of women's Choice.[14] Such a charge also ignores the rhetorical situation and the place of the medical issues in the argument.

The medical issues were not central to the legal doctrine of Choice but rather were related to the conditions taken to be *previously* impinging upon the women's right. This is evident in the fact that the medicalization content has gradually withered away, leaving the much more substantive part of the decision to stand.[15] Indeed, the Court sought to overturn these precedents with this rhetorical device of historical narrative only because it found that women had a fundamental right that both prevented intrusion upon their lives by the state governments and justified the interference of the federal judiciary in state law. This was the heart of the contest.

Freedom of Choice

The *Roe* decision and its subsequent elaborations and clarifications involved one of the most difficult problematics that arise for the judiciary. The Court was required to adjudicate a claim of competing fundamental rights for which there were no clear right-granting precedents. Neither the Right to Life of the fetus, developed as a claim by the pro-Life movement and supported by states' attorneys, nor the Right to Choice of women, articulated through the women's movement and urged in Court by the women's attorneys, had ever been explicitly incorporated into the legal discourse. The Court was asked to decide here if either of these claims, developed in the broader realm of public discourse, had constitutional legitimacy, and if so, what their relationship to each other would be.

This position made it impossible for the judges to work exclusively from precedent and statute, as conservative legal theory holds they should. According to these legal theories, judges should strive to operate in a closed legal vocabulary where nothing new need gain status. However, this conservative premise is rendered incompetent in cases in which the judges must operate from the Constitution's

Ninth and Fourteenth amendments. These amendments dictate that there are fundamental individual rights, not all of which have been previously enumerated, that a state can disregard only in extreme cases.[16] In such instances, the Supreme Court walks a careful line between the limiting constraints of precedent and statute—legislatively established—and fundamental rights—constitutionally established.

Although it is occasionally contested, one of the techniques the Court has adopted for this balancing act is the doctrine of "scrutiny." The Court may invalidate state laws under two carefully proscribed conditions.[17] First, the Supreme Court may declare unconstitutional any law that violates a fundamental right, unless the state has a "compelling interest" in overriding that right. In cases of fundamental rights, the Court employs "strict judicial scrutiny," relying on its own judgment—not that of legislative bodies—to assess the validity of the violation of individual rights. Second, the Supreme Court may declare unconstitutional laws that violate less fundamental rights only where there is no "rational state purpose" motivating the law. These latter cases allow the Court a less active role in scrutinizing the soundness of legislative decisions. *Roe* therefore involved assessment not only of the nature of the competing rights involved but also of how fundamental they were. If fundamental rights were involved, the Court was required to protect them from the assaults of state legislatures; if the rights were less fundamental or nonexistent, the Court was required to uphold state law.

For reasons we will explore shortly, the majority of the Court decided that the pro-Choice vocabulary was constitutionally legitimate—that women indeed have a *fundamental* Right to Choose. Blackmun repeatedly employed the precise vocabulary from the pro-Choice discourse, citing a "fundamental right to choose" (pp. 122, 129, 153) and "freedom to choose." However, since the Right to Choose had been a public term, not yet a legal one, Blackmun had to legitimize this right by demonstrating its linkage to legal vocabulary. Had sexism and the legal tendency to subdivide and over-categorize not dominated legal thought, Blackmun might simply have described this right as a clear instance of the right to Liberty. Instead, because the Court subconsciously continued to see pregnancy as in some way different from and derivative of sexual practices, it employed the subsidiary terminology of "right to privacy," which had most recently been articulated in regard to another issue concerning procreative freedom—birth control.[18]

The Court's use of the privacy doctrine has been attacked from both the Left and the Right. Socialist feminist scholars and lawyers have argued that privacy is undesirable as a key term to protect women's rights for two reasons. First, these opponents charge that the privacy doctrine creates a space, especially around the "family," in which women cannot be protected from abusive patriarchs (in a variety of ways).[19] However, nowhere in the *Roe* text did the Court place privacy in the hands of the patriarchal family; it clearly placed it in the woman's hands.[20] Second, feminists argue that the privacy doctrine entailed later decisions in which financial resources for abortion were denied because the state has no responsibility to support "private" decisions financially.[21] The text of *Roe* itself again contradicts this argument. All of the Court's descriptions of the need for a Right to Choice indicated that the Court saw this as a substantive right. Moreover, in the *Harris* v. *McRae* case, so important to the funding issues, it was not the doctrine of privacy that led to the Court's decision against protecting funding. Instead, it was precisely the Court's interpretation of the discrimination doctrine (which the socialist feminists generally prefer) that allowed the Court to avoid the issue on the grounds that poverty was not a "suspect classification."[22] Thus the Congress and later arguments, not *Roe*, defined Choice in this manner.[23]

The legal bridge provided by "privacy" has also been attacked by pro-Life forces. This attack is one of political convenience rather than true legal principle, and it is distressing that pro-Life advocates would be willing to sacrifice a basic liberty simply because it provided part of the bridge to abortion rights. The persuasiveness of their claim rests solely on the fact that the Court's rhetorical task of collection of a large group of previously identified rights and a set of unenumerated but widely cherished rights into a single category labeled "privacy" was executed with something less than eloquence. However, as the Court pointed out in *Griswold* v. *Connecticut* (381 US 479, 1965), privacy, although newly named, was hardly a new right. It had always been clearly fundamental to the American "way of life." The Court's recognition of a "fundamental right to privacy" was based in part on the example of several constitutional amendments that explicitly protected specific types of privacy (for example, the Fourth Amendment right to "be secure in their persons, houses, papers, and effects," the Third Amendment right to have one's home a private domain in which soldiers cannot be quartered, the First Amendment right to self-expression, and other rights of "privacy and repose," including the right to privacy in marriage and birth control cited in *Griswold*).[24] Most important, the Court traced the right directly from the *explicit* constitutional assertion that the intent of the entire form of government was to protect the "liberties" of all citizens (*Roe*, p. 152, and later elaborated by Justice Douglas in a concurring opinion, pp. 210–13). Given the assumption of an individualist government, for both men and women, the maintenance of "zones of privacy" is absolutely essential to maintaining Liberty—the rights of individuals against the state. The anomaly rests in the fact that the Court has never before been forced to make these rights explicit.

Telling evidence of the breadth of legal consensus on the privacy right is close at hand. In *Roe* both the *amicus* brief of the National Right to Life Committee and the attorneys for the state of Texas appeared to recognize the woman's right to privacy.[25] Thus the opposition to this right on the grounds that it was new seems to be little more than a retroactive smokescreen aimed at public persuasion rather than legal argument.

Pro-Life activists could, nonetheless, still argue that the "right to privacy" did not include a right to abortion—a position that continues to be disputed. However, even the legal consensus that "privacy" does provide the legal and rhetorical bridge for "choice" in abortion became ever more complete as the Court began to clarify its decisions in this area. By 1985 the smaller but more entrenched Court majority articulated the private Right to Choose as an instance of the larger term *liberty* in clear and eloquent form. In the case of *Thornburgh* vs. *American College of Obstetricians and Gynecologists* (54 USLW 4618), the decision read:

> Our cases long have recognized that the Constitution embodies a promise that a certain private sphere of individual liberty will be kept largely beyond the reach of government. . . . That promise extends to women as well as to men. Few decisions are more personal and intimate, more properly private, or more basic to individual dignity and autonomy, than a woman's decision—with the guidance of her physician and within the limits specified in *Roe*—whether to end her pregnancy. A woman's right to make that choice freely is fundamental. Any other result, in our view, would protect inadequately a central part of the sphere of liberty that our law guarantees equally to all. (P. 4625)

Crucially, by the time of this 1985 decision, *even the dissenting justices* had come to accept *not only* the existence of the privacy right *but also* its application to abortion. Justice White (with Rehnquist) noted, "I can certainly agree with the proposition—which I deem indisputable—that a woman's ability to choose an abortion is a species of 'liberty' that is subject to the general protections of the Due Process Clause" (p. 4629). White and Rehnquist's primary objection was simply that the right was not fundamental enough to allow the Court to censure the decisions of the state legislature. White continued, "I cannot agree, however, that this liberty is so 'fundamental' that restrictions upon it call into play anything more than the most minimal judicial scrutiny" (pp. 4629–30). The dissenters indicated, in general, that they thought the Court had overstepped its bounds because the Right to Choose, although a constitutional right, was not adequately fundamental to allow the judiciary to protect it from the "reasonable" decision-making processes of legislatures.

How does one decide how fundamental a right might be? It is at this point that the characterizations from the public argument are embedded in a most crucial and inevitable manner in the law, and it is at this point that we can see the nontechnical motives that led the jurists to a legal doctrine legitimating Choice through privacy.

In determining whether or not a right was fundamental, Justice White held that only those rights which were "implicit in the concept of ordered liberty" might be considered fundamental. His dissent indicated that "it seems apparent to me that a free, *egalitarian* and democratic society does not presuppose any particular rules or set of rules with respect to abortion" (p. 4630, my emphasis). The question thus became, what kind of human needs are essential and must be met to produce a world that is free, egalitarian, and democratic? This ultimately depended on the mythic views of women and motherhood held by the justices on both sides of this issue.

In *Roe* v. *Wade*, the dissenters described abortion and motherhood precisely within the characterizations used by the pro-Life movement. They employed the pro-Life descriptions of the reasons for abortion— "convenience, whim, or caprice of the putative mother" (p. 222). They hinted that perhaps abortion statutes might credibly require that abortion be allowed for the life or health of the mother but that any other cause would not be fundamental. In other words, only a woman's survival and health, not the *conduct* of her life, presented fundamental Freedoms.

The most apparent reason for this is that the conservative judges also shared the pro-Life movement's general assumption that *motherhood was the essential definition of "womanhood."[26] Indeed, they explicitly repudiated abortion choices for all the reasons that represented a challenge to the traditional characterization of motherhood. Specifically, they opposed abortions for "convenience, family planning, economics, *dislike of children*, the embarrassment of illegitimacy, etc." (*Roe*, p. 221, my emphasis). Only if one conceives of motherhood as essential to "womanhood" is it possible to classify family planning as unessential. Only if one cannot imagine women as other than mothers is the right to reject children because one dislikes them not a fundamental right of an individual woman. It is not accidental that the dissenters preferred the term *mother* to the term *pregnant woman*, which was employed more frequently by the majority. In sum, the dissenters continued to understand women and their goals as primarily devoted to childbearing. Hence, issues of timing or "dislike of children" were inadequate or inconceivable reasons for women to choose the course of their own lives.[27]

The majority, operating from a different characterization of women, believed that, for an *egalitarian* society, the right of women to Choose was indeed fundamental. The fact that the United States had not allowed legal abortion in the last hundred years did not deny its necessity. After all, the United States had not allowed *Equality* for women in those years. An egalitarian government, by the majority's definition, then, could not have "ordered liberty" without recognizing the fundamental importance of this choice for the conduct of women's lives.

The role of basic characterizations was as essential to this majority view as it had been to the minority view. The majority repeatedly indicated its acceptance of the broad new re-characterizations of women that expanded their choices beyond motherhood. Drawing from the larger social discourse directly and through the appellant's briefs, the majority's decision gave official recognition to the fact that pregnancy could in fact be "distressful," saying that "maternity, or additional offspring may force upon the woman a distressful life and future. Psychological harm may be imminent. Mental and physical health may be taxed by child care" (p. 153). Issues of "illegitimacy" and the problem of "unwanted children" were also listed. Directly, then, the view that motherhood was either incumbent on, or necessarily positive for, women was denied in the legal system by the majority in the *Roe* decision. Once the system recognized that women had reasons for choice, the Right to Choice was virtually inevitable, if we have a Constitution that protects the rights of human beings to make the significant decisions in their own lives.

The first half of the dispute over abortion was the question of whether women had a fundamental right to Freedom of Choice. The legal parties agreed that there existed a right to privacy that covered abortion. They disagreed over how *fundamental* that right was. Since this decision rested on basic characterizations of women, the final decision was inevitably a consequence of the political positions on womanhood held by the justices who happened to be in the majority.

This was not, as critics of the decision would have it, a matter of judicial error, but rather a social necessity. The justices on both sides ultimately rested their decisions on the concrete level of characterization because in order to be effective legal discourse must always rest ultimately on public characterizations of the people its rules will constrain. To understand a justice's characterization of the sociopolitical world is therefore as essential as to understand her or his legal philosophy.

The second half of the judicial issue of abortion was also a matter of characterizations negotiated between the public and legal vocabularies and it was of equal importance. Even having admitted the right of women's Choice, the Court's decision might have been dramatically different if the Court had also constructed a legal right of the fetus to Life.

A Right to Life?

The attorneys for the state of Texas argued both that the fetus had a Right to Life that outweighed the woman's right to privacy and that the state had a valid interest in protecting the life or potential life of the fetus.[28] The centrality of this issue for the Court was evident in the oral arguments. The justices asked attorneys for both sides if the status of the fetus was the determining issue. They queried Weddington, "If it were established that an unborn fetus is a person, with the protection of the Fourteenth Amendment, you would have almost an impossible case here, would you not?" and she replied, "I would have a very difficult case."[29] To Flowers, the question was, "Do you think the case is over for you? You've lost your case, then, if the fetus or the embryo is not a person? Is that it?" to which the attorney replied, "Yes, sir, I would say so."[30]

That the Court believed the personhood of the fetus to be a pivotal issue was also explicitly stated in Blackmun's decision. He argued that "if this suggestion of personhood is established, the appellant's case, of course, collapses, for the fetus' right to life would then be guaranteed specifically by the [Fourteenth] Amendment" (p. 157).

The manner in which this issue was decided was initiated in the briefs and heightened in the oral arguments. The justices began, quite appropriately, with legal precedent. They asked the attorney for Texas, "Do you know of any case, anywhere, that's held that an unborn fetus is a person within the meaning of the Fourteenth Amendment?" and Flowers responded, "No, sir. We can only go back to what the framers of our Constitution had in mind."[31] The justices immediately turned to the Constitution, to point out that the Constitution referred, in its only explicit reference, to persons "born" in the United States. After that point they noted that if a fetus were *legally* a person the Texas statutes—along with those of most other states—would be inconsistent, because they did not treat abortion as murder nor punish the pregnant woman for inducing abortion.[32] Moreover, the justices suggested that the precedent established by these statutes clearly indicated that the fetus had never been treated legally as a person.[33] The attorneys for Texas offered no response to any of these substantive points.

If the justices had confined themselves strictly to this logical, legal framing of the issue, Texas would have lost immediately. Instead, they gave the appellees the opportunity to characterize the fetus as a "human person," based on evidence from other realms. Here, too, the pro-Life attorneys replied weakly. To begin with, the justices asked Flowers how they ought to decide the issue. He suggested medical criteria, but, crucially, by his own admission he was unable to provide a medical source that clearly described a fetus as a human person from conception.[34] He then suggested that the issue was reasonably one for the Supreme Court, but when he was trapped by the judges into admitting that the precedent of the law did not establish the fetus as a person, he returned to the claim that the matter was appropriately one for the state legislatures, not the Courts. Here the justices again caught him in a contradiction when he admitted that if the fetus were a person, then the state legislatures would not have a right to decide to take its life—thus framing the issue squarely as a constitutional one that only the Supreme Court could decide.[35]

In the process of oral argument, therefore, three things became clear: (1) that the only thing that could possibly outweigh a woman's Right to Choice would be another person with an independent and more fundamental Right to Life, (2) that the status of the fetus was clearly a constitutional issue which the Court had the *necessity* of deciding, and (3) that to label a fetus a person entailed legal and logical inconsistencies the law could not tolerate, absent a well-argued reason external to the law for doing so.

The issues broached in oral argument were faithfully enshrined in the final decision. Most important, Blackmun noted that the *legal* meaning of person does not include a fetus. Utilizing an argument presented in an *amicus* brief, he carefully cited each use of the word *person* in the Constitution and concluded that "in nearly all these instances, the use of the word is such that it has application only post-natally. None indicates, with any assurance, that it has any possible pre-natal application" (p. 157). For example, he emphasized that a citizen was defined as a person *born* (or later naturalized) in the U.S. He suggested further that if the law really held the fetus to be a person state laws such as that of Texas would be self-contradictory because they allowed abortion in order to save the pregnant woman's life and did not prosecute as murderers women who obtained abortions (pp. 157–58). Given the technical requirements of the law, such open and evident self-contradiction was impermissible, and so neither the Court nor the state could find a fetus to be equivalent to a person. Similarly, he indicated that most state laws at the time protected the rights of fetuses only if the child was eventually born (or in some cases where the fetus was viable at the time of injury). Strict adherence to deductive logic and legal precedent led the Court to deny that a fetus was legally a person and had a Right to Life.

Significantly, the dissenting justices did not challenge this framing. In direct contrast to the public criticism of the *Roe* decision, the dissenting justices did not argue that a fetus was a person and/or had a Right to Life. In fact, in order to maintain that the matter was one for state legislatures—the point that constituted their major argument—they could not have maintained that either the fetus or the woman had fundamental rights at stake. Legally, therefore, the pro-Life movement was in an untenable position. Their only hope was to get the Court to decide the issue of the status of the fetus on non-legal grounds.

The final decision gave clear consideration to the broader social argument about the personhood of the fetus. However, Blackmun's decision was constrained by the particular relationship between the law and public discourse. First he responded to the technical medical argument, elaborated fully in briefs, that the science of biology had irrefutably established the fetus as a human person. Consistent with the development of the issue in oral argument and with his medical background and research, he indicated that medical criteria did not, in fact, establish that a fetus was a human being from the instant of conception, and that, instead, coming to be a human being was a process. He cited "new embryological data that purport to indicate that conception is a 'process' over time, rather than an event" (p. 162). The technical grounds of medicine did not, therefore, provide definitional grounds for the law to treat the fetus as a person. Consequently, the potential life of the fetus was to be integrated into the decision, but only to the extent that a fetus represented a substance of value, not a full person with a fundamental right.

Blackmun also responded to the public component of the pro-Life definitional argument. Essentially, he argued that public persuasion could only influence a judicial decision when there was real consensus (and the difference between the decisions made in *Plessy* v. *Ferguson* and *Brown* v. *Board of Education* suggests the longer-term pattern of the role of public consensus in background characterizations). Blackmun pointed out that there was no consensus about when life began in the broader, non-legal sense. He deferred the issue, saying, "When those trained in the respective disciplines of medicine, philosophy, and theology are unable to arrive at any consensus, the judiciary, at this point in the development of man's knowledge, is not in a position to speculate as to the answer. It should be sufficient to note briefly the wide divergence of thinking on this most sensitive and difficult question" (pp. 159–60).

In other words, the Supreme Court refused to legislate an empirical meaning to unsettled social definitions; Blackmun recognized that the judiciary could not legislate a factual meaning for controversial public terms. Only if there were consensus about a term could the social meaning produce a dramatic alteration of the legal meaning, overturning the presumption of precedent or other substantiated rights.

The Court decision in *Roe* v. *Wade* thus accepted the pro-Choice movement's claims and integrated their key terms into the legal discourse, establishing that a woman's "right to privacy" protected the *Choice* of abortion. The Court rejected the feebly argued pro-Life claim that a fetus, from the moment of conception, had a Right to Life that would override the woman's right. The Court arrived at this position because of the particular constellation of public characterizations and legal precedent and the relative skill with which these had been presented. The coercive power of the state was therefore shifted from the pro-natalists to the women and their interests.

The policy consequences of this decision were a bit more complex than a simple win for the pro-Choice faction, however. Because of the substantive value of the fetus, the Court backed off from acknowledging an absolute right to abortion. As with any personal right (including life, free speech, religion, etc.), the Court holds the communitarian or statist position that compelling state interests might overrule these rights. The justices found that the reproductive Freedom of women was limited by state interests in protecting women's health and—borrowing the residual argumentative grounds of the pro-Life movement—the "potential life" of the fetus after it was viable.

The limits on abortion derived from the health issues were, primarily, decided on empirical medical criteria, as interpreted by the judges. Given the relative safety of abortions at different stages of pregnancy, states were authorized to exert different degrees of control in the first, second, and third trimesters. The limits on abortion deriving from the state's interest in the "potential life" of the fetus were decided to be *compelling* only after the fetus was viable. Consequently, the states were free to restrict abortion in the third trimester, except at the cost of the woman's life and health (broadly defined).

In the end, therefore, the Court constructed a compromise from the strongest substantive arguments offered by both sides. The *value* of the fetus (as it became materially more substantial in the later stages of development) and women's Liberty (through the "freedom of choice") were both conserved. The compromise was unique. It did not specify what purposes for abortion would be acceptable nor place control of abortions in outside committees, as other Western countries had done; instead, it reflected the liberal American tradition, recognizing women as individuals with rights that could not be violated for "the good of the community" except in extreme cases.

Historically, this liberal individualism was probably essential to allow women a right to abortion in America. Otherwise, as the dissenters and opposing attorneys directly argued, the state interest in encouraging women to engage in the un-waged, extremely demanding effort of childbirth would simply override most reasons for abortion. And this was precisely the argument used in the decisions denying protection of funding for abortions: states could conceivably have a "rational purpose" in pro-natalism. Nonetheless, this kind of individualism exacts a clear price. Acceptance of the premise that the independent and unique existence of each individual entails the need for that individual to be the center of personal choice-making can be construed to mean that individuals are also economically responsible for all such choices. This component of traditional American liberalism also was employed to shape the meanings of the new abortion vocabularies, but this time the narrowing occurred in the national legislature.

The Congress Restrains "Choices"

If White and Rehnquist's reaction was strong—so strong as to call the decision "an exercise of raw judicial power" (p. 222)—that of the pro-Life public was nearly apocalyptic. The Court's decision was, however, only one component of the "legal integration" of the pro-Choice and pro-Life vocabularies into the legal system. If we focus solely on the Court decision, we are likely to conclude that the pro-Life discourse gained much less public sanction than it actually did.

In comparison to the considerations of the legislature, the decisions of the Supreme Court are appealingly simple. Legislative decisions never offer any single rationale for their mandates—only dozens of votes and policies, committee hearings, and hours of discussions. Legislative intent is, therefore, even more difficult to interpret. However, because of this complexity and variability, because of the sheer increase in the "representativeness" of the legislature, and because legislatures deal more with pocketbooks than with rights, legislative decisions reveal far more clearly the negotiation and compromise inherent in situations in which competing interests work to influence the law.

The most notable abortion issue that faced the Congress was the "Hyde Amendment," which in various forms bedeviled the national legislature, especially between 1976 and 1978.[36] The amendment and its relatives went through a plethora of wording options and breadths and were attached to a wide range of options, seeking to limit public funding of abortions as stringently as possible. Most centrally, the amendment cut off Medicaid funding for abortions but not for childbirth. The strictest versions included all abortions. Other versions made exceptions for the life of the woman, rape, or health. Such amendments included or accompanied restrictions against federal spending for abortions on military bases and Indian reservations, for foreign service officers abroad, and in federal medical plans. In each case, the arguments were similar, and revealing.

On the "pro-funding" side, four major types of arguments were advanced.[37] First, the bills' opponents insisted the measure would force poor women into illegal abortion, which would result in carnage. Second, they protested that the measure was "discriminatory" and violated the "equal protection" clause, because it prevented poor women from enjoying a constitutional right to abortion while allowing affluent women to do so. Third, they stressed the various social costs of the limitation, including the economics of supporting welfare instead of abortion, and the costs in human suffering of "unwanted children" and "unwanting" teenage mothers. Finally, they addressed the procedural impropriety of using a funding rider in this manner and, early on, of flaunting the Courts. In short, the pro-funding legislators presented a microcosm of the discourse developed in the pro-Choice movement, complete with truncated narration of the tale of the horrors of illegal abortion, the *regulative ideograph "discrimination," and the *substantive ideograph Right to Choice. The pro-Choice legislators simply asserted that their previously elaborated grounds (accepted by the Supreme Court) covered this area as well. They lost this argument resoundingly and repeatedly; federal funding for abortions was drastically curtailed.

The discourse of the pro-Life advocates offers two arguments that might justify or explain the defeats. The first argument, heard repeatedly, held simply that abortion represented the killing of an innocent life and hence was intolerable. Some members of Congress urged that "the issue we face in this debate is the right of defenseless human life to exist."[38] The sponsor of the funding restrictions, Henry Hyde, was frequently supported in his insistence that this was the Congress's opportunity to limit the number of "killings." For these legislators, abortion was clearly and painfully immoral and ought to be prohibited.

In spite of the fact that this argument was vigorously and insistently repeated, there is reason to believe it was not directly the determining factor in the voting. During the same time period the Congress was considering the issue of a Constitutional amendment to prohibit abortion. This measure never received majority support in the House or Senate (nor in the public opinion polls).[39] The general lack of enthusiasm for the constitutional measure in the face of grand enthusiasm for the funding limitation suggests that legislators were attempting to "split the difference." They were seeking to negotiate the two vocabularies by making compromises that would recognize and incorporate some of the interests of both constituencies. The discursive manner in which these interests and vocabularies were negotiated came from the second major argument of the congressional pro-Life coalition.

The fervency, frequency, and persuasiveness of the Right-to-Life argument indicated that the pro-Life vocabulary and interests had to be dealt with in some manner. The discursive grounds on which the pro-Life interests were allowed to claim the funding limitations as a concession owed them, however, was a careful manipulation of the pro-Choice ideology against itself. The anti-funding advocates insisted that if abortion were a matter of individual conscience, and if there were no consensus about the beginning point of human life, then the Congress had no business forcing taxpayers whose consciences compelled them to oppose abortion into paying for the abortions of others. Mrs. Lloyd of Tennessee said that "it is discrimination of the worst kind against any taxpayer who opposes abortion to force that individual to finance an act toward which he or she has a deep personal, moral aversion. . . . Congress has no business using its power to tax to collect funds for this purpose."[40] Two years earlier, Mr. Paul had said:

> Civil libertarians must oppose tax dollars for abortion if they choose to be consistent. The use of tax dollars for abortion flaunts the first amendment protection of religious liberty. The advice I give to the pro-abortionists is "Do not use the dollar of citizens with devout religious beliefs against abortion to carry out this procedure. This is like waving a red flag in front of a bull and providing an incentive for the antiabortionists to organize and rally with great strength."[41]

The advocates further backed their claims by indicating that, to this point in American law, medical procedures were not themselves treated as an inherent right and that the government had always picked and chosen various coverages. Medicaid, Rep. Obey pointed out, did not pay for dental work; it need not pay for abortions.[42] The argument was extended to indicate that government did not and could not pay for every right it allowed: poor women could not exercise all the "vices" of the rich.[43]

The issue, of course, received some rebuttal. Pro-funding legislators argued that anarchy would result if constituents could choose, individually, to refuse to support specific government programs by withholding their taxes (especially in wartime). The pro-Life group was not, however, positing an *individual* right to refuse to pay taxes. They were arguing for a strong, impassioned minority, and they were holding their opponents to argumentative consistency: if the issue was one of personal conscience, by definition, then it was a matter in which everyone ought to be able to act only according to conscience. Essentially, therefore, the issue seems to have come down to Mr. Kindness's conclusion that "governments are, in the first place, established in order that we may live together peaceably without imposing upon one another. And yet we are confronted with the question today of whether the Government should tax dollars and pay for an act which is particularly offensive to many people from whom those taxes are taken. These people cannot, as a result, have a respect for that government."[44] The vocabulary of Choice was thus turned back against itself as a limiting condition.

Legal Conclusions

Over the next fifteen years the Supreme Court and state and national legislatures were to entertain a wide variety of subsidiary issues related to regulation of and support for abortion.[45] The pattern they established was fairly consistent. Many state legislatures attempted repeatedly to limit abortion rights and to discourage abortion through "nuisance" requirements demanding pro-natalist counseling for women contemplating abortion, physician reporting requirements, parental and spousal consent requirements, emergency equipment requirements, and so forth. The state and national legislatures by and large also worked to cut off all conceivable funding of public abortions. The Court overturned virtually all of the nuisance requirements (except certain consent measures) but supported the funding limitations.

The result was a redefinition of the Right to Choice. The pro-Choice vocabulary was adopted as a legitimate component of the national repertoire; the coercive power of the state was no longer to be employed to prevent women's choices. The women's vocabulary of "choice," however, was translated from a substantive demand for real choices in one's life to a permissive liberal demand to prevent active government interference in whatever choices one might economically, socially, and personally have.[46]

As a matter of political philosophy, we could describe the transformation of the women's vocabulary as the inevitable result of the limitations of liberal discourse that bases its demand for change on individual rights. We could place the liberal component as inherent either in the vocabulary of Choice or in the social system into which it was integrated. We would thereby describe either the pro-Choice movement or the social system as inherently incapable of providing substantive (instead of permissive) rights. Such an internal problematic is not simply a matter of "liberalism." however, for in whatever manner a woman's demand to "control her own body" is framed, to do so requires resources, and those resources must come either from her own efforts ("individualism") or from the efforts of others ("socialism") who, in good conscience, might well object to being involved in her actions. The substantive demand for real choices for women that had been granted legal standing by the Court was trimmed back by the legislature to a simple permission because of the continuing disagreements about the standing of abortion.

As a matter of communication theory, the transformation takes on a different character. In public discourse, one must appeal to some form of majority or consensus group of "others" who constitute the social system. Where one is successful, one's vocabulary will be integrated into the public discourse, and thereby one's actions and interests enabled. However, where there are competing discourses that also gain legitimacy with a sizable and powerful segment of the populace, the way in which one's discourse is integrated into or "translated into" the public repertoire will be seriously constrained by the opposing discourse and interests. The result may well be a compromise of the sort evident both in *Roe* v. *Wade* and in the actions of the legislatures and popular referenda.[47] Consequently, in order to see one's vocabulary and interests fully enacted, one must not only persuade the public of the appropriateness of one's own terms but also refute or respond to the terms of the opposition. This is not always done by movement rhetors, and in some cases it cannot be done.

On this account, it was not primarily a philosophical deficiency— not the "essential liberalism"—of the vocabulary of Choice or even of the social system that was limiting. Rather, it was the existence of competing interest groups and a sparse and largely ineffective refutation of their discourse that resulted in a "compromising" of the pro-Choice movement's full goals. As a consequence, the vocabularies of both Life and Choice became partially entrenched in the law, although in different ways and covering different territories.

This compromise, articulated in the formal realm of legal discourse, was tightly interwoven with the compromises worked out in the less formal mass discourse. In chapter 7 I trace the extension of the legal compromise to the cultural realm by examining prime-time television's portrayals of abortion. In chapter 8 I will describe the even more dire consequences of the failure to respond to the pro-Life discourse which occurred with the production of minority violence to replace the State's coercion.

NOTES

1. *Roe* v. *Wade* 410 US. 113 (1973) and *Doe* v. *Bolton* 410 US 179 (1973).

2. The decision is defended by Philip B. Heymann and Douglas E. Barzelay, "The Forest and the Trees: *Roe* v. *Wade* and Its Critics," *Boston University Law Review* 53 (1973), 765–84. The initial reactions on the right are summarized and cited by Basile J. Uddo, "A Wink from the Bench: The Federal Courts and Abortion," *Tulane Law Review* 53 (1979), 398–464. The language of some of these reviews is far from confined to legal scholarship. Robert Byrn, for example, states the issues quite emotionally. However, the central pretext of his argument concerns legal ways of reasoning. See "An American Tragedy: The Supreme Court on Abortion," *Fordham Law Review* 41 (1973), 807. Additional critical defenses are contained in Sylvia A. Law, "Rethinking Sex and the Constitution," *University of Pennsylvania Law Review* 132 (1984), 955; Laurence H. Tribe, "The Supreme Court 1972 Term; Forword: Toward a Model of

Roles in the Due Process of Life and Law," *Harvard Law Review* 87 (1973), 1 (later partially repudiated); Donald H. Regan, "Rewriting Roe v. Wade," *Michigan Law Review* 77, no.7 (1979), 1569, and other articles, same volume.

3. Feminists have recently mounted serious attacks on the adequacy of "privacy" for providing women with substantive life choices. This issue is dealt with more fully below, but see Ruth Bader Ginsberg, "Some Thoughts on Autonomy and Equality in Relation to *Roe v. Wade*," *North Carolina Law Review* 63 (January 1985), 375–86; Rosalind Pollack Petchesky, "Introduction: *Amicus Brief: Richard Thornburgh* v. *American College of Obstetricians and Gynecologists*," *Women's Rights Law Reporter* 9 (1986), 3–6; "Privacy or Sex Discrimination Doctrine: Must There Be a Choice?" *Harvard Women's Law Journal* 4 (Spring 1981), ix–xvi. An additional series of pivotal articles are compiled in the citations in Susan Frelich Appleton, "Doctors, Patients and the Constitution: A Theoretical Analysis of the Physician's Role in 'Private' Reproductive Decisions," *Washington University Law Quarterly* 63 (1985), 183–236.

4. An extensive body of research is developing on the different rules of rationalist and sound argument in different fields of discourse (e.g., law, science, business, ethics, politics, religion). See the work by Stephen Toulmin, *The Uses of Argument* (Cambridge: Cambridge University Press, 1958), and several essays by a variety of authors in *Proceedings of the Summer Conference on Argumentation* (Annandale, Va.: Speech Communication Association, 1981) and in *Argument in Transition: Proceedings of the Third Summer Conference on Argumentation* (Annandale, Va.: Speech Communication Association, 1983), and see Josina M. Makau, "The Supreme Court and Reasonableness," *Quarterly Journal of Speech* 70 (1984), 381, and W. Lance Bennett and Martha S. Feldman, *Reconstructing Reality in the Courtroom: Justice and Judgment in American Culture* (New Brunswick, N.J.: Rutgers University Press, 1981), and Chaim Perelman, *Justice, Law and Argument* (Dordrecht, Holland: D. Reidel, 1980).

5. This claim does not deny that the discourse in criminal trials and civil cases is understood by juries through narrative frames (e.g., Bennett and Feldman). The claim does indicate that the legal structure has attempted to replace such narrative rationality with conventional propositional rationality for its professionals—appellate judges. The argument does not violate the claim of several theorists that narrative form is pervasive and essential to human understanding; it merely indicates the efforts of various "elite" or "expert" groups to subordinate that form. Compare to Walter Fisher, *Human Communication as Narration: Toward a Philosophy of Reason, Value, and Action* (Columbia: University of South Carolina Press, 1987).

6. Roe's complaint was joined by a physician and a married couple, but their cases were not ruled to have standing and be justiciable.

7. Rehnquist argued that the stage of Roe's pregnancy was unclear and that this resulted in an overbroad ruling. 35 L Ed 2d 147, p. 197.

8. *Landmark Briefs and Arguments of the Supreme Court of the United States: Constitutional Law Edition,* vol. 75, ed. Philip B. Kurland and Gerhard Casper (Arlington, Va.: University Publications of America, 1975).

9. *Landmark*, p. 787, oral arguments.

10. The judges called this statement "eloquent" (*Landmark*, p. 788). Although they originally denied the *legal* importance of this argument, suggesting that she get to "Constitutional" issues (p. 788), they were clearly later influenced by this explanation of the cruciality of the issue. None of the judges, even the dissenting judges, directly challenged these claims, either during oral argument or in the written decisions and responses. However, the conservative judges did not accept these claims as 'fundamental,' even though they accepted them as existent. See below.

11. The *Roe* decision elaborates some of the case law here, p. 161. The appellee's briefs and their *amici* attempted to portray the situation differently, but they generally do not make the distinction between the rights of the fetus at the time of injury, inheritance, etc., and the rights of the fetus contingent on its eventual birth or the parental rights in the fetus, but see "State Protection of Future 'Persons'" *Connecticut Law Review* 18 (Winter 1986), 429–58.

12. First, the admission of serious, sustained, perhaps sexist, error is particularly difficult for a Court that sees itself as a last arbiter of major conflicts. Second, even those who are not strict constructionists find it difficult to believe that new fundamental rights can be created. At best, the argument is made that the rights had not previously been contested. It is important to remember, in this regard, that the rights articulated in the Bill of Rights and elsewhere are not equivalent to the only fundamental rights the framers and ratifiers intended to protect. They are, rather, the particular rights that were directly under assault at the time. The right to privacy was not a major concern in the age when every framer's plantation was *his* castle. No one asked Thomas Jefferson for a urine sample. In contrast, from contemporary perspectives, the provision against quartering troops in the home represents a right no more fundamental than the privacy rights in the bedroom, but the founders were not concerned about birth control infringements, and so the former, perhaps less fundamental, right was explicitly enumerated while the latter was left unarticulated but arguably protected by the Ninth Amendment, which declares, "The Enumeration in the Constitution of certain rights shall not be construed to deny or disparage others retained by the people."

13. See chapter 3, and also John T. Noonan, Jr., "An Almost Absolute Value in History," in *The Morality of Abortion*, ed. John T. Noonan, Jr. (Cambridge: Harvard University Press, 1970). In oral arguments, see *Landmark*, pp. 800–801.

14. Compare Appleton to Andrea Asaro, "The Judicial Portrayal of the Physician in Abortion and Sterilization Decisions: The Use and Abuse of Medical Discretion," *Harvard Women's Law Journal* 6 (Spring 1983), 51–102.

15. Asaro describes the shift and Appleton admits to it on p. 188.

16. This interpretation of the Ninth Amendment is vigorously resisted by conservatives who claim, among other things, that the intent of the framers was to limit this to states' rights. Given the clarity of the amendment and its omission of any explicit states' rights language, the intent of a few isolated

framers is irrelevant. The large number of persons responsible for *ratifying* the document would have interpreted without these special intentions but in terms of the clear language it presented then as now. This framing of the issue in terms of public discourse is related to the legal framing of the issue in terms of "strict constructionism." The "strict constructionist" holds the former premise—preventing the judiciary from adding anything "new" to the constitution—hence avoiding legislative-type action. However, given that the Ninth Amendment *explicitly* indicates that there *are* other constitutionally protected rights that the Court must safegaurd, even though they are not expressly elaborated in the document itself, a strict construction position should not be taken, as it so often has been by White and Rehnquist, to mean that no other rights may be protected as fundamental. This move is predicated on their political conservativism, rather than their judicial conservativism, because they argue that any right that has not previously been recognized must not be fundamental. The alternative, of course, is that there can be fundamental rights that have not been previously challenged by an ever-more-intrusive government, or that new rights can become more fundamental in changed social circumstances, or—as in the case of *Brown* v. *Board of Education*—that the Court previously was wrong.

17. There is a middle tier applied to discrimination cases, which I do not discuss here because of its tangential relevance. See Makau, "The Supreme Courts." As with all the legal doctrines discussed here, this one is, of course, not uncontested.

18. Key decisions include *Griswold* v. *Connecticut* 381 US 479 (1965); *Eisenstadt* v. *Baird* 405 US 438 (1972); *Loving* v. *Virginia* 388 US 1.

19. See Petchesky; Appleton.

20. The extent to which the Court has *not* placed privacy in the familial context is evident in Meera Werth, "Spousal Notification and the Right of Privacy," *Chicago Kent Law Review* 59 (Fall 1983), 1129–51. Additionally, it is arguable that the Court has made a progressive move by eliminating patriarchal family rights which controlled issues of sexuality and abortion without much explicit legal sanction and replacing them with more equitable privacy rights granted independently to women and men. Furthermore, the reverse case of Chinese law, in which women do not have a "zone of privacy" surrounding their bodies and therefore can be literally invaded by the state, suggests the need to achieve women's liberation from familial (and economic) constraints in ways other than by discarding privacy. On the Chinese problem see Ann S. Anagnost, "Magical Practice, Birth Policy and Women's Health in Post-Mao China," public lecture, University of Illinois, Urbana, fall 1988; John S. Aird, "Coercion in Family Planning," Congress of the U.S., Joint Economic Committee, *China's Economy Looks toward the Year 2000* (Washington, D.C.: Government Printing Office, 21 May 1986), 184–221, or, most accessibly, Julian L. Simon, "China's 'Voluntary' Population Initiative," *Wall Street Journal*, 29 February 1988, p. 19. I believe that the underlying animus of these attacks is a basic displeasure with private property which I do not share. The utility of the privacy argument on the international scene is argued by Aaron E.

Michel, "Abortion and International Law: The Status and Possible Extension of Women's Right to Privacy," *Journal of Family Law* 20 (January 1982), 241–61.

21. Appleton; Petchesky.

22. The role of the equal protection/discrimination pitfall is made evident in Larry P. Boyd, "The Hyde Amendment: New Implications for Equal Protection Claims," *Baylor Law Review* 33 (Spring 1981), 295–306. On the positive role of equal protection in the Court's decision see Tribe, p. 3.

23. Ginsberg admits that, to this point, the Court has not ruled in other equal protection cases in a fashion that would lead to the desired outcomes if equal protection were the primary grounds and that the Court has moved to establish the right as fundamental for women through the current line of argument; Ginsberg, pp. 376–79.

24. *Roe*, p. 152.

25. In oral arguments (*Landmark*, p. 823) Flowers accepts that he is "balancing against the Ninth Amendment rights of the mother." He does not argue that the woman does not have those rights but merely that they are outweighed by the right to life of the fetus.

26. See Ginsberg.

27. Another alternative is that the justices admitted the importance of this right to women but took an extreme statist position that would, on analogy, have required them to uphold state laws prescribing occupations, housing, or travel undertaken by men.

28. *Landmark*, pp. 821, 823, 802, 803.

29. *Landmark*, p. 817. She had earlier been asked a similar question and evaded it by focusing the issue on the specific context of the way the case had been framed (p. 813).

30. *Landmark*, p. 822, re-argument. A similar line of questioning was pursued on argument, p. 803.

31. *Landmark*, p. 819. On original argument, see also Floyd, p. 803.

32. *Landmark*, pp. 819–20.

33. The Court asked, "Mr. Flowers, doesn't the fact that so many of the state abortion statutes do provide for exceptional situations in which an abortion may be performed—and presumably these date back a great number of years, following Mr. Justice Stewart's comment—suggest that the absolute proposition that a fetus from the time of conception is a person, just is at least against the weight of historical legal approach to the question?" Flowers replied, "Yes, sir, I would think, possibly, that that would indicate that." He then went on to argue for the suggestion that the states just never properly considered the issue. *Landmark*, p. 828.

34. The Court's query comes at *Landmark*, p. 818. The medical discussions are on re-argument, pp. 826 and 827, on initial argument, pp. 804–5.

35. *Landmark*, p. 827.

36. For a summary of the legislative history see Peg O'Hara, "Congress and the Hyde Amendment," *Congressional Quarterly Weekly Report,* 19 April 1980, pp. 1038–39. See also Eva R. Rubin, *Abortion, Politics, and the Courts: Roe v. Wade and Its Aftermath,* rev. ed. (New York: Greenwood Press, 1987).

37. See, for example, *Congressional Record: House*, 95th Congress, 2d session, 13 June 1978, pp. 17258–270, or 10 August 1976, pp. 26781–792 (hereafter, *Congressional Record* will be abbreviated *CR*). The first full-scale debate on an abortion rider was in 1974. See *CR: Senate*, June 27, 1974, pp. 21687–695. After Senate Judiciary Commitee Hearings on Abortion in 1974 and 1975, there was an open debate on the Hatch Amendment (SJ Res 3) in the 98th Congress, 1st session, March and April, 1983, and on the Helms position, 28 April 1976, SJ Res 178.

38. Rep. Oberstar, *CR*, 13 June 1978, p. 17261.

39. In brief, the polls indicated that most people made distinctions about the appropriateness of an abortion based upon the time in the pregnancy and the reasons for the abortion. Earlier abortions and more serious reasons generated more support for legalization. A large majority strongly opposed a constitutional amendment to ban all abortions except to save the pregnant woman's life. For more detail on the polls, see chapter 8.

40. Rep. Lloyd, *CR*, 13 June 1978, p. 17261.

41. Rep. Paul, *CR*, 10 August 1976, p. 26787.

42. Rep. Obey, *CR*, 12 October 1978, p. 3692.

43. Ibid.

44. Rep. Kindness, *CR*, 10 August 1976, p. 26787.

45. See Rubin.

46. As yet, the pro-Choice advocates have not presented much evidence that these funding restrictions have had any significant impact by reducing the use of the abortion option. Using figures for the first year after the Hyde Amendment was enacted, Frohock argues that 94 percent of the Medicaid-eligible women wanting abortions were able to fund them through other sources (p. 24). However, according to Nanette J. Davis this may have meant seventeen deaths from illegal abortions resorted to because funding was not available between 1975 and 1979 (*From Crime to Choice* [Westport, Conn.: Greenwood Press, 1985]). Arguably, as long as the economic system is providing for the execution of these rights for the overwhelming majority of women through indirect means, it will not be forced to confront the provision of services through direct means. I specify the persons at interest here as wage-laboring women, because this is the group that consciously shares the "choice" vocabulary, according to studies of activists in the movement by Kristin Luker, *Abortion and the Politics of Motherhood* (Berkeley: University of California Press, 1984). Marilyn Falik, *Ideology and Abortion Politics* (New York: Praeger, 1983), p. 124, reported that 100 percent of pro-Choice activists in her sample were employed outside the home, while 70 percent of the married, female anti-abortion activists indicated "housewife/mother" as their occupation (88 percent were married).

47. By and large, state referenda have not tended to support the pro-Life vocabulary.

CHAPTER SEVEN

Prime-Time Abortion
Rhetoric and Popular Culture
———— 1973-85 ————

Legal fenceposts can establish only the outer limits within which social practices are conducted. The understanding of abortion as an actual practice in real lives—the social norms about abortion—would be negotiated in the more fluid and multiplicitous realm of *culture. In America, in the last half of the twentieth century, prime-time network television has been the most widely accessed cultural medium. As David Thorburn has argued, television is the contemporary medium of "consensus narrative,"[1] the primary source of "shared stories" that explain "life as an American" to those holding the dominant vision in the culture as well as to a large number outside that dominant vision in some way.[2] An examination of prime-time television is therefore essential to understanding the ways in which public, explicitly political, discourse made the crucial transition into the cultural vocabularies of everyday life.[3]

Historically, the political-cultural discursive work done in network prime-time depictions of abortion practices followed, rather than led, the public argument and legal change; almost all of the episodes dealing with abortion occurred after *Roe* v. *Wade*, and most of them were not aired until 1984–85.[4] Consequently, the programs visibly reveal the influences of the public argument. However, television reworked those discourses in line with the medium's own characteristics to produce a unique compromise of its own.

Creating an Abortion Culture

The earliest televised depictions of abortion were most single-sided— that is, most rhetorical.[5] Episodes of the *Defenders* in 1962 and of *Maude* in 1973 relied on relatively strong cases for abortion. In the case

123

of the *Defenders* a doctor crusaded for legalized abortion and a woman sought abortion to rid herself of a rapist's child, thus presenting one of the most rhetorically compelling cases possible. In *Maude* the central character was old enough to make pregnancy plausibly undesirable for her, and she was assertive enough to convey the message of her life and experiences powerfully. Mimicking the early public story of illegal abortion, these early programs most clearly participated in a rather explicit argument for change.

This apparent stridency resulted in direct political retaliation—economic sanctions by opponents of liberalized abortion laws. In the case of the *Defenders*, all three of the original sponsors pulled out of the program, and the Catholic magazine *America* urged its readers to write the replacement sponsor with their comments.[6] In the *Maude* case, a decade later, the Catholic opposition was even more fully organized. *Time* magazine noted that "Roman Catholics were mounting an intensive—and remarkably successful—campaign" against the program.[7] Thirty-eight CBS stations canceled the episode, moved the segment, or provided response time.[8]

The particular charges made against the program were of consequence. Right-to-Life advocates specifically labeled Maude's decision a "convenience abortion" and bemoaned that it "preached individual selfishness."[9] By drawing particular attention to the *reasons* for Maude's abortion—by condemning her motives rather than abortion per se—they inadvertently created ground for negotiation. In the future, television would not back off from televising abortion but rather would portray the motives for it in more careful and complicated fashion.

This early conflict over televised abortion reveals itself as even more patently rhetorical and political when we consider the fact that the *Maude* episode grew out of a prize offered by the Population Institution (a Methodist-linked organization) for television programs that dealt with population matters.[10] Direct political and rhetorical input into the content of television programs through economic means becomes quite clear on both sides of the issue. At this early stage economics, sanctions, and discourse generated by different political interest groups clearly shaped the admission of abortion into American mass culture.

These direct, visible, and vehement sanctions should not be taken as the sole causal agents affecting the absorption of the political arguments into the cultural medium. The direct economic sanctions were merely signs of the broader economic and political pressures acting on television programmers. Television is always somewhat responsive to the political tastes and concerns of its potential audiences. The particular way in which television responds—the particular portrait of a cultural practice given *presence for the national viewing audience—depends upon several key characteristics of the medium. These characteristics and their consequences become visible when we look closely at the range of abortion practices presented on television.

The Prime-Time Practice of Abortion

Three distinctly different types of entertainment programs focused on abortion.[11] The first set of programs featuring abortion as a central problem in the plot addressed the relationship of legal and medical professionals to legal abortion. "Liberal" doctor and police programs affirmed the necessity for professionals to adhere to the new laws by providing support for abortion practices.[12] Episodes of *Hill Street Blues*, *Cagney and Lacey*, and *St. Elsewhere* fell in this "pro-*Choice*" category.

A second set of programs, primarily family series, constituted what I shall call the "false-pregnancy" programs. In these episodes central female characters found themselves with "unwanted pregnancies," discussed abortion, decided against it, and yet were saved from the consequences of carrying the pregnancy to term by miscarriages or by the discovery that they were not pregnant after all. This "anti-abortion" formula was included in episodes of *Call to Glory*, *Webster*, *Magruder and Loud*, *Dallas*, and *Family*.

In a final category of "pro-abortion" programs, central female characters actually decided to have abortions and explicitly or implicitly went through with them. *Spenser for Hire*, *Maude*, *Defenders*, *Buffalo Bill*, part of the *Cagney and Lacey* subplot, and a second *St. Elsewhere* dealt with abortion in this manner.

Prime-time television thus offered three apparently contradictory positions on abortion. This diversity was increased by the fact that, in each of the program types, different characters were assigned to recite different portions of both the pro-Life and pro-Choice arguments in some detail. At first glance, therefore, the integration of the public discourse into the cultural realm seems nothing more than a virtually unaltered transference of the public disagreement into the cultural realm. The words of the movement advocates were funneled into the characters' mouths and their values and worldviews were funneled into the characters' actions. Entertainment programming appears to have allowed its audiences to "take sides" in the controversy, selecting pro-Choice, pro-abortion, or pro-family positions. Actually, however, through cautious assignment of roles and arguments the three program types cooperated, if inadvertently, to produce a much more integrated and shared set of interpretations of acceptable abortion in American culture. The outlines of this cultural portrayal emerges through detailed exploration of each of the program types.

Professional Choices

In the "professional regulation" programs of the eighties programmers dealt with the underlying political struggle in several ways. *Cagney and Lacey, St. Elsewhere,* and *Hill Street Blues* all featured doctors and law enforcement officials counteracting the effects of extra-legal violence directed against legal abortion practices. Regardless of the dictates of their personal consciences, the doctors and lawyers were forced to take a stand in support of the law. Detective Sergeant Chris Cagney, in spite of her Catholic background, protected and assisted an indigent woman who sought an abortion and tracked down and confronted an abortion clinic bomber. The *St. Elsewhere* team provided an abortion to a mentally retarded woman, featured an abortion by the girlfriend of an internist, and treated the victims of an abortion clinic bomber. The *Hill Street* crew dealt with an abortion clinic demonstration in which a pro-Life activist caused the death of a fetus by violently shoving its mother.

Each of these cases presented the issues as contested and controversial; particular characters who clearly represented different interest groups argued about them. In two lengthy scenes, Cagney and Lacey argued out the issue of "choice," and in another Cagney re-argued the issue with her recalcitrant Catholic father. These disputes were clearly phrased in terms of the interests and beliefs of "women" vs. "the church." This episode provides a clear example of the particular way prime-time television positioned these vocabularies for private lives.

The key points of the pro-Life argument in the *Cagney and Lacey* episode were presented by two minor characters—one woman and one man. Early in the program the pro-Life position was articulated by Arlene Crenshaw, the leader of the local pro-Life group. As Cagney and Lacey attempted to restrain a picket line so that women could pass through into the clinic, Crenshaw accused Cagney, "How can you help murder unborn babies?" She continued, "Sergeant, human beings are being murdered here every day. . . . If you were in

Nazi Germany and you saw lives being taken by the thousands, wouldn't you do everything in your power to stop that?"

Throughout the program, Arlene was portrayed in a basically inoffensive manner.[13] She was firm and sincere, if a bit "straight-laced" or severe. Her argument—that abortion was the taking of human life—was presented publicly, as a matter of reasonable conviction. It was, however, indirectly contrasted with the argument offered by the male pro-Life character—Cagney's father. Playing pool in a bar one evening, Cagney and her father had a conversation in which he urged her to ask to get relieved from the case because the "big boys" downtown—Irish Catholics—would not look favorably on the investigation.

father: This whole thing makes me sick anyway. I mean, when an abortionist used to be a dirty word. Just because the times have changed doesn't change anything, you know. It's still a mortal sin.

Cagney: Are you so sure of that?

father: Chrissy, that is the way I was taught. It's the way you were taught and it's the way I believe. People a lot smarter than me have spent a lot of time figuring this thing out.

Cagney: Yeah, what if I was pregnant and I didn't want to marry the guy? Or he was married and I couldn't and I didn't want to raise the baby by myself?

father: We . . . we . . . we'd figure something out. You know. Adoption . . . your brother. Something.

Cagney: Well, what if I didn't want to?

father: Hey, what are you asking me these questions for? It's not a man's problem, you know. Sheee . . . I'm sorry . . . that's not what I meant. What I meant was. . . . Boy, this is some conversation for somebody who once wanted to be a nun. But it's not going to happen, so please. It's your shot. . . .

This "private" conversation gave voice to the assumptions of the pro-Choice worldview about the private motivations of the pro-Life movement—that it was a religious (Catholic) matter and a matter of male vs. female.[14] In thus re-articulating the arguments the cultural program retained the pro-Life group's *universalized argument based on Life but revised it by portraying it as dependent on private motivations. The pro-Life position thus retained the moral ground, but that morality was recast from universal to religious and private. The ramifications of that portrayal should become evident shortly.

This episode of *Cagney and Lacey* also presented a series of characters enacting and articulating specific components of the pro-Choice discourse. "Mrs. Herrera" initiated the contáct between the detectives and the clinic by requesting assistance from the police to get through the picket line. She was apparently of Latin American descent, and she expressed a highly rhetoricized motivation for seeking an abortion. In the police car with Cagney and Lacey she answered a question about her husband, saying, "He's on disability. . . . They can't make me have this baby. I see my friends my age. They have babies. They can't work. They can't go to school. The only thing they can do is watch TV all day." Mary Beth then asked her, "Will your husband be able to go back to work?" and Mrs. Herrera replied, "Who knows when. I don't want to be on welfare. I want to finish business school."

Mrs. Herrera thus represented and articulated the economic motivation for abortion for lower-class women. Through this means the program enacted and restated a major component of the pro-Choice position. However, the program also transformed that argument into a "pro-abortion" rather than "pro-Choice" position in two ways. First, because Mrs. Herrera was a temporary, secondary character, she was put in the position of justifying her abortion to the representatives of the social order (the detectives). The dialogue provided the middle-class auditors an economic reason (welfare costs) for supporting abortions for the poor rather than for supporting choices for the poor women per se. In addition, through negation the dialogue built the assumption that women whose husbands could support them did not need or should not have abortions. The dramatization thus limited the appropriate realm for Choice in a second way.

This limiting of Choice was reinforced by the male physician from the abortion clinic, who gave two "speeches" on abortion. In his first contact with the detectives he angrily ranted: "They're so worried about the unborn. What about the babies that are already here? Do you think those people were picketing City Hall when day-care funding was cut?" He then turned to Detective Mary Beth Lacey, asking, "What month are you in?

Lacey: Fifth.
Dr.:   That's wonderful.
Lacey: Yeah.
Dr.:   You got a ring on your finger. You got a good paying job. A lot of
        the women who come in here aren't so lucky.

In re-articulating the consistency challenge to the pro-Life movement, the doctor once again raised the issue of the social costs of giving birth to children for parents who had only marginal economic self-sufficiency. He also described Mary Beth as the opposite of a woman seeking abortion, thereby again identifying a type of woman who should *not* seek an abortion. Both of these topics framed the issue as a matter of support for specific types of abortions, rather than as a matter of support for the principle of women's Choice.

The doctor's articulation of the "pro-abortion" position was particularly powerful because of the authority physicians carry (in both social and dramatic life). Unlike Mrs. Herrera, who "justified" her abortion to the detectives, the doctor *lectured* the detectives, somewhat righteously. This authority was crucial, as he defined even the pro-Choice rationale for the pro-abortion position, not as a matter of morality or principle but as a matter of sympathy and social necessity. After his clinic had been bombed, he met Cagney and Lacey in the rubble and commented: "You just look through some of these records. We had twelve-year-olds—children—who came here pregnant. Now what brand of compassion forces a child—hell, anyone—to go through an unwanted pregnancy?"

Cagney: Well, apparently there are people who disagree with you.
Dr.:   Well, that's hard to see when you're standing in my shoes. It wasn't that long ago that I'd see women who had literally mutilated themselves. They were that desperate.

The doctor, replicating the physicians' role in the entire abortion controversy, here presented himself as an expert witness giving first-hand testimony. He did not propose that the Right to Choice was a matter of principle. Instead, he described Choice as a pragmatic necessity, given the fact that women would otherwise mutilate themselves, leaving doctors to deal with the messy consequences. This would prove to be a consequential acquiescence to the pro-Life claim to own the higher moral ground.

The physician, Mrs. Herrera, Cagney's father, and Arlene Crenshaw articulated and modified the public argument on abortion in the cultural realm by embodying the lived positions of those who might inhabit particular social conditions. Each of these characters was, however, placed in opposition to the main characters. The physician, as a male, occupied a suspect category in this pro-women program, and he lectured the detectives as if they were the opposition. Cagney's father enacted a similar male, authority-figure opposition to Cagney. Mrs. Herrera and Arlene Crenshaw both confronted the detectives making demands upon them in their "line of duty."

Cagney and Lacey were therefore positioned against these characters to provide a "resolution" of the social conflict. This occurred in two separate encounters.

The most dramatic of the pro-Choice discourses in the episode was the retelling of the tale of illegal abortion by the visibly pregnant detective, Mary Beth Lacey. One night in bed with her husband, Harvey, Mary Beth reflected on the day's events at the clinic, assisting Mrs. Herrera.

Lacey: I'm the luckiest lady alive. I've got my health back. I got you and the boys. I got new life in me. [She then contrasts her position to that of Mrs. Herrera.]

Harvey: That's what birth control's for. People shouldn't have kids if they can't take care of them.

Lacey: Who knows what she was dreaming would happen. I mean, it's easy to judge when it's somebody else you're talking about. It's different when it's you that's pregnant and you've got nowhere to turn.

Harvey: It's a long time ago, Mary Beth. It's over. [Long pause]

Lacey: I was nineteen years old, Harvey. I thought he was the man of my dreams. For him it was a little experiment and then time to move on.

Harvey: He was a bum, Mary Beth. Any guy that would not stand by you. Make you go through that by yourself.

Lacey: I couldn't tell anybody. Not even my mother.

Harvey: You did what you had to do.

Lacey: Well, I wasn't going to bring a kid into this world without a father. That's too hard, never knowing your father. [Mary Beth had been raised without her deserting father.]

Harvey: I know, babe.

Lacey: I snuck around like a criminal. Got some guy's name. Somebody said he'd been a medic in the army.

Harvey: It's OK.

Lacey: And one Sunday afternoon I went to where he lived in the Bronx—this little room over a grocery. In the corner was a table and he pointed to it and he said, "Lie down!" like I was a dog. No better than a dog, Harv.

Harvey: OK, Mary Beth. You said it.

Lacey: And you know I almost let him do it to me. I stood there and I thought about it. . . . There's people that want us to go back to that, Harv.

Harvey: It'll never be that way again.

Lacey: It'll be exactly like that. The only reason I could walk away was 'cause the money I saved for second semester. I made a choice right there. Take that money and go to Puerto Rico. Have it

done. . . . My college money. How many women do you
think he butchered on that table, Harv, huh?

In this dialogue, Mary Beth not only recounted a personalized
version of the tale of illegal abortion, she also provided the deepest
defense of the pro-Choice position—the inability to judge others and
the consequent requirement that they be allowed to make their own
choices. She also recognized that a system that disallows Choice
intensifies the economic disparities between women. In providing
this argument, however, Mary Beth was concerned not with a particular moral argument about the intrinsic desirability of Choice as a
moral fact but rather with the desirability of permissive laws. She did
not define abortion as a right or as a moral action available to women
on principle; instead, she simply refused to pass moral judgment on
other women. Like the public positions articulated by Mrs. Herrera
and the physician, her point of view did not contest the moral ground
claimed by anti-abortionists. Moreover, she described, once again,
the situation in which a woman would not want to have an abortion—
if she were married with good financial support.

Lacey's personal, and clearly private, position on abortion was not
an adequate resolution to the public conflict, but it did set up the
grounds for compromise. Throughout the program Lacey was positioned as the pro-Choice advocate; Cagney, in contrast, was placed as
the pivotal figure—uncertain about abortion, reluctant to help Mrs.
Herrera, willing to listen to Arlene Crenshaw. It was therefore Lacey's
confrontation with Cagney and their shared discourse that constructed a "resolution." That event took place in the half-public, half-
private space of the women's locker room. Mary Beth finally confronted Chris's reluctance:

Lacey: Chris, the woman is entitled to make up her own mind about
         her own body. . . .
Cagney: Mary Beth, please don't lecture me. I live what you're talking
         about.
Lacey: Pardon?
Cagney: I was raised Catholic. This is a hard one for me.
Lacey: [with sarcasm] Oh, I see.
Cagney: [softly] No, you don't.
Lacey: Women like Mrs. Herrera are wrong. They don't have a right
         to make their own decisions.
Cagney: I didn't say that. But there are other choices besides abortion.
Lacey: No one should tell Mrs. Herrera to have a child she doesn't
         want.
Cagney: [very softly] You're right, Mary Beth. I am pro-Choice. You

know. I've never lived my life any other way. But that doesn't mean I'm . . . I'm also pro-Life.

Lacey: So you're on everybody's side? You have to take a stand on this one, Christine. Otherwise you're walking a fence.

Cagney: [very softly] O.K., I'm walking a fence.

Lacey: How would you feel if you were raped and you got pregnant?

Cagney: Oh, I don't know; it would depend on the guy.

Lacey: Ahh!

Cagney: Well, please, that is the most stupid thing you ever asked me.

Lacey: OK, let's forget about rape victims and teenage girls and women carrying around severely *damaged children.* [Italic type represents talking over each other.]

Cagney: *I don't forget. I do not forget anyone.*

Lacey: *What if* it were you, Christine? A thirty-eight-year-old woman having to conspire with her doctor to commit a crime. That's humiliating, and what if they changed the law back and you don't have a choice any more?

Cagney: Then stop. I'd hate it. All right? I'm just trying to tell you my feelings. [softly] I don't know when it's murder.

Lacey: Abortion is not murder. It's not even a person yet.

Cagney: Well, tell that to your belly.

Lacey: My belly is my business. Same as Mrs. Herrera's belly is her business.

Cagney: I don't want to argue anymore, OK, Mary Beth? For the record, no one should take away anyone's right to make their own choices about anything. But this one feels wrong. Let's stop.

Lacey: Really, abortion is wrong but birth control isn't? You do use birth control, Christine?

Cagney: [softly and regretfully] Nobody's perfect.

This dialogue is a complex negotiation of meaning. The two women jump back and forth between public and private perspectives. They employ the key terms of the movement—*Choice* and *murder*—but they end up relating them in a specific and unique way. Mary Beth challenges Cagney to avoid "walking the fence"—that is, to come up with a resolution of the terms and the public/private dilemma. Cagney's answer is to support public Choice but to suggest that the private decision ought to be against abortion as a moral sin. The resolution is deepened by the birth control analogy: Cagney admits the difficulty of living up to one's own moral prescriptions, let alone the problematic of enacting those moral prescriptions into law.

In *Cagney and Lacey*, therefore, the public argument was translated into the cultural realm in two ways. First, characters enacted the life conditions alleged by the public dialogue to be lived by real people in "real life"—the woman who had an abortion as a teenager, the doctor who treated victims of illegal abortion, the financially destitute minority woman who lacks the resources to raise a child, and even the male Catholic who makes the issue one of tradition and abstraction while denying himself contact with the experiences of the female world. Second, these characters spoke the discourse of the social movement activists, but they did so in a carefully narrowed and re-personalized fashion. Through these two mechanisms, the program gave meaning to "abortion" and the surrounding vocabularies in private conditions rather than as general social abstractions.

This double assimilation gave access to meanings of the new public vocabulary that could be directly appropriated in everyday life. In doing so, however, it encouraged a particular, circumscribed cultural meaning for the practice of abortion, supporting legal Choice as a pragmatic necessity but defining abortion as a morally undesirable act. Abortions were "justified" only in a particular range of conditions—where a woman was too young or too old, unmarried, or financially destitute. The prime-time interpretation thus provided a resolution fully consonant with *Roe* v. *Wade:* individuals shall make their own moral choices. However, it endorsed only a limited range of such choices and accepted the pro-Life position that the practice of abortion is morally problematic.

The construction of the meaning of abortion in this depiction was not, of course, universally persuasive. The program, like pro-Choice programs before it, was boycotted by Catholics and the Right-to-Life movement. However, the definition of the practice of abortion created in this program was consonant with those in the other programs in the category and in the other program types. The uniformity of depiction created the presence of a somewhat singular vision of abortion in televised American culture. This largely uncontested presence, over the long term, carried persuasive impact.

Although generally less artistic, less sensitive, and less profound, the other programs in the professional genre similarly constructed a permissive, but limited, definition of abortion. *Hill Street Blues'* outcast female public defender gleefully based the defense of a pro-Life activist who had caused a miscarriage on the claim that the fetus was not a living human person. Her definition, however, was rejected and constrained both by the more moderate responses of the acceptable professional woman (Joyce Davenport) and by the willingness of the pro-Life, religious male to accede to legal penalties rather than betray his public principles by accepting the heretical defense for private protection. The right to "impose your morality on others" was again denied (violence to prevent abortion was chastised and legal abortion supported), but moral strength was portrayed as resting on the pro-Life ground.

The *St. Elsewhere* episode likewise supported this proscribed meaning of abortion. It featured vigorous argument from a male (Jack) that abortion is wrong. There were relatively lengthy discussions in the doctors' lounge, airing many pro-Choice and pro-Life claims. In these discussions the interests of pregnant women were explicitly defended by female doctors-to-be and young career women in opposition to Jack's masculine defense of the fetus's rights. In the end, the mentally impaired woman—lacking both choice and moral judgment—was aborted by a medical establishment that defined the operation as a morally regrettable necessity. Another episode of *St. Elsewhere* similarly negotiated the discourse on abortion through a plot focused on a fanatic pro-Lifer threatening the hospital with violence.

As a whole, the professional programs produced a fairly narrow range of portrayals in which professionals supported legal Choice but regarded abortion itself as morally undesirable—neither an "easy choice" nor a replacement for birth control and positively inappropriate for happily married women. Perhaps it is not surprising that the constraints of the liberal professional/personal programs tended to produce fairly similar transformations of the public discourse, resulting in a fairly unified enactment of abortion across different episodes and programs. However, in the other two categories of prime-time programs, very different struggles and portrayals produced similar outcomes.

False Choices/False Pregnancies

In the "false pregnancy" programs, central female characters discovered themselves to be pregnant against their wishes. Their dominant reasons for not wanting a child centered on the desire for a career or a life of "one's own"—factors described as "convenience" by pro-Life advocates (*Dallas*, focusing on a Down's Syndrome fetus, provided the only exception). The episode of *Call to Glory* provides a typical example. Vanessa Sarnouk was in college, studying electronics. She had just been offered a job about which she was excited, if frightened, when she discovered she was pregnant. She was crushed but terrified to admit that she did not want the child. When an older female family member asked her "What about school? What about your job?" Vanessa refused to answer. A female friend finally forced her to confront the issue, rather than merely going along with the inevitability of pregnancy:

Friend: Yeah, but do you *want* it?

Vanessa: Rainer's very happy.

Friend: Rainer's not pregnant. His life isn't going to change one tiny bit. Yours is. Doesn't that make any difference to you? [pause] I made that choice. Three years ago. . . . It wasn't a dirty back room. It was a modern clinic. Right across the border. American doctors . . . I didn't feel too great about it. I don't think anybody ever does. But I went ahead with the life I'd planned.

Vanessa: I don't want to hear about this.

Friend: You have the right to make that choice.

Vanessa: [angry look]

Later, at the restroom of a pizza parlor, the friend came in to find an agitated, crying Vanessa. Vanessa sobbed to her, with anger and despair: "I'm going to have this baby. I'm going to love this baby. It's all right. I'm all right."

Like Vanessa, the other women in these "false pregnancy" programs were portrayed as giving up career for family, deciding to have a child rather than an abortion. Their explicit discourse reaffirmed the value of motherhood and family over career. This explicit rationale and "choice" was, however, in each case revealed as inauthentic; after making the anti-abortion choice each of these women had a miscarriage or discovered that she was not really pregnant at all. The women then expressed great regret and even guilt, simultaneously tying their own motivations back into the decision process. Vanessa, for example, said to her husband, "I didn't want it. . . . It must have known."

In these programs the dramatic structure and the underlying politics of television series worked together to constrain very tightly the cultural enactment of the practice of abortion. The specific "characters" that inhabit television have a restricted range of probable actions open to them, limited by the nature of the mass audience and their politics and life experiences.[15] The identity given modern female characters in these television programs was incompatible with returning to (or assuming) motherhood if it meant sacrifice of career. Consequently, even though the scriptwriters overtly affirmed the choice of motherhood, they subsequently negated that choice by relieving the women of its character-destroying consequences.

These programs reached this conclusion because of problems of narrative coherence. They were unable to provide an answer to the problematic presented by abortion because they were faced with the fundamental abortion problem: although women's lives include alternatives to pregnancy, women's biology presents the difficult-to-control fact of pregnancy. Specifically, the women of the programs lived late-twentieth-century lives, with careers and other-than-maternal interests. To bear the children (whether to become mothers or to adopt out the children) would have destroyed their character types, which were fundamental to the coherence of the plot and the series identity for the mass audience. These same constraints also prohibited these family-oriented women from having abortions. The dramatic resolution fit the persuasive limitations of the situation, defined by the limits authorized by the competing special-interest groups, but it did not provide complete role-models successfully blending traditional values with contemporary life patterns.

Additionally, even these "family" programs could not directly present the central discourse of the pro-Life movement itself. Because television uses narrative form focused on individuals while the pro-Life public argument focused on ideographs, social heritage, fetal images, and scientific discourses, television entertainment programming could not present a dramatic enactment of the pro-Life claim. The best it could do was to shift the discursive ground back to "family" (a focus the movement itself had generally avoided because of its anti-feminist and pro-natalist overtones).

Like the pro-Choice programs, therefore, the family programs did not represent the discourse of a single side of the controversy as a pure enactment of the practice and meaning of abortion. In the pro-Life programs characters could endorse the pro-Life discourse of "family" and choose explicitly against abortion, but they could not *act* on those discursive motivations. Once again, refusal of abortion by married women was portrayed as the moral choice, but once again, the need to permit abortion (or at least its effects) was enacted. Moreover, to get to this enactment, the family programs had to endorse the concept of women's Choice in the first place. In all cases, it was the women who made the decision whether to continue the pregnancy. This was, indeed, a mixed introduction to the practice. It depicted moral disapproval of abortion, support for the concept of women's Choice, and endorsement of family but no authentic alternative such as resources for and commitment to child-raising.

Pro-Abortion?

The same range of meanings emerged yet again through slightly different images in the last of the program types. Five programs featured women having abortions. As indicated above, the *Maude* and *Defenders* episodes were early and more rhetorical, but in the three cases of *Spenser for Hire*, *St. Elsewhere*, and the subplot of *Cagney and Lacey* abortion was not introduced in a simple pro-abortion fashion. In these programs, the women's reasons for choosing abortion fell into the "acceptable" range charted out in the "false pregnancy" and "pro-Choice" programs. The *Spenser for Hire* episode illustrates the texture of these programs. Spenser's girlfriend, Susan, discovered that she was pregnant, and they discussed it during a walk in the park [I have underlined the explicit discourse from the political controversy]:

Susan: Saying it out loud makes it sound so *selfish*, but dammit, this is just the worst time for this to have happened.

Spenser: Worst time? Do you think there'd ever be a perfect time, Suse? . . . *Convenience*, is that what we are talking about here? I love you, and I know you too well to think that your motives would ever be *selfish*. . . . [He goes on to interpret her reluctance as a fear that he would not be able to be a good father. She denies that and continues.]

Susan: What I'm really talking about is *independence*. All my life I've depended on someone. First my parents, then Frank. I'm finally at a point where I can stand on my own and feel some *control over my own life*—make decisions based on what I *want*. If I have a baby now I'll lose that. So maybe it is *selfish*.

Spenser: Susan, I understand about independence. About people making decisions. About being controlled or forced. But this decision is not yours alone. It's mine, too. I've got a responsibility here. . . . I want it. I'm prepared for it. . . . *This baby has a right to live.*

Susan: *What if I don't think it's a baby yet?* What if I think there is still a *choice?*

They continued walking and arguing:

Susan: You're very lucky to be so sure. 'Cause the only thing I know right now is that I love you.

Spenser: So you think the ultimate harmony in the world comes from us knowing we're independent creatures? [no answer] If it were my decision, I couldn't do it.

Susan: If I do, what about us?

Spenser: I don't know.

In the end, Spenser brought her flowers at the hospital to begin the process of healing the relationship. The discourse of this "pro-abortion" program, however, clearly did not frame abortion as a practice simply in terms of the public pro-Choice arguments. It articulated both sides of the issue at several levels, including the Right to Life vs.

"control of my life" and Choice. Additionally, the characterization of motivations as "selfish" was explored—with the characters cooperating to accept the pro-Life label here. Moreover, the abstract moral premise of the pro-Life attack—that the pro-Choice position recognizes no higher value than the individual—also was presented with greater presence than its opposite. In the end, the choice occurred, the character enacted the pro-Choice position, but only in the face of its definition as a highly problematic personal and moral action. The "convenience" abortion was thereby defined and derogated even as it was enacted.

The portrayal of abortion as an act entailing moral guilt and personal regret pervaded the "pro-abortion" programs. The episode of *St. Elsewhere* deepened this coloration of abortion by displaying the actions of a woman after an abortion. In this episode Jack's girlfriend, Clancey, managed to fend off his sexual fondling in the doctor's lounge long enough to inform him that "the rabbit died." She told him of her intent to have an abortion and the reasons for it:

Clancey: I'm not going to have it. . . . I don't want to complicate our lives. . . . There's no room in my life for a kid right now. . . . I'm not being callous about this—just practical. I've given it a lot of thought. You've got to trust me here, Jack. It makes perfect sense. I have to get to class. Bye.
Jack: Clancey, I think what you're doing is wrong.

After the abortion she returned to him, crying.

Clancey: I love you and someday I would like to have your baby. It's just that now wasn't the right time. That's all.
Jack: Well, when is?
Clancey: Jack, I'm so unhappy.
Jack: That's a natural post-operative depression.
Clancey: No. I was unhappy before the abortion 'cause, for all my talk about being in control, I'm not as grown-up as I thought. I didn't take precautions to keep from getting pregnant.
Jack: Well, that's as much my responsibility as yours.
Clancey: The problem with making choices is that you have to live with them. Hold me, Jack. I need to be held.

Thus even in the pro-abortion programs the depiction of the practice of abortion was tightly constrained. Abortion emerged as a practice which, because it was morally problematic, entailed personal regret and moral guilt and should be avoided through birth control. It was sanctioned only when it did not conflict with the values of family and motherhood—for the unmarried or those in otherwise seriously problematic situations. In none of these cases, nor to my knowledge in any television program in this time period, did a woman in a "family situation" (that is, married, with a husband who could support her, and of normal childbearing age, say twenty to thirty-five) abort a healthy fetus.[16] Lacey talked about an abortion she had as a teenager, unmarried and with little economic support. She defended that right but did so even as she was pregnant with a child she very much wanted. Spenser's girlfriend was also unmarried, as was Clancey in *St. Elsewhere* and the mentally retarded woman in a separate *St. Elsewhere* episode. While both Jack and Spenser offered to marry the women with whom they were involved, marriage-only-to-bear-a-child was disparaged as wrong in itself. Additionally, even these apparently "pro-abortion" episodes included vigorous argument against abortion and in favor of having and dealing with the baby.

Even in the strongest cases, therefore, the mass cultural medium of television admitted abortion only as an ambiguous and constrained practice. Legal permission was not translated into unmitigated cultural sanction, and abortion certainly was not endorsed as a casual method of birth control. Although the three different types of abortion episodes presented abortion practices in noticeably different ways, in the end they constructed a relatively unified depiction of the practice of abortion in American mainstream culture. Simply stated, abortion in the world of network prime-time television was a woman's choice but morally undesirable, especially as a practice for women in financially secure traditional marriages. The positive worth of abortion as an act to achieve specific goals for specific women was portrayed but overlaid with a set of evaluations that described abortion as an action to be avoided wherever possible.

The televised boundaries around the practice of abortion were, in many ways, very much in tune with the larger non-televised cultural practices. Eighty percent of abortions are by unmarried women, and in the television series the percentage was very similar.[17] In addition, most of the reasons given for considering abortion related to the woman's life-style—her career and educational goals, her existing family, and so on—rather than to rape or fetal deformity. This too was representative of American abortion practices, and that similarity was unlike the discourse of the larger public argument.

In addition to being representative of cultural practices in some ways, the programs also strove mightily to remain within dominant cultural values. Most of the episodes explicitly highlighted the values of childbearing, family, and mothering in the face of the potential threat to these values abortion represents. It was the happily pregnant

Lacey who defended abortion rights, not the "still"-unmarried Cagney. *Spenser for Hire* featured a subplot of two orphaned children that Spenser and his girlfriend cared for lovingly. *Magruder and Loud* included a side-plot showing their love and care for a young child, as well as one emphasizing the dangers of a bad marriage. Webster's mom reaffirmed her love for him, even as she fretted over whether to go through with her pregnancy. The "false pregnancy" programs all strongly affirmed the value of children. In addition, in all these cases the men involved were very supportive of bringing the pregnancy to term. The cultural practice of abortion was in this way hemmed in by other values and practices.

The abortion practice was also, however, defined by omissions. The networks created an image of abortion that addressed a presumed dominant audience. Although one-third of all abortions are done on teenagers, there was no enactment of the practice of abortion for teenagers. Similarly, the programs did not portray the questions abortion brings for minority women. Mrs. Herrera, the only minority person seeking abortion, remained a secondary character who served as an excuse for Cagney and Lacey's involvement rather than a person whose real life experiences, within her own culture and situation, were framed and explored in any detail.

The characteristics of television and the mass audience it addresses were, once again, influential here. Programs directed at teenagers (largely science fiction, action programs, and situation comedies) are not "appropriate" for dealing with a controversial issue like abortion. Moreover, the methods of dealing with teen pregnancy are still too controversial for extended address. Similarly, the medium is not much involved in attracting small minority cultures as audiences, and so the problem of abortion for minority women could gain no space for a hearing.

There were many other important omissions as well. In general, although the programs presented the major claims of each side, they did not articulate the grounds supporting those claims. They did not include visual images of aborted fetuses, philosophical or scientific arguments about the status of the fetus, or even coverage of the experience of having an abortion. The programs did not generally depict either adoption or contraception as alternatives.

As a whole, television focused more closely on the purposes of representative individual women and the stories of their lives than had the political discourse. The compromise on abortion framed in the cultural medium therefore featured significant similarities to and differences from the compromises reached in the political realm. Like the Supreme Court, the cultural compromise placed the *decision* for abortion in the private realm. Unlike the Court, it made an explicit moral evaluation of the practice. Like the popular opinion (analyzed in the next chapter), the television programs made the reason for abortion an important factor in determining the acceptability of abortions. Unlike the popular opinion, the programs ignored the stage of the development of the fetus and preferred instead the nature of the relationships between men and women.

Conclusion

In absorbing the public argument and the new legal formation generated by *Roe* v. *Wade,* prime-time television generated a limited range of portrayals of the cultural practice of abortion. The particular characteristics of prime-time network television—its narratives, its genres, and the economics of its audiences—shaped the elements of the public discourse that would be included and the manner in which they would be combined. Ultimately, television portrayed a compromise of both vocabularies, but the practical, cultural compromise was somewhat different from the legal-political one.

Television's depiction of a culture of abortion therefore was of great consequence. As the public argument moved from the distant realm of politics into the realm of people's lives, this pervasive cultural medium helped to translate the abstractions of political discourse into terms of real life practices. It did so by enacting abortion in ways that showed clear signs of both pro-Choice and pro-Life influences. It was a compromise generated by the fact that a new discourse (the language of Choice) had been accepted without direct refutation of the old governing terms (the discourse of pro-Life).

The generation of such compromises is of great importance for social and moral theory. The development and general acceptance of a compromise position on the abortion issue controverts the claims of social pessimists such as Alasdair MacIntyre, who label such issues "incommensurable."[18] These conservatives have joined the ranks of the leftists in suggesting that we live in an age in which public discourse cannot produce satisfactory political decisions. The case of abortion refutes this claim. For the majority, the social practice of abortion generated by the prime-time portrayal was perhaps not optimal, but it was at least satisfactory.

The issue for the conservatives hinges, however, upon the rational character of the compromise. There is, of course, no way to defend the compromise solely from the principles of either the pro-Choice or the pro-Life movement. The televisual enactment abandoned or transformed the principle of Choice and the claim to a Right to Life for the fetus. The various components of the compromise were not arrived at through "argumentation," and therefore, it would be difficult to justify its particular elements argumentatively. The compromise was, however, both discursively and rationally generated. The discursive form was narrative and the rationale was that of a response to the material realities of the audience's lives. It was a working compromise, a pragmatic resolution rather than a philosophical one. Perhaps that suggests more clearly than anything the limits of philosophy for governing or understanding public life.

Not all persons living in the nation accepted either the legal or cultural compromises reached by the dominant culture. The lack of decisive refutation encouraged activist adherents to pure forms of older vocabularies. When they found their vocabulary displaced and modified by new laws and new cultural enactments, these activists (seeking their own version of philosophical purity) moved to restore the full potency of their words. Given the increasingly stabilized public discourse, their failure to understand reasons against their position, and their own distance from the dominant discourses of the political and cultural realm, they shifted the attack from rhetoric to violence.

NOTES

1. David Thorburn, "Television as an Aesthetic Medium," *Critical Studies in Mass Communication* 4 (June 1987), 161–74; however, I disagree with Thorburn's argument for a primary emphasis on the aesthetic dimensions of these narratives.

2. Thorburn's view is often taken to be in opposition to the current arguments in favor of the "polysemic" qualities of television. I do not believe this is an accurate opposition. It is simply the case that, in most cultures, consensual narratives have always served primarily the dominant coalitions. Theories of consensuality in public narratives are similarly not destroyed by the fact that there might be a certain range of different and somewhat incompatible narratives within the medium. Absolute identity is not essential for a consensual narrative to do its social work. Compare to John Fiske, "Television: Polysemy and Popularity," *Critical Studies in Mass Communication* 3 (December 1986), pp. 391–408, or David Morley, *The "Nationwide" Audience* (London: British Film Institute, 1980).

3. The relationship between change-bearing public argument and entertainment television has not yet been adequately accounted for in theory or in current methods. Dissecting a single program, describing a genre, or even

charting a particular strip of viewing cannot reveal the way in which television, as a central cultural medium, processes specific legal changes or public
arguments. Nor would a resort to a closed theoretical explanation about the
"means of production" in the television industry tell us *how* this process
occurred at the discursive level (though it might illuminate why). Instead, the
entire range of programs concerning a given political issue must be analyzed
as a set. Given the quantity and disorder surrounding the medium, I cannot
claim to have examined all the regular television episodes that featured
abortion practices. However, the set of programs discussed herein at least
provides a sample of adequate depth and breadth to insure that all of the
major trends and forces are represented. A bibliography of television studies
is available in Caren J. Demming and Bruce E. Gronbeck, *The (Not Quite)
Comprehensive Bibliography of Broadcast Criticism* (Iowa City: University of Iowa,
1985), disseminated to Television Conference participants. The classic collection of critical essays is Horace Newcomb, ed., *Television: The Critical View,* 2nd
ed. (New York, Oxford: Oxford University Press, 1979). See also Arthur Asa
Berger, *Media Analysis Techniques* (Beverly Hills: Sage, 1982); Robert Ruther-
ford Smith, *Beyond the Wasteland,* rev. ed. (Annandale, Va.: SCA, 1980);
Horace Newcomb, "Prime Time as a Cultural Forum," paper presented at the
68th Annual Meeting of the Speech Communication Association, Louisville,
Ky., November 4–7, 1982. And see, especially, recent issues of *Critical Studies
in Mass Communication.* For a study that does an excellent job of following an
issue through the mass news media, see Daniel C. Hallin, *The "Uncensored"
War: The Media and Vietnam* (Oxford: Oxford University Press, 1986). I am
deeply indebted to Lawrance Bernabo for his work in collecting videotapes of
various prime-time television programs that depicted abortion. The programs
I have personally viewed include one episode each of *Cagney and Lacey, Spenser
for Hire, Dallas, Magruder and Loud, Call to Glory, Webster, Hill Street Blues,* and
Family, along with three episodes of *St. Elsewhere* (actually, two episodes
dealing with one abortion story line and two episodes dealing with separate
story lines). In addition I have received plot summaries for *Maude, Defenders,
Buffalo Bill* and a third episode of *St. Elsewhere.* I have information that early
episodes of the following programs also covered abortion, although I have not
been able to find further information on them: *The Bold Ones, Marcus Welby,
M.D.,* and *A Brand New Life.* Apparently, the latter two were "pro-Life" and
the former was more "pro-Choice." Other programs, including an episode of
Mike and Jack, featured unplanned pregnancies (which ended in miscarriages)
but did not explicitly discuss abortion. *Choices,* a prime-time made-for-televi-
sion movie, also fits the descriptions I use here; however, because it is not a
serial, I have not directly included it in the analysis.

4. Revised characterizations of women in television programming may
have actually led to legal changes and made the public argument more
compatible with the pro-Choice position. However, I have no proof that this was
the case, and much further empirical examination of characterizations of
women in this pre-1970 era would have to be done. Most role studies post-
date this period.

5. See John Louis Lucaites and Celeste Michelle Condit, "Reconstructing Narrative Theory: A Functional Perspective," *Journal of Communication* 36 (1986), 90–108. Lucaites and Condit indicate that there are three functions for narrative (rhetorical, dialectical, and poetical—i.e., "entertainment"). They suggest "one-sidedness" as one of the distinctive formal characteristics of narratives that primarily serve the rhetorical function.

6. "CBS on Abortion," *America*, 5 May 1962, pp. 193–94.

7. "That's Entertainment," *Time*, 27 August 1973, p. 630. The furor was generated at the rerun of the program. The reports indicated that earlier programs had dealt less sympathetically with abortion, including, in 1970–71, *The Bold Ones* and anti-abortion programs on *A Brand New Life* and *Marcus Welby*.

8. Robert R. Beusse and Russell Shaw, "Maude's Abortion: Spontaneous or Induced?" *America*, 3 November 1973, pp. 324–26.

9. Beusse and Shaw.

10. Ibid.

11. It is sometimes argued that, because audiences do not all interpret programs in the same fashion, it is useless to try to describe themes that are preferred by programming; audiences can make what they will of program content (see Fisk). Indeed, we cannot specify precisely how different audience members might react to a text, for the reasons given. We can, however, describe the limits a discourse *attempts* to impose, and we can do so in an empirically verifiable manner by noting what has been left out—what is not depicted. Moreover, I believe that it has not yet been established that the reading of dominant audiences is unpredictable or that their readings are not important for social processes, regardless of what some non-standard reading practices might produce. See Celeste Michelle Condit, "The Rhetorical Limits of Polysemy," *Critical Studies in Mass Communication* 6, no. 2 (forthcoming). Related arguments are developed by Philip Wander in "Cultural Criticism," in *Handbook of Political Communication*, ed. Dan D. Nimmo and Keith R. Sanders (Beverly Hills: Sage, 1981), pp. 497–528, and Wander, "The Third Persona: An Ideological Turn in Rhetorical Theory," *Central States Speech Journal* 35, no. 4 (Winter 1984), 197–216. I suggest that, rather than analyzing the specific "persuasiveness" of a given piece of discourse, when we look at any unified message constructed across a powerful medium, we should be concerned about its mere *presence. Sheer presence exerts important kinds of social forces, regardless of how persuaded individual audience members are by a specific discourse.

12. These programs are all MTM-related—either direct products of this company or products of producer/writers and other staff who got major experience through MTM productions. MTM has been noted for its clear "liberal" orientation. See Jane Feuer, "MTM Enterprises: An Overview," and "The MTM Style," in *MTM: "Quality Television,"* ed. Jane Feuer, Paul Kerr, and Tise Vahimagi (London: BFI, 1984), esp. p. 22.

13. In a study of the reactions of a pro-Life and a pro-Choice leader to this program, the pro-Life activist identified Crenshaw as the most positive

character in the program. The pro-Choice activist identified her as somewhat negative. Both respondents identified their reaction as based primarily upon what she stood for, but they also cited some of the character details I note.

14. The material in this book, along with many others, suggests both that the pro-Choice advocates routinely insinuated that these were the real motives of the pro-Life rhetors, and that, for a large group of pro-Life rhetors, these motives were in fact important. See, for example, Fred M. Frohock, *Abortion: A Case Study in Law and Morals* (Westport, Conn.: Greenwood Press, 1983).

15. Here the direct sanctions of special-interest groups merge with the persuasive dimensions of mass-mediated narratives. TV writer/producers generally seek narrative coherence. They try to produce programs within which the actions of "sympathetic characters" make sense to the mass audience. Given the existing repertoire of the "public consciousness," certain actions do not make sense (cops refusing to enforce legal abortion or career women giving up "outside lives" to have "second families"). Given the public arguments of competing interest groups, other actions destroy the "sympathy" with a character (e.g., because abortion has been characterized as a "selfish" act, *Call to Glory*'s apple-pie-loving mom cannot choose it, although acerbic Maude can). The interaction of these direct sanctions and indirect demands of narrative probability (which themselves interact with the public arguments produced by the special interest groups) produces a particular range of definitions for abortion practices. Narrative probability is thus one of the most vivid and direct links between the realm of public arguments (politics) and that of cultural enactments.

This concept of persuasion and probability may, at first blush, sound rather like the old industry claim to "give the people what they want" or to simply reflect the culture, but it is not that. For, indeed, the cultural media are required to participate in an active way in creating a cultural definition that enacts and accepts the boundaries placed by the special interest groups. It is not simply what the *public* wants that the culture industry produces. It is what the public will accept from the limited repertoire allowed by the special interest groups. Polls, in fact, indicate that the public has a great deal of ambivalence on the issue and might find a broader range of enactments plausible.

The persuasive boundaries of the public vocabulary, related as they are to particular interest groups, set the limits of what the mass cultural media can "say" about abortion—how they can enact it—but they have active complicity in the construction. The desire for maximal economic payoffs encourages them to participate within the boundaries, but participate *actively* they do. They could try alternate definitions of abortion, or resist depictions of abortion altogether. They choose, however, to perpetuate the game by complicitly constructing the cultural images that make vivid and legitimate the compromises possible from interest group struggles.

16. Programs outside the time frame of this study pushed the boundaries of acceptable abortion somewhat further. A later *St. Elsewhere* featured a

program in which a woman chooses abortion because of a *potential* defect in a fetus. An episode of *Heartbeats* presented an abortion of two out of four fertility-drug-induced quadruplets in order to safeguard the health of the two survivors.

17. Melinda Beck, Diane Weathers, John McCormick, David T. Friendly, Pamela Abramson, Mary Bruno, "America's Abortion Dilemma," *Newsweek*, 14 January 1985, p. 24.

18. Alasdair MacIntyre, *After Virtue: A Study in Moral Theory* (Notre Dame, Ind.: University of Notre Dame Press, 1981).

CHAPTER EIGHT

Mass Compromise and Minority Violence
Rhetoric and Ideology
——— 1978–85 ———

> When the history of this period is written, it won't be the pickets or letter-writers who will be the heroes. . . . It's going to be the bombers.
>
> —John Burt, founder
> "Our Father's House"[1]

As the eighties lumbered into view, America's ideologically mature controversy over abortion moved into a complex new stage—resolute schizophrenia. The populace gradually began to integrate the new laws, rhetorics, and practices of legalized abortion into a unique compromise within the "American way of life." Given the continued presence of the powerful image of the fetus, however, this routinization of compromise simultaneously spurred activists to polarization and violence. Both the mass compromise and the violence were, in part, consequences of the particular formation taken by the new discourse about abortion.

The Populace Compromises

Determining whether the compromises enacted in the American legal and cultural establishments between 1973 and 1985 truly represented popular opinions about abortion cannot be done with great precision. The sole tool for answering such a query is opinion polling, and such surveys have been criticized on a wide variety of grounds.[2] They may tend to "construct," rather than reflect, public opinion; they must always rely on slanted questions; and they tend to over-homogenize the variety of opinions held by the wide range of any populace.

Although these objections to polling data can never be fully overcome, they can be somewhat mitigated. No single question can tell us the shape of public opinion, and digital (favor/oppose) polls can tell us only about crude forced-choice majorities. If, however, we ask a wide range of questions, not in some supposedly neutral vocabulary but alternately in the vocabularies of both sides of a controversy, we can gradually get a reading of the contours of public sentiments. The outcomes will be much more like a rugged curve than simple digital majorities and minorities. Examining a wide range of polls gives a surprisingly consistent picture of popular opinion on the new range of abortion practices and vocabularies.

During the seventies and eighties the actual *changes* in *popular opinion about abortion were relatively slight, indicating that the actions of the Court and the cultural establishment had little impact on the development of arguments in the *public realm. Nonetheless, to the best of our ability to ascertain, the personal or private opinions of the majority of Americans seemed consonant with the resolutions adopted in their laws and mass culture. The popular opinion included a wide range of beliefs, but by and large these attitudes incorporated elements of both the pro-Choice and pro-Life rhetorics. This compromise is delineated in three different outcomes of a wide range of popular opinion polls.

As early as 1972, 64 percent of those polled on the statement that abortion should be a decision between a "woman and her physician" and agreed with the pro-Choice group's argument for Privacy and Choice in several different polls and forms.[3] At the same time, however, more than half of those polled felt that life began before viability and more than 85 percent felt that life began before birth.[4] Even if "person" were substituted for "human being," more than two-thirds believed that the fetus was a person before birth; more than half, before viability.[5] The public thus accepted the major grounds of both pro-Choice and pro-Life advocates: women should have the Choice to control their own bodies, *and* fetuses were persons well before birth.

The incorporation of the competing values was also evident in the tendency of those polled to differentiate between permissible and impermissible motives and stages for abortion. The majority of the populace accepted neither the claim that all abortions should be permissible nor the claim that no abortions should be permissible (although around 20 percent of the populace endorsed each of these two polar options for almost two decades).[6] Instead, the majority of Americans cautiously judged that abortion was acceptable only if the purposes carried enough weight. Thus, abortion to save the pregnant woman's life got 77 percent support in 1965 (as it did in 1978). Apparently the populace compared adult life to nascent life and found the woman's life to be the first concern.[7] Similarly, in 1965, 54 percent supported the abortion of a potentially deformed child but only 45 percent did so in 1977, reflecting the changing values surrounding deformity in the culture and an increased acceptance of individuals with handicaps.[8] Also, in 1978, 65 percent felt that abortion should be permitted in cases of rape or incest, due perhaps to the stressful nature of such pregnancies or to the fact that the women could not be held "responsible" for becoming pregnant.[9] In 1978 support for abortions to prevent severe damage to physical health (54 percent approved) and to protect mental health (42 percent approved) reached a high-water mark. But still only 16 percent supported abortion for economic reasons, reflecting a reluctance to balance life against money.[10] By weighing the purposes for abortion, Americans thus negotiated a range of compromises between the pro-Life claim that the fetus's Right to Life was absolute and the pro-Choice claim that the woman's Right to Choice was all-inclusive.

In addition to considering the motives for abortion, the polls indicated that the populace was also extremely sensitive to the stage of fetal development. The rhetoric of "absolute Right to Choose" called for a Right to Choose abortion at any stage of fetal development. The rhetoric of "absolute Right to Life" prohibited abortion at any stage. The populace, in contrast to both of these views, judged the correctness of abortions based on the fetus's development. For example, in 1978 willingness to choose the pregnant woman's life over that of the fetus dropped from 77 percent in the first trimester to 60 percent in the third trimester. Willingness to permit abortion for rape or incest dropped from 65 percent in the first trimester to 38 percent in the second and only 24 percent in the final trimester, and so on for each category of motives and stages.[11] The populace showed more concern for the Life of the fetus as the fetus grew closer and closer to full term. Thereby, they rejected the pro-Choice tendency to ignore the fetus and the pro-Life tendency to fail to make developmental distinctions.

If we examine the wide range of polls available, we have fairly good grounds for concluding that American popular opinion on abortion covered a fairly wide range, with no single position holding complete dominance. Between the late sixties and mid-eighties there were only slight variations from a general curve. Around 20 percent tended to want to ban all abortions and around 20 percent tended to want to permit all abortions; the other 60 percent would have permitted only some abortions, but they did not have much consensus about exactly which abortions, varying their decision by stage of fetal development and by the motive for the abortion.

Perhaps because the populace was sensitive to this wide variety of positions, the polls also seem to indicate that (at least until 1985) Americans had reached one other compromise of a very fundamental sort. Pollees tended to separate what they thought they would do personally in an abortion situation from what they thought the law should be about abortion. In 1978, for example, only 24 percent polled would have recommended abortion to a hypothetical fifteen-year-old daughter, even though polls near that time showed that less than a fifth of the populace disapproved of legal abortion in all circumstances and a later poll reported that 75 percent opposed a constitutional amendment to prohibit abortion.[12] That result was not much different from the 1972 NBC-TV poll of New Yorkers which, in the face of reasonably strong support for legalized abortion, showed only 34 percent of the women claiming they would have an abortion in case of an unwanted pregnancy, while 50 percent indicated they would bear and raise the child and 7 percent claimed they would put it up for adoption.[13] Thus, Americans seemed, continually, to make a distinction between their personal dislike of abortion, their personal actions with regard to abortion, and their willingness to allow it to be legal.

This distinction between public law and private morality parallels the compromises constructed in both the legal and cultural realms. It suggests, once again, the unique character of discourse as a carrier and arbiter of conflicts among different interest groups (including genders, ethnic groups, and economic enterprises). Any one individual's experience of life might make either the pro-Life or the pro-Choice vocabulary personally descriptive, expressive, or advantageous. According to both Kristin Luker and Marilyn Falik, most activists on each side of the controversy found themselves in this position:[14] unmarried professional women without children constituted the majority of pro-Choice activists, while married housewife-mothers tended to constitute the pro-Life activists. However, for a large number of other individuals, the material experiences and advantages of a particular vocabulary were not overwhelming. In such cases the "majority" either find utility in both vocabularies and therefore integrate them or they judge the issues more abstractly on the arguments, images, and ideographs themselves and, again, integrate them. The discursive realm thus adds considerable complexity to simple models that describe all social change primarily in terms of unidimensional economic or demographic shifts.

The "American attitude" in the seventies and the first half of the eighties thus held abortion to be a more or less acceptable choice depending on one's situation, motives, and the stage of development of the fetus. Mass opinion seemed to indicate that abortion might often, perhaps even in the majority of cases, be a morally wrong choice. Certainly in almost all these cases contraception or, for some, abstinence, would have been morally preferred. But the populace also seemed to accept that the guilt was a private one, because the decision had to be a private one. Indeed, the state could neither know enough about each case to make rational and informed decisions nor legislate the woman's own morality. Hence, the public law permitted the private woman to decide.

Polarization to Violence: Pro-Life?

Not all Americans accepted this compromise. In fact, the more the mass consensus accepting abortion seemed to solidify, the more frustrated and active became the minority of those who accepted the unalloyed pro-Life discourse. For them, the image of the unborn child continued to dominate the meaning of abortion. Gradually, throughout the eighties increasing percentages of these pro-Life activists began to shift away from the sanctioned American method of adjudicating disputes through persuasion toward the methods of coercion, law-breaking, and violence.

The first step toward coercive action was the rise of picketing of abortion clinics and legal buildings such as the Supreme Court—a fairly sustained and widespread effort in the eighties. All across the country, in small and large cities, on virtually any day of the year, at least one picketer could usually be found in front of any medical facility responsible for a large number of abortions. While most pro-Life activists preferred non-violent means to *persuade* the women who walked past their lines not to have an abortion, many were perfectly willing to *intimidate* them into not having an abortion instead.[15] In some instances this picketing escalated to pushing and shoving, resulting in assault charges—a minimal act of violence but a crucial step nonetheless.[16] Finally, the picketing frequently led to harassment of women who had abortions and of clinic personnel. They were telephoned late at night or had placards stuck on their lawn; here coercion through intimidation became the clear goal. In some cases, clinics were closed through coercion.[17]

The picketing of clinics gradually escalated into two other related strategies, one non-coercive but illegal, the other both dramatically coercive and illegal. In the eighties civil disobedience was increasingly used to gain public attention. Picketers would intentionally trespass (entering abortion clinics or the Supreme Court building) in order to

These Salem, Oregon, picketers joined others on the 1985 anniversary of *Roe v. Wade*, employing demonstrations to support the pro-Choice movement. Photo by Harry Demarest.

be arrested and to make news. The use of such non-violent civil disobedience is widely viewed as legitimate as long as protesters are willing to serve their sentences, but the move nonetheless polarizes. The other strategy, the use of "mock" abortion clinics, was more covert and therefore more sinister.

Pro-Life activists set up offices that advertised as abortion clinics. When women came to the clinics asking for abortions, they were not told that the clinic was a pro-Life propaganda center. Instead, they were pressured to observe pro-Life films and look at pro-Life materials. Of course, the basic strategy here included a persuasive element, but when one coerces someone to read one's persuasion, one is coercing nonetheless. In Texas, the proprietors of one such "clinic" were tried and convicted, but the strategy was not eliminated.[18]

This catalogue of coercive, violent, and illegal pro-Life activities reflected the intensity and activism of pro-Lifers in the eighties. Although troubling, it is hardly an exceptional list for any social movement. It is the bombing and burning of abortion clinics that most definitively put the protest "over the line" from public persuasion to violent coercion. In order to understand the move to violence, a detailed exploration of a clinic bombing will be useful.

The Gideon Project

On 25 December 1984 bombs exploded at three facilities that provided abortions in Pensacola, Florida. No one was hurt, but a half-million dollars worth of damage was inflicted. The local newspaper coverage of the incident reflected clearly the split between the majority and the minority who had been moved to violence. The Pensacola papers portrayed the "average" uninvolved citizens of Pensacola as concurring with Robert Cronemeyer, who said, "Yes, it's terrorism and no, there is no justification."[19] A series of virtually unanimous quotations from "people off the street" suggested that the general public was overwhelmingly opposed to such political violence. Quotations from pro-Choice activists reinforced these sentiments. The physicians who operated the clinics and the representatives of N.O.W. emphasized that the bombings would not stop abortions and re-emphasized the rights of women and their need for abortions.[20]

The majority of the public pro-Life discourse appearing in the news media also opposed the bombings. The dominant initial response was summed up in the newspaper headline, "Church leaders condemn Christmas-morning violence." Mainline churches, especially the Catholics, were depicted as in opposition to the bombing. Catholic

In Pensacola, Florida, pro-Life activities ranged from demonstrations to bombings. Photos by Gary McCracken

Bishop Symons was quoted as saying, "These people have nothing to do with our effort for the dignity or respect for human life. . . . We have ways, under our Constitution, to express our views, and there are other ways than using violence."[21] His comments were seconded by other religious and pro-Life leaders. These mainline activist rhetors, involved in trying to persuade Americans that abortion was wrong, felt their credibility was damaged by violence.

There was, however, at least a subsidiary current of support for the bombers in this ocean of opposition. Near the end of this first article, and increasingly in later articles, a more tolerant position toward the bombings by a different group of pro-Life activists was heard. A substantial group of fundamentalists had long stirred and manned a visible pro-Life activism in Pensacola—an activism that often bordered upon coercion.[22] These idealogues saw the bombing in a different light. The Reverend David Shofner of the West Pensacola Baptist Church admitted that bombing was not God's way but went on to say, "Bombings and fire will certainly stop it [abortion]. . . . Picketing doesn't. You might stop one or two girls every now and then or help them change their minds [by picketing], but certainly there won't be any babies killed in these three clinics for a while." He was joined by John Burt, a man the newspapers described as a religious leader, reformed KKK member, and anti-abortionist, who was quoted as saying, "If there is an element of our society that does that, and no one is hurt, I'm glad the killing [of babies] has stopped."[23]

This supportive community had created the violent mentality adopted by four young people under twenty-one years of age—Jimmy and Kathryn Simmons, Mathew Goldsby, and his fiancée, Kaye Wiggins. Taking as their model the biblical story of Gideon, an intensely faithful religious character who served God by destroying the shrine of the false god Baal under cover of night, they undertook the bombings they called "the Gideon Project." Kathryn and Kaye were convicted of conspiracy, and Jimmy and Mathew were each convicted of conspiracy to build a bomb and three counts of making a bomb and of damaging a building with a bomb.

The trial of these four would-be heroes presents us, as it did the jury, with a serious question: why would four young American Christians turn to bombing in their own land? There are both material and discursive answers. To begin with the material factors, the story is one of four all-too-typical young people. As their defense attorney suggested, precisely their "ordinariness" and "virtues," not their vices, would get them convicted.[24] The four high school graduates were working-class kids with typically troubled backgrounds. Goldsby had grown up without a father. Simmons's father had died when Jimmy was eighteen, and his family had "disassembled," sending Jimmy, small and thin, to a Marine boot camp whose training he did not complete. Wiggins had been traumatized by watching her older brother drown when she was nine, her parents had divorced, and her church had recently dissolved. Kathryn Simmons had married to escape an extremely rigid family who had kept her away from outsiders, refusing even to let her play with other children.[25]

These young adults faced the difficulty of growing up in a rapidly changing South, in which an invasion of Yankees and modernization was challenging the traditional value systems. These young working-class adults dealt with these regional problems, their class problems, and their personal problems through religion and a fantasy of the "knights of the round table."[26] When their religious affiliation exposed them to intensive pro-Life discourse, they believed that they heard God's voice telling them, under the "Code of Chivalry," to act.

The dimension of direct action was important. The bombings were originally designed not simply as a "publicity stunt" (a rhetorical motivation) but as an attempt at direct, effective, local action (a coercive motivation). The bombers and their partners were not trying just to draw attention to the issue, for they had had little involvement in public discourse on the issue previously. Goldsby had described picketing and such public persuasion as "not his bag."[27] Instead, they believed that the bombing would stop local abortions immediately and directly. As Jimmy Simmons said, "If one baby lives out of all of this, then it's worth it."[28] In his confession Goldsby told the ATF agents that they did it "to stop abortions," and that "if he spent the rest of his life in jail, if he saved one life, then it was worth what he had done."[29] Consequently, when Wiggins felt that "they haven't made the people stop abortions," she also concluded that "there was no good purpose for the bombings."[30] Although later, after they noted the national attention the bombings garnered, they expressed satisfaction with the attention the bombings directed to the issue, the local particular action was itself one primary motivation for them. On these grounds their local action was at least partially effective; one of the bombing victims, Dr. William Permenter, announced he would discontinue performing abortions.[31]

The major belief that drove the quartet to this direct local action against particular abortions was, as any examination of the periphery of the pro-Life movement would have predicted, the conviction that God opposed abortion as murder and that God had told them to act to end abortions. As Kaye Wiggins said, the group thought of the bombings as "a gift to Jesus on his birthday."[32] God's command to bomb the abortion clinics, in Jimmy Simmons's words "just hit us . . . almost like a supernatural knowledge came to us and built [the bombs]."[33] Goldsby agreed, telling the ATF agents that "he and God carried out the bombings."[34] In the trial, Wiggins reasserted the claim: "He felt like . . . it was God's will for Jimmy and he to do that," she said. "He did feel like God played a big part in it."[35]

The source of this conviction (if not of the final claim that God had spoken to them) was the evident Christianity within which the four defined their universe. The Christian devotion of each of these young adults was the central topic of all those who gave a public appraisal of the quartet. As the Rev. James Courtney, who had known Goldsby for years, said, "He was such a nice young man, a real Christian and a very quiet fellow."[36] Wiggins's mother reinforced that description, emphasizing, "He's an exceptionally fine Christian boy. . . . In fact, I don't ever remember him missing a church service. He's not just a Sunday Christian, he's an everyday Christian."[37] Similar comments were made about the others. A former high school teacher described Wiggins as "a very genuine person with strong Christian convictions."[38] Simmons's mother-in-law said of him, "He's a good strong Christian and, my, he loves his Jesus."[39]

The living force of this Christianity ran deep: it was evident in the reactions, not only of the four but also of their mothers. Ruby Menard, Kathy's mother, answered a reporter's queries by saying, "I don't know anything right now except she needs a lot of prayer."[40] Similarly, Rhoda Goldsby averred that "whatever happens . . . I'm contented in my God."[41] God was, for these families, the locus of action and causality; it was not surprising that "He" was the source of the decision to bomb.

In addition to the general orientation Christianity provided, their Christian contacts that they developed—both at church and at home—shaped their anti-abortion perspective. Through church groups they viewed anti-abortion movies such as "Assignment Abortion," which one psychiatrist described as crucial to Jimmy's anti-abortion bombing. They also received vivid anti-abortion pamphlets through these sources.

Thus in both the particular sense of a "command from God" to bomb abortion clinics and in the general sense of an understanding of a world in which God was a central and coercive authority, the Gideon quartet was ideologically motivated by Christianity. Labeling themselves the "Protectors of the Code," they spoke this motivation clearly and proudly. All Christianity, however, does not simply and inevitably lead to violence. It was a particular brand of Christianity that focused their efforts.

The basic values in their version of Christianity were those generally associated with the *traditional family. As Simmons told the ATF, his "motivation was love for 'God, my country, my family—that's about it.' "[42] One of the dominant features of this Christian, patriotic, familial value set was a view of women as subordinate and passive, primarily designed for child-rearing. Not surprisingly, Goldsby's favorite song was "I've Never Been to Me," a top-forty, "easy-listening" tune that told the story of a woman who had lived an exciting life but felt lost because she had never had a baby.

In part, this component of the ideology was made vivid through the group's fantasy of the "code of chivalry," which portrayed women as "damsels in distress" and men as "knights in shining armor." As Kathryn Simmons put it, when asked about her role in the bombing, "Women are not allowed. . . . It's white knights. We're not allowed. We're the damsels in distress."[43] Similarly, Wiggins emphasized that Kaye could cry about the bombings, but Goldsby couldn't because he had to provide strength and support because "he was a knight of the Round Table."[44]

As the attorneys pointed out, however, this Round Table imagery was itself firmly grounded in the Bible. Attorney Kasun said that her client, Simmons, had merely "believed St. Paul when he said, 'Submit unto your husband as unto the Lord.' "[45] Attorney Shimik emphasized of Wiggins that "she merely remained loyal to Goldsby as the Bible requires."[46]

The ideology and values from which the foursome acted were clearly Christian and anti-feminist. This ideology was, in its pure form, the underlying ideology of the Right-to-Life movement as a whole. Such a hierarchical, authoritarian, coercion-focused, and militarist discourse is a partial pre-condition of violence. Yet, most of the official spokespersons for the movement in Pensacola repudiated the violence, even though they shared the ideology. Ideological content may enable, but it is not a sufficient cause of violence. Additional discursive conditions were required to activate this coercive ideology.

Two separate factors, each manifesting a similar problem at a different level, were instrumental in the transformation of four young Christians into the Gideon quartet. Both at the public level and in the private discourse of the youths, the *pro-Life* discourse had moved beyond persuasion or rhetoric to a closed ideological discourse. By the 1980s the bombers and their partners, along with many other activists, had become ideologues concerned with enacting and enforcing their/God's beliefs rather than persuaders seeking to convince others that those beliefs were true. That discursive closure, that rejection of persuasion as the fundamental mode of human influence, was the crucial link in the move to violence.

On the public level, the move away from rhetoric, toward closed ideology, was facilitated by the rise of a new dominant discursive strategy—the widespread use of the argument of "over-weighing." The rhetorical tactic of over-weighing is a basic comparison strategy. With it, rhetors attempt to show that the values and interests on their side carry more weight than those of the opposition. The strategy became widespread for two reasons.

First, the Right-to-Life movement in the eighties became increasingly disillusioned; it had failed to alter the permissive legal policies enacted in the previous decade. While public opinion polls registered some slight changes and state and local activities produced some results, apparently the national political movement had stalled.[47] A constitutional amendment did not seem plausible; the Supreme Court reaffirmed and strengthened its *Roe* v. *Wade* decision; voters in several states rejected referenda limiting abortions; and the Congress showed willingness only to modify related bills (e.g., Family Planning legislation), not to change fundamental law. The movement's central objective—making abortion illegal—seemed unattainable through current means. Since the values of their opposition had, to some significant extent, been accepted, their primary persuasion could no longer be directed toward disallowing the opposition's discourse or toward developing their own values but instead had to show how their values were more important than those of the opposition—over-weighing them.

Second, in general the strategy of over-weighing becomes widespread when two well-developed ideologies clash without making any significant attempt to refute points of disagreement. At such a point late in a public argument, seasoned movement advocates are well aware that the audience is familiar with the strong points in the opposition's case. If they are also unwilling to adopt a compromise position that takes into account those strong points, then "over-weighing"—the claim that one's values outweigh those of the opposition and so necessitate a complete sacrifice of the opposing values—is virtually the only strategy open. The abortion controversy in the eighties increasingly presented precisely such a case—refutation had been lacking and the activists on both sides were unwilling to settle for compromise.

Hence, in this stage Right-to-Life activists argued that Life was more important than Choice. Some activists indicated, for example, that "just as civil rights take precedence over property or state rights, so does the right to life of an unborn infant take precedence over proprietary rights of a woman over her own body."[48] Similarly, Haven Gow echoed the signs of many picketers, proclaiming that a woman should not be " 'free to choose' to kill."[49] Others noted that "a woman has the right to control her own body . . . but not at the price of another life."[50] Pro-Life rhetors similarly over-weighed the claim presented by the "abortion tale" by drawing on the testimony of one woman who, after having an abortion from which the fetus lived for a short while, concluded that "nothing is worth the hell of abortion."[51]

Ultimately, the political compromise between public and private views was also directly attacked by the over-weighing strategy. Pro-Life advocates noted that "the left repeatedly insists that those opposed to abortions are free to have them or not, which is to miss the whole point of the conflict, namely, their belief that the life of another party is at stake."[52]

The over-weighing strategy was the dominant new discursive force in the late seventies and early eighties. It was, as I have suggested, a predictable strategy, given both the stage of the controversy and the American political system, which relies on partisan activists. Such a strategy, however, also harbors some serious dangers.

Those who choose to over-weigh rather than to seek compromise write off any competing claims and move into a uni-dimensional understanding of the world unbounded by other restraining principles, terms, and factors. Once a set of activists decides that the opposition's values are outweighed by its own, *and can therefore be totally ignored*, they can easily depict opponents as devil figures and supporters as saints. One's own grounds become the sole values; therefore, any means are justified to secure those ends. The dominance of the over-weighing strategy was thus the necessary rhetorical component which led pro-Life activists away from the sanctioned American method of persuasion and toward coercion, law-breaking, and violence.

It was in this general social context, supportive of closed perspectives, that the Pensacola conspirators found themselves. Kaye, Jimmy, Mathew, and Kathy were exposed to a minority group discourse which suggested that (1) the opposition had no argument and were merely resisting God with sheer power and (2) the value of the group (fetal Life) outweighed major constraining values (e.g., Law, Property, or peace). An understanding of the world in which the resort to violence was a reasonable option was therefore ready to hand. It required, however, an additional factor—their personal experience of discursive closure—to generate the final step toward violence.

Essentially, the quartet refused to participate in discourse outside their own closed set. They did not picket or counsel or argue with others. They maintained a closed communication circuit which turned into a fantasy world. Speaking only together, without any external constraining discourses, they built for each other an ideology in which God literally called them to violence.

The underlying claim that supports this interpretation is that a communication process closed and directed only to like-minded individuals results in dramatically different consequences (i.e., a higher potential for violence) than does open, persuasive discourse directed at a disparate audience. That claim depends on a finding of empirical differences between ideological discourse and persuasive discourse. The case of the Pensacola bombings provides a unique opportunity to compare the products of two such processes.

Two days after the bombing the *Pensacola News-Journal* received, and published, an anonymous letter claiming credit for the bombings (full text in Appendix B). Dramatically different from the discourse produced by the bombers themselves, the letter claimed that the bombing was done by a woman, primarily because after having an abortion late in pregnancy she had later discovered that this meant she had killed her child. The letter's author emphatically denied a religious background, saying, "It was not because of religious fanaticism . . . I don't even go to church."[53] Finally, the letter claimed that the purpose of the bombing was to help women, "to prevent any more lives from being ruined," as much as to "put an end to the murder of babies." It also provided a legal justification for bombing itself, saying that "it is a well-established principal [*sic*] of justice that force, even deadly force, is justified in order to save innocent lives if necessary."

As rhetoric, the letter was not much more skilled than were the ideologically based justifications of the bombers. The letter's attempts at justification were too blatant and harsh to be truly convincing. The difference here, therefore, is not simply a matter of naive vs. skilled persuasion. Several contrasts between the discourse of the letter and of the bombers mark the difference as one of rhetoric vs. ideology.

First, where the bombers relied on their Christianity and the command from God as justification, the letter-writer vigorously denied religious motivation. The denial of religious motivation is a common topos among the national advocates of the pro-Life movement. Prominent Catholic and fundamentalist leaders, such as John C. Willke or

John Noonan, spend a great deal of effort to deny that their cause is a religious one, for that religious cast would mark their discourse as partisan rather than universal.[54] The persuader emphasizes publicly shared values and grounds, avoiding the taint of partisanship. The ideologue, confident in the total rightness of her or his beliefs, emphasizes those partisan values, ignorant of, or hostile to, an audience that does not share them.

The letter's author and the bombers also differed visibly in their gendering of the agents of change. The letter claimed to be from a woman and claimed the bombing to be the act of women. Although no woman had previously been charged with any of the many clinic bombings in America, such a move was rhetorically apt, for it confounded the pro-Choice claim to represent a "woman's movement." It denied or submerged the largely unpopular pro-Life characterization of women as confined to the "soft" role of mother and hence incapable of forceful action. In contrast, where the letter spoke with a female voice, the bombers acted with a male hand. They did not allow the women to be directly involved, and they made public justification based on the subordination of women.

In addition to these central, ideologically based differences, the ideologue and the rhetor focused on distinctly different kinds of abortion. The letter-writer, like most pro-Life advocates, focused on late-term abortions, where the pro-Life case was most persuasive.[55] The bombers opposed all abortion; they bombed clinics that, almost exclusively, performed first trimester abortions.

Finally, the letter-writer recognized that "she" had broken the public compact against violence. Therefore, she carefully justified her action from a shared public legal tenet and on the basis of the prevention of greater violence. The Gideon quartet was sensitive to this public compact only after they realized the public stir they had created. Even then, it was not until the very end of their trial that they produced a public, legal justification. Until that point they relied on the force of God's command to overrule the public compact.

In almost every point the letter-writer sought a persuasive ground, shaping the discourse to what appeared most likely to be credible to the public audience. This resulted in a dramatically different discourse from that produced by the ideologues, who explained their action completely from their own ideology, largely ignoring the potentially different beliefs of the audience.

The implications of these different contents are dramatic. The persuasive discourse offered several potential grounds for compromise.

By emphasizing late-term abortions it created the possibility to negotiate over stage of development. It acknowledged the importance of the interests of women and the condition of their lives in making such decisions. And it recognized the inappropriateness of religious belief as a ground for shared public action. The ideological discourse of the real bombers offered no such grounds, assuming that, since compromise or persuasive victory were impossible, violence was the only alternative to alienation.

The discursive conditions that enabled the clinic bombings were, therefore, partially the result of a shift to a strategy of over-weighing in the public discourse, along with the particular closed form of discourse used by the bombers themselves. On both levels, the agents refused the possibility of interaction of beliefs and values—refused the *mutuality* of persuasion.[56] In the largest sense, this problem is generated by the otherwise desirable American tolerance toward religious groups. In particular circumstances, American courts have ruled that religious groups can be exempted from American laws that force them to share in the public discourse (for example, permitting special, non-accredited schools for religious sects). The courts allow groups their ideological discourse. This mandate of tolerance has generally been relatively unproblematic because those seeking exemption from the public discourse have not, in turn, tried to influence the larger society. In closing off influence from outside, they have also repudiated the right to attempt to influence the outside world. When a group seeks to influence the outside world but refuses to be open to persuasion itself, however, the rights to free speech and religious belief become distinctly more problematic. If this combination of cultural isolationism and political imperialism continues, increasing violence is a probable result. It may be important to insist that free speech is only possible when it is open speech, constituted by a two-way flow of ideas and argumentation.

This is more or less what the jury in the Gideon case found, as it faced the task of dealing with the ideological discourse and its violent consequences. The defense lawyers tried very hard to put abortion on trial in place of their defendants.[57] They relied heavily on a presentation of the Christian ideology of the defendants as a legitimate motivation for their behavior. The jury found them guilty but assessed very light sentences. The jury's decision seems to have been highly sympathetic to the motives of the group, but, in the end, the representatives of the American people insisted on the necessity of argumentation and persuasion as the mechanism to enact even the best of goals.

Pro-Choice?

In the eighties an extremist minority of the pro-Life group put themselves outside of the public process of persuasion and moved to violence. Their position was grounded, however, in the rhetorical strategies of the mainstream pro-Life movement (the tactic of "over-weighing"). Although it did not share the move to violence, the pro-Choice movement of the period shared the over-weighing tactic and the tendency toward discursive closure.

The pro-Choice group in the eighties continued to insist on the adoption of their vocabulary and their vocabulary alone. Facing rhetorical conditions that virtually mirrored those of the pro-Life rhetors, pro-Choice activists also moved to a rhetorical strategy of over-weighing. Lance Morrow, for example, claimed that "the risks of making abortion too easily available are outweighed by the risks of making it too difficult or impossible to obtain."[58] Similarly, Mary and Scott Reed argued that their value-weighing process led them to this conclusion: "We believe that abortions are abhorrent, but feel the liberation of America's poor has higher priority."[59] The most typical version of this strategy was the chant, often appearing on posters, that "A Woman's Life Is a Human Life."

Because the law allowed most abortions as a legal option, for the pro-Choice advocates the over-weighing strategy did not lead to bombings or to other acts of overt coercion. The basic ideological grounding in Choice probably also prevented the move to coercion where it might have been appropriate (in seeking to force doctors and nurses to provide abortion services). The weighing strategy was, however, accompanied by a form of ideological closure similar to that of the pro-Life movement. Until about 1985 many pro-Choice advocates systematically refused to engage the arguments of the Right-to-Life movement. In public speeches, debates, and articles, they did not address the violence being done to the fetus and they only rarely refuted the argument that the fetus is a human person. Instead, when pushed on this issue, they argued that everyone has a right to decide.

The deferral to the individual's right to decide was ideologically consistent with the full position of the pro-Choice group, but it was not an adequate public argument. The pro-Life analogies to slavery or murder, even though logically imprecise, had broad persuasiveness. Individuals in the American community have not generally been given the right to decide whether they are hurting someone else by their actions (with the contestable exceptions of parental care of children and spouse abuse). This has been a community responsibility. To make the fetus a special case would require both justification far more detailed than had been given and destruction of the near consensus that a fetus was a human person at least by viability.

Because the public pro-Choice discourse did not adequately answer the major concerns of pro-Lifers, pro-Choice activists appeared to shut off the dialogue. In the eighties that appearance lent increasing plausibility to the claim that the issue of abortion was nothing more than a matter of power politics. In such circumstances, the resort to violence was far easier to justify.

The pro-Choice advocates' use of polarization as a strategy of power also risked the loss of important ground in the long run. At pro-Life meetings the speakers were frequently challenged by pro-Choice activists: "Are you saying we should ban all abortions? What about rape or incest?" Indeed, the rape case was compelling for most hearers. But such a pattern of challenges, based solely on extreme cases, endangered the larger case. They produced the discursive climate for laws that would ban all abortions *except* in cases of rape or incest and to save the pregnant woman's life. Such pro-Choice rhetorics may have been constructing the conditions of their own eventual defeat.

The same problem existed with the other major rhetorical move of the later period—"Speak Outs," in which victims of back-alley abortions or abortion prohibitions gave testimonials in favor of abortion. A central strategy of pro-Choice advocates in this late stage, the Speak Out sought to "replace" the image of the fetus with the image of needy women.[60] This move to "over-weighing" at the visual level similarly cut off consideration of all of the available grounds for decision and policy-making. As chapter 5 indicated, because the image of the "innocent" fetus was far more potent than that of the woman as victim (if for no other reason than the complexity of the tale), such a move was likely to be a rhetorical failure.

Finally, by relying on available legal power and the over-weighing strategy instead of extending the argument to stave off the opposition, the national pro-Choice movement risked allowing its discourse to become "wrong." It endangered its ability to deal with a series of issues and challenges that might require self-modification to preserve the internal consistency of feminism. Recent objections to the large-scale female feticide, which arises from the power to determine fetal sex and to abort females selectively, rest on a more complex understanding of the status of the fetus than the ideological rigidity the pro-Choice movement has hitherto allowed.[61] These cases are similar to the challenges brought by disabled feminists on behalf of "deformed" fetuses.[62] Even when it is not an invitation to violence, closing off dialogue is always a move away from the ability to make "best choices." Thus the polarizing moves of the pro-Choice discourse were also of serious concern.

Summary

Between 1980 and 1985, the American discourse on abortion settled into two distinct and very different tracks. The mass public opinion began to work out and live a compromise that integrated the values and argumentative grounds presented by both sides of the issue. However, the activists on each side continued their insistence on the dominance of their own ideology in pure form.

These dual tracks were partly engendered by the form taken by persuasive processes in America. In national debate activists usually come from partisan groups that have a fervent ideological commitment or a large economic stake in a polar outcome of the issue. Therefore, the primary speakers on any issue are generally unwilling to listen to the other side or to reach caring compromises, and they are tempted to turn to coercion to gain their ends. Fortunately, in many instances the political and cultural process eventually takes the decision-making out of the hands of activists and places it in the hands of a larger audience with more diffuse interests. Moreover, in the best cases the act of persuading also requires activists to abandon their own narrow views of the world, to address the audience in its own terms, and often to learn in the process (as was the case when American Catholics' defense of Life led them to reconsider their position on capital punishment). Thus the persuasive process makes possible "good" decisions that articulate the widest possible range of interests and values.

By 1985 the contemporary American abortion controversy had traveled a path long and difficult for all its sincere, caring, hard-working participants. The movement had begun with the stories of women; it now found itself with an uneasy truce in which the public accepted grounds from both groups. The peace was marked by occasional violence on one side and closed-minded hostility on both sides. In the public realm, tactical changes and small battles would continue. Perhaps, in the long term, changes in technology or perspective would bring more major realignments. For women, in their private lives, however, the discourse had reached a stasis of great potential consequence. To put the public discourse process into perspective, I conclude with a consideration of the inter-relationships between the path of public discourse and the private lives of women.

NOTES

1. John Burt, quoted by Jon Nordheimer, "Bombing Case Offers a Stark Look at Abortion Conflicts," *New York Times*, 18 January 1985, p. A12.

2. The major argument against public opinion polling is that it artificially creates a singular "public opinion" that does not really exist except in the answers to the poll itself (thus, it is not a valid indicator of any external construct). This occurs because polls force people to make choices among particular policies or beliefs that they might be able to hold (even in contradiction) simultaneously and, by forcing them to articulate opinions, actually create opinions where none existed previously.

3. George H. Gallup, *The Gallup Poll: Public Opinion, 1972–1977* (Wilmington, Del.: Scholarly Resources, Inc., 1978), p. 54; Judith Blake, "The Abortion Decisions: Judicial Review and Public Opinion," in *Abortion: New Directions for Policy Studies*, ed. Edward Manier, William Liu, and David Solomon, p. 65. Other polls included in this survey are all published Gallup Polls during the period of this study, along with various Harris, U.S. Commission on Population Growth and the American Future, and AP/NBC News polls. See "Rallies Mark Court Ruling on Abortions," *Des Moines Register*, 23 January 1982, pp. 1, 6A; Eric M. Ulsaner and Ronald E. Weber, "Public Support for Pro-Choice Abortion Policies in the Nation and States: Changes and Stability after the *Roe* and *Doe* Decisions," in *The Law and Politics of Abortion*, ed. Carl E. Schneider and Maris A. Vinovskis (Lexington, Mass.: D. C. Heath, 1980); Gerald Lipson and Dianne Wolman, "Polling Americans on Birth Control and Population," *Family Planning Perspectives* 4 (January 1972), 39–42; Richard J. Neuhaus, "Figures and Fetuses: Findings of New York TV Surveys," *Commonweal*, 24 November 1972, pp. 175–78; "American Adults' Approval of Legal Abortion Has Remained Virtually Unchanged since 1972," *Family Planning Perspectives* 17, no. 4 (July/August 1985), p. 181; "Newsweek Poll: Divisions and Growing Doubts," *Newsweek*, 14 January 1985, p. 22.

4. Gallup, p. 54; Blake, p. 65.

5. Blake, p. 65.

6. See Gallup or "Newsweek Poll: Divisions and Growing Doubts," *Newsweek*, 14 January 1985, p. 22.

7. Gallup, *Public Opinion, 1935–1971* (New York: Random House, 1972), p. 3 (the first poll does not specify trimesters, the second poll specifies first trimester).

8. Ibid.

9. Gallup, *Public Opinion, 1978*, p. 33. See also "Newsweek Poll," which indicated that in 1985, 58 percent of the respondents favored "a ban on all abortions except in the case of rape, incest or when the mother's life is endangered" (p. 22). The idea that women are held responsible for their pregnancies is further reflected by the fact that this poll reports that substantial majorities of people favor banning most abortions, even though they realize that this would cause many women to be harmed in illegal abortions and many more unwanted children. The key fact is that 62 percent of the

public also believed that such a ban would mean that "people would practice better birth control." Only 26 percent thought that such a revision would also improve the "moral tone" in America.

10. In 1965 only 18 percent supported abortion if the parents could not support another child financially. Gallup, *Public Opinion, 1935–1971*, p. 1985; Gallup, *Public Opinion, 1978*, p. 33.

11. Blake, pp. 62–64; Gallup, *Public Opinion, 1978*, p. 33. This trend is even more pronounced among obstetricians and gynecologists. A poll of the American College of Obstetricians and Gynecologists shows that, since 1971, there has been overwhelming support for legalized abortion but that this has been clearly divided between purposes and fetal stage of development. In 1985, 91 percent supported abortion for fetal abnormality in the first trimester, 84 percent beyond; 93 percent supported it for rape and incest (first trimester), 68 percent beyond; 94 percent for physical health (first trimester), 75 percent beyond; 83 percent for mental health (first trimester), 56 percent beyond; 71 percent for financial difficulty (first trimester), 36 percent beyond; 75 percent personal choice (first trimester), 36 percent beyond. See "ACOG Poll: Ob-Gyns' Support for Abortion Unchanged since 1971," *Family Planning Perspectives* 17, no. 6 (November/December 1985), p. 2.

12. Gallup, *Public Opinion, 1978*, pp. 29, 33. AP/NBC News poll, "Rallies Mark Court Ruling on Abortions," *Des Moines Register*, p. 1 and esp. 6A, col 4.

13. Neuhaus, p. 176.

14. See Kristin Luker, *Abortion and the Politics of Motherhood* (Berkeley: University of California Press, 1984), and Marilyn Falik, *Ideology and Abortion Policy Politics* (New York: Praeger, 1983).

15. Joseph Scheidler is probably the most noted advocate of this "any means necessary" philosophy. For example, he reflected this attitude in his public lecture at the University of Illinois, Urbana, 7 October 1986, and in other publications, including *Closed: 99 Ways to Stop Abortion* (Lake Bluff, Ill.: Regnery Books, 1985).

16. For example, an off-duty police officer was convicted of shoving two women at an abortion clinic picketing. The conviction was later overturned by a judge and was being appealed at this writing. See, for example, "Conviction Upset in Officer's Case," *New York Times*, 18 December 1985, II, 2:1.

17. See Scheidler.

18. E.g., "Conviction on Abortion Ads," *New York Times*, 8 October 1986, I, 16:1.

19. "We Asked You," *Pensacola News*, 26 December 1985, p. 1A. This account as a whole is taken from several issues of the *Pensacola News*, the *Pensacola Journal*, the *Pensacola News-Journal*, other national papers and national magazines, as well as discussions with reporters. Henceforth, only direct quotations will be cited, since most of the material is readily accessible in the Pensacola papers and is repeated several times in various papers.

20. Dave Goodwin, "Victims: This Won't Stop Anything," *Pensacola Journal*, 26 December 1984, p. 1A, quoted victims of the bombings and representatives of N.O.W.

21. Cindy West, "Church Leaders Condemn Christmas-Morning Violence," *Pensacola Journal*, 26 December 1986, p. 5A.

22. "A Chronology: Local Anti-Abortionists Protest Frequently," *Pensacola Journal*, 26 December 1984, p. 4A.

23. West and Dave Goodwin, "Pro-Life: Anti-Abortionists Frown on Bombs, But Not Unhappy," *Pensacola Journal*, 26 December 1986, p. 2A.

24. The attorney, T. Patrick Monaghan, called them "four outstanding young people," and everyone interviewed by the press agreed they were devout and hard-working, clean-cut kids. The attorney also said, "We're going to be looking at young people whose virtues have gotten them into this courtroom, not their vices." Ginny Graybiel, "Trial Focuses on Conflict: God's Law vs. Man's Law," *Pensacola News*, 17 April 1985, p.10A.

25. Barbara Janesh, "Psychiatrist: Defendants Obsessed," *Pensacola News-Journal*, 21 April 1985, p. 3A.

26. Ginny Graybiel, "Goldsby Fiancée Says She'll Stand by Her Man," *Pensacola News-Journal*, 1 January 1985, p. 1A.

27. Chris Cooper, "Guilty," *Pensacola News*, 24 April 1985, p. 3A.

28. Chris Cooper, "Witnesses: Goldsby Told Agents He Wasn't Insane," *Pensacola News*, 18 April 1985, p. 1.

29. Chris Cooper, "Goldsby Appears Scared and Strangely Detached," *Pensacola News*, 31 December 1985, p. 2A.

30. Graybiel, "Stand by Her Man," p. 2A.

31. "Reaction," *Pensacola Journal*, 31 December 1984, p. 4A.

32. Chris Cooper, "Suspect's Fiancée: Clinic Bombings 'A Gift to Jesus,'" *Pensacola News*, 3 January 1985, p. 1A. The ideological treatment of the women is interesting here, given that Wiggins herself is a "suspect," yet she takes status only as a fiancée.

33. Cooper, "Witnesses."

34. *Pensacola Journal*, 18 April 1985, p. 14A.

35. Chris Cooper, "Trial," *Pensacola Journal*, 20 April 1986, p. 4A.

36. "Agents: Suspect Admits Bombings," *Pensacola News*, 31 December 1986, p. 2A.

37. Craig Pittman and Dave Goodwin, "Pro-Life Leaders Say Heat's Off," *Pensacola Journal*, 31 December 1985, p. 1A.

38. Tom Hall, "Shocked Exclamations Follow Women's Arrests," *Pensacola Journal*, 3 January 1985, p. 1A.

39. Chris Cooper, "Suspect's Friends Shocked at Arrest," *Pensacola News*, 2 January 1985, p. 1A.

40. Hall, "Shocked," p. 3A.

41. *Pensacola Journal*, 16 April 1985, p. 1.

42. Jon Nordheimer, "Bombing Case Offers," p. A12.

43. "Judge Reassessed Bombing," *Pensacola Journal*, 19 April 1985, p. 14A.

44. Craig Pittman, "Aftershock," *Pensacola News-Journal*, 6 January 1985, p. 2A.

45. Chris Cooper, "Guilty: Four Convicted in Clinic Bombings," *Pensacola News*, 24 April 1985, p. 3A.

46. Barbara Janesh, "Jury Deliberates Bomb Case Today," *Pensacola Journal*, 24 April 1985, p. 12A.

47. The *Newsweek* poll reveals a slight shift in public opinion toward the pro-Choice position between 1981 and 1983 and then back toward the pro-Life position between 1983 and 1985. The percentage saying that abortion should be illegal in all circumstances was, in 1981, 21 percent; in 1983, 16 percent; and in 1985, 21 percent. The percentage saying abortion should be legal in only some circumstances was, in 1981, 52 percent; in 1983, 58 percent; and in 1985, 55 percent. The percentage saying abortion should be legal in all circumstances was, in 1981, 23 percent; in 1983, 23 percent; and in 1985, 21 percent. It has been claimed that the finding that 58 percent favored a law to make abortion illegal except in cases of rape, incest, or endangerment of the mother's life reflected a major shift in momentum, but this is not the case. That precise question was not asked previously, and similar results could be compiled in many previous years from the polls which asked people under which conditions they would favor legalized abortion.

48. Thomas A. Prentice, "Letters from Readers," *Progressive*, December 1980, p. 37.

49. Haven Bradford Gow, "Abortion and the Abuse of the English Language," *Mademoiselle*, July 1979, p. 39.

50. Andrew Hacker, "Of Two Minds about Abortion," *Harpers*, September 1979, p. 16.

51. Milton Rockmore, "Are You Sorry You Had an Abortion?" *Good Housekeeping*, July 1977, p. 163.

52. "Abortion, Religion and Political Life," *Commonweal*, 2 February 1979, p. 37.

53. "Letter," *Pensacola Journal*, 28 December 1984, p. 1.

54. For example, John C. Willke, head of the National Right to Life Committee, public lecture, University of Illinois, Urbana, 6 February 1987; John Noonan, public lecture, University of Iowa School of Law, 1981.

55. Consider the polls cited above, but also consider the strong emphasis on late-term abortions by the Right-to-Life advocates—e.g., Noonan, lecture, University of Iowa, and "ACOG Poll, note 12."

56. For a discussion of the mutuality of persuasion see Douglas Ehninger, "Argument as Method: Its Nature, Its Limitations and Its Uses," *Communication Monographs* 37 (June 1970), 101–10, and "Validity as Moral Obligation," *Southern States Speech Journal* 33 (Spring 1968), 215–22.

57. For a discussion of the discourse in the trial itself, see Celeste Michelle Condit, "Rhetoric and Ideology in the Pensacola Abortion Clinic Bombings," paper presented at the Speech Communication Association National Conference, Boston, November 1987.

58. Lance Morrow, "Of Abortion and the Unfairness of Life," *Time*, 1 August 1977, p. 49.

59. Mary and Scott Reed, "Letters from Readers," *Progressive*, December 1980, p. 37.

60. Nanette Falkenberg, executive director of National Abortion Rights

Coalition, said, "I wanted to find a way to treat the issue so that when people think of abortion, what they see in their mind is not a fetal picture but the face of someone they know, someone who is not a murderer," quoted in Dudley Clendinen, "Abortion Choice Defended in Capital," *New York Times,* 22 May 1985, p. A18.

61. Viola Roggencamp, "Abortion of a Special Kind: Male Sex Selection in India," in *Test-Tube Women: What Future for Motherhood,* ed. Rita Arditti, Renate Duelli-Klein, Shelley Minden (London, Boston: Pandora Press, 1984).

62. Anne Finger, "Claiming All of Our Bodies: Reproductive Rights and Disabilities," in Arditti, Duelli-Klein, and Minden, pp. 281–97.

CHAPTER NINE

Public Rhetoric and Private Lives

The manner in which Americans spoke in the public space about abortion changed markedly between 1960 and 1985. They expressed new interests and thus enabled new laws and cultural practices. Although these new words and ways were not universally endorsed, nor were women's interests fully represented, a new public consensus arose.

In important ways the meaning we impute to this consensus depends upon the impact this flooding torrent of public discourse had on the actions and thoughts of real persons. Surely, such verbal hurricanes disturb even "individuals" huddled inside their private dwellings and cultural enclaves, out of the main currents of the public gale. As yet, however, there have been virtually no attempts to illuminate the precise relationships between such public discourse and private life. Having discarded "hypodermic needle" models and "limited effects" denials as oversimplifications, we are left without theories of the verbal commerce between public and private realms.[1] No single work could fill such a void in our understanding. In order to place the American controversy into a concrete perspective, however, this concluding chapter provides a preliminary exploration of the ways in which changes in public talk and private lives were related to each other.

How to Compare Public and Private?

The major difficulty in comparing public discourse and private lives is the fact that, by definition, any attempt to bring the "private" into the realm of scholarly discourse tampers with the very character of "privateness." Consequently, access to private discourse and private lives not only is difficult to obtain but also is never available to academic analysis in a "pure" form. (Appendix C explores these methodological issues more fully.) Scholars are left with severely limited sources of "data."

Despite such limitations, a few collections of texts from private individuals can provide some partial access to some private lives. In the abortion controversy Katrina Maxtone-Graham has provided a set of personal narratives that supply the grounds for useful comparisons. Her book, *Pregnant by Mistake,* includes edited transcripts of interviews with seventeen women talking about what they did when they found themselves with "unwanted pregnancies" and why they acted as they did.[2] Most of the women had abortions, but some had children whom they put up for adoption, and a few kept "unwanted children." Some of the women, at different times in their lives, took more than one of these options. The women, interviewed by Maxtone-Graham between February 1971 and October 1972, came from varying income levels, age groups, and ethnic backgrounds. Although they cannot be fully representative of the experience of all women, their stories certainly provide an initial wide slice for our edification.

In analyzing these discourses, I compared those portions of the transcripts that dealt directly with childbearing decisions to all the mass-circulation magazine articles that made a direct argument in favor of reforming or repealing abortion laws (as indexed in the *Reader's Guide to Periodical Literature*) for the years 1960–61, 1964–65, and 1970–71. To use these two discourse sets to explore the interaction of public and private requires first an extended comparison of their character.

Potent Differences
Purposes, Characters, and Moral Principles

The broad outline of the public and private discourses shared some common grounds. Most important, for both, "the woman's story" was a key component. These stories, however, conveyed different textures of meaning. The public accounts, especially in the early period, told of women who experienced dangerous or deadly illegal abortions or who bore children into horrid circumstances. The public narratives sought to arouse horror or sympathy, and they defined these women's experiences as "representative" through accompanying statistics. The magazine articles then discussed reasons for and against new abortion laws, generally expressing preferences for "reform." During the discussions the "opponents" and "supporters" of abortion were clearly characterized. The supporters of more lenient laws were depicted as the heroic figures: doctors, lawyers, and ecumenical clergy dominated their ranks. The villains were Roman Catholics, conservatives, men, and "hypocrites," all living in an archaic value structure.

The private discourse was less sure-footed. The seventeen women who told their own stories in *Pregnant by Mistake* usually began with a discussion of their birth control practices or their life situation at the time of their pregnancy. Next they talked about their discovery of pregnancies they had not planned. Gradually, they wove an explanation of their reasons for choosing abortion. The framework of these accounts was formed by life situations, personal goals, and beliefs. Emotions, incidents, and responses filled out the shell.

Each woman described the experience of seeking an abortion and the abortion itself—whether it was legal, clean, and safe or illegal, dirty, and dangerous. About half these women then generalized from their feelings, universalizing their experience to others, suggesting that abortion, though it was to be avoided through birth control when possible, was a needed, regrettable, last resort. Even though they were not skilled verbal artists, their stories emerge through the interviews as full human dramas. As a result, typical readers of this book would probably come to feel that they understood the real and often tragic feelings and needs of these struggling human beings. Such "understanding" bridged occasionally on "identification" with the women—a sense of being their friend or wanting to help. This was a far different feeling from the distant "sympathy" created by the public discourse. These different textures were created primarily through the portrayal of the purposes, characters, and moral principles of the women.

Private Purposes

In *Pregnant by Mistake,* the fifteen women's stories that included abortion decisions featured widely varying circumstances and therefore described abortions undertaken for a variety of purposes.[3] Some of the women had chosen abortion because they were destitute, some because the males involved coerced them into it, and one because her first child was severely asthmatic, tottering between life and death. In general, however, the women based their choices on a constellation of factors subsumable under the term *life-style* rather than on a single cause. The women described themselves as living in an aggregate of conditions that made having a child what they repeatedly called "impossible." They stated simply and forcefully that they did not "want" another child—in one woman's terms "at any cost" (343). In the interviews the accumulated detail of their life circumstances helped to make the "wants" of these women appear important and credible. While a pro-Life advocate reading the stories might still have asked these women to "make the sacrifice for the baby," it is difficult to imagine someone telling Catherine that she is acting for "mere convenience" after she responds to the possibility of keeping the child by exclaiming: "No, absolutely ridiculous! I was already supporting five kids! You're out of your bloody mind! I was working full time and going to school and conducting my political life; I slept four hours a night, sometimes three" (293). Similarly, it is hard to call Sandy's decision a "whim" when she tells us that "abortion, in my case, saved my life as my life is. It left me so that I could still communicate with my family. I could still have a job. It didn't totally destroy everything I was" (132).

As with Sandy and Catherine, most of these women's purposes were not of the stereotypically "forgivable" type—rape, incest, eugenics, life- or health-threatening conditions. Nonetheless, the women's purposes came to have *force* through their individual complexity and reality. In addition to the weight of detail that constitutes "real lives," that reality was created through the characters of the women.

Private Characters

Readers of these stories would come to know the character of these women through a variety of means. Powerfully, the women told of their goals in life and the moral principles they lived by. They recounted a good bit of their lives' histories, and, not surprisingly, such histories were troubled and trying, full of the difficulties and tragedies which all human beings must face. In addition, each woman revealed her character through the manner in which she spoke—the words she chose, the grammar she employed, and the topics she selected. In each case, for different reasons, typical readers would probably have judged that the narrator's character made moral condemnation inapplicable.

One set of women explicitly represented themselves as morally "correct." They argued that they responsibly used birth control and that they had made a prior consistent decision about abortion, unaffected by the emotions of the moment. These women matched a general sense of "moral entities" acting in a moral way. Even if they did not live up to a particular reader's moral principles, most readers would be hard-pressed to challenge their moral *intentions*.

Another set of the women characterized themselves as psychologically incompetent, labeling themselves "messed up." Their language and their traumatic personal histories made such self-analysis credible. Consequently, readers might come to feel that berating these women for immorality would be a futile exercise.

Although the last set of women did not plead incompetence, they appeared young or naive and incapable of assessing their world in a way that made traditional categories of morality functional. Again, then, the typical reader would be most likely to judge them not as morally deficient but as simply unequipped to live by standards of morality that depend heavily upon rational assessment and the ability to take personal responsibility.

Although the characterizations might not have invited approval, in Maxtone-Graham's interviews the complex, detailed, tangled discourse about private abortion decisions would lead a typical reader to understanding, sympathy, or pity rather than hostile moral judgment. At the least, the women's decisions were expressed in such a way that they appeared to have been based on vivid and forceful conditions in their lives, as well as upon a sense of what was "best" that included both others (a moral component) and their own "wants" (an individual component). The case is quite different in the public discourse.

Public Characters and Purposes

The stories of the seventeen women took an entire book to tell. Moreover, a reader would have to get well through *Pregnant by Mistake* to absorb enough detail about the women's lives to sense the force, complexity, and vividness of the "real life" this discourse expressed. In stark contrast, the mass media's stories—representing all women's experiences—often averaged less than two hundred lines. These brief accounts simply could not convey to a mass audience the same variety with any force. Consequently, reporters and public advocates resorted to an alternative rhetorical device: they selected for portrayal stories of women whose purposes for seeking abortion were culturally most persuasive—victims of rape, incest, eugenics, and extreme youth.[4] Such cases could, in the briefest number of words, convey the forcefulness of the problems facing women who chose abortion.

The same reduction of private complexity to narrow public forms occurred with regard to "character." Where readers of the private interviews came to know their subjects through a variety of means that gave reality and force to their individual and flawed characters, the publicly presented women were reduced to mere roles and forms. In the early period, a few adjectives, a few of the women's own statements, and a few indications about their behaviors told the reader something of the women, but even here their character was essentially their "purpose"—the situation in which they found themselves. In one version of the Sherri Finkbine story, she was "a healthy and happily married Arizona woman, mother of four children . . . star of . . . *Romper Room* [who feared that her fifth child] might be hideously deformed as a result of her [unknowingly] taking the sleeping pill thalidomide."[5] As the years went by, magazines and newspapers eliminated even these adjectives, statements, and behaviors. The women became nothing more than their purposes, built from their situations: "A married woman has six children, all that the parents can possibly support; another child would impair the family's stability. . . . A woman on the brink of menopause feels that at her age she cannot care adequately for the expected child. . . . A young girl is pregnant as the result of incest or rape. . . ."[6]

In the most extreme cases even these hasty depictions of purpose disappeared into accounts of "getting the abortion."[7] The multiple, demanding realities of women's lives were thus lost in the translation to public justification. The public discourse did not take into account the full range and complexity of individuals' lived experiences. The serious consequence of this omission can be found in the public moral code constructed from this discourse—a morality distinctly and importantly different from the moral code the women constructed for themselves.

Moral Principles

In their private discourse the women interviewed by Maxtone-Graham used moral principles to different extents, and they applied a variety of rules. One set of moral criteria most frequently applied was threefold. First, in order to have moral grounds for an abortion, they indicated, *you should use birth control as a first line of prevention.* Betsey, for example, justified her decision by noting that "I also felt that I *was* using contraceptives, and that it was a contraceptive failure" (64). Second, the women indicated that *you should be consistent about your decisions and values.* They had decided, *before* finding themselves pregnant, that they would have an abortion in case of unwanted pregnancy. Carole emphasized the importance of such consistency as a sign of sincerity, concluding "whatever your reasons might be. I don't think that anyone's reasons really need to be questioned. If someone is really sincere in wanting an abortion" (100). Finally, the women indicated that *you should consider the interests of all those around you,* encompassing a broad range of factors that should be weighed against each other. Several times the women noted that "your whole life situation plays a big, big part" (7) or that "there were many factors" (232). Carole indicated the ways she finally balanced these interests, saying, "So I just feel that it's better for me, and it's better for the children, and better for my husband" (104).

Another group of women presented an alternative, quite different, moral set. Rather than assuming that any abortion must be justified as a "special case," they indicated that *having* a child required justification. They argued that it would be "fair" to bring a child into the world only under certain conditions. Most centrally, *you must provide a loving, stable environment.* Alex, for example, insisted, "Kids should be desired. . . . A child should be wanted and brought into an emotional climate . . . that can accept him and *wants* him" (189). Acting otherwise, indicated Samantha, "it's really unfair to the child" (36). Applying these rules to her own pregnancy, Annie suggested that it took "courage" to surmount her own fears and feelings in order to live up to this morality. She said, "I'm pregnant now, but, my God, will I bring a child into the world simply because I'm afraid of having to face my *feelings*? No, we are too strong. We love each other too much. Our children. The whole philosophy of: we affirm life; and so, therefore, we cannot treat it in such a shabby way as to say we are not strong enough to have an abortion" (121).

This moral principle—that children should only be born wanted, that unwanted pregnancies should not be brought to term—was also extended to cover adoption. Catherine, for example, insisted that "you have no right to do that to another human being. I don't think you have any right at all to create a human being and *give it away*" (292). Allison expressed a similar view: "There are very real reasons for a woman not to keep a child, but then she shouldn't have *had* it! She should have had an *abortion*" (86).

The most abstract of these moral statements consciously *disapproved* of the alternate morality expressed by "the society." Samantha challenged the correctness of the dominant public morality, saying, "People like me shouldn't be made to go through undiluted hell. Because of a FLUKE that's happened" (47). Louise also consciously challenged the existing view: "I'm not a prude, and I do believe in abortions. . . . Okay, some people call it murder. But I think that there's a lot of murder going on in young girls who have nowhere else to turn; and who perhaps ruin their lives by going through with a pregnancy, or by having an illegal abortion in which they're butchered" (327). Antonia concurred: "It really bothers me how they feel you can *force* someone to go through with it; and even worse, you know, to have unmarried girls go through with it and then give it up for adoption. How—how can you be so cruel?" (31).

From such challenges to the existing moral system, the women drew an alternative moral principle. Having concluded that the options of "forcing someone to go through with it are cruel," Antonia constructed the moral principle, "having an abortion should be the woman's choice" (31). In Annie's version, "People ought to be in control of their own bodies . . . we all have to work toward allowing people to do what they know they must do. . ." (120).

Thus, the women applied varying moral systems. Some provided a set of conditions under which abortion was "permissible" and indicated how their decisions met those criteria. Others described an alternate moral system in which abortion was morally the best option, rather than one in which abortion must be "excused." Whether finding moral grounds to "excuse" an abortion, or elaborating a system in which abortion was a moral "necessity," most of the women applied moral principles and gave a good bit of attention to these maxims.

This is a somewhat different finding from the popularly publicized claims of Carol Gilligan, who argues that men make moral decisions on the basis of principles or fixed rules (of "justice"), while women decide on a more diffuse morality of "care," which requires more complex moral "weighing" processes.[8] Instead, this analysis suggests that Gilligan may have simply accepted male definitions of what *count* as moral principles. Women operate on moral principles, but (at least in the area of abortion) they are different principles than those used by men because women tend to have different interests on abortion issues.

Men's employment of "rules" appears to be a simple process of "applying principles," rather than the more complex endeavor of "weighing," only because the male "rule-system" has become the dominant *public* rule-system. Men therefore do not have to negotiate between their own interests and the public moral system, because these two sets are largely identical. Male moral decision-making therefore has the appearance of being neater and cleaner—more purely rule-governed.

Women, in contrast, must work harder in their justification process: they must both account for these dominant rules *and* make a case for their own rules and interests. Therefore, their decision-making appears more complex—not because they "lack principles" or use an inherently different *process* of moral valuation but because their rhetorical position imposes a particular way of talking about their moral principles. Most women face two rhetorical exigencies that differ from those of most men.

As American society and public discourse have been constituted, women must *justify* their own moral principles *as they apply them* because these principles and the female interests they represent have not become publicly accepted maxims. (This condition may be changing rapidly: many of my young female students today seem to have no trouble with a quick and easy citation of the maxim "It's my body, isn't it"). Secondly, women must then negotiate between "their" principles and the dominant principles. No wonder their discourse looks complex and entails complicated "weighings." The "different" sound of women's "voice," however, may result not from any inherent characteristic of women (neither nurturance nor a peculiar capacity for responding to rules and principles) but from their current, historically specific situation in American society—a position shaped by the dominance of alien male principles, the absence of public endorsement of female principles, and women's need to negotiate among these in articulating their moral justifications.

Foundations of Morality in Experience

To this point I have described the dramatically different ways in which public and private discourse portrayed women's "character" and "purposes." I also have shown that women constructed and applied clear moral principles to justify their abortion decisions. Finally, I have suggested that male/public moral principles are fundamentally at odds with those of the women. By exploring the foundations of these principles in their supporting rhetoric, we can see the way in which the exclusion of the women's voice and the consequent exclusion of their interests founded the differences between public/male moral discourse on abortion and the private/female stories. That will provide the last preliminary to an exploration of the interaction of these two realms.

As we have seen, the women in this sample held themselves responsible for a pregnancy only if they knew about and had access to birth control but did not use it when having sexual intercourse. In contrast, in the *public* discourse the moral rule held that women were "excused" from pregnancy only if they were not "responsible" for having intercourse or if the outcome of the pregnancy might be socially undesirable (as in deformities threatened by measles). An article in *Christian Century* in 1961 provides a typical example when it concludes that the laws should be restructured but only so as not to "compel the bearing of children conceived through rape, incest and irresponsibility by minor or mentally incompetent girls."[9] The authors were equally clear that the decision process was not to rest with the women or be addressed to their interests. They directly excluded the pregnant women from the decision-making process, saying "the limits of legalized abortion should be drawn by the mutual agreement of the law, medicine and the church"—no mention of the women.[10] In fact, women's views were dismissed as "whims" and expressly ruled out as grounds.[11] The institutions sought to retain control, unshared with individual women, to set the legal and moral rules. The institutional rules dictated that once a woman knowingly acquiesced to sex (and hence, to marriage), she accepted the responsibility of bearing and raising any healthy child (because she admitted the possibility that birth control would fail, or simply that intercourse could result in conception). Because she "voluntarily" took the risk, she was held to be morally bound to give up all her own interests in favor of the potential child.

These moral weightings arose, most basically, because it was perceived as in the public interest for women to bear and caringly raise children (so that society might perpetuate itself). Consequently, society had an incentive to count each sex act as in some way voluntary (the strong force of sexual drive in women was routinely discounted, and manifestations of it were branded as signs of deviance and evil). Supporting this, the value of the fetus was understood in an abstract manner. Fetuses were classified in a digital fashion as either sacred or disposable on grounds of their "soul," "potential," "genetic structure," or "personhood." Because women's interests were partially different from these abstract systemic concerns, the women's articulations of principles concerning sexuality and the fetus were different.

Sexuality

Individual women must live with their own biological nature—that is, their own sexuality. As a consequence, most of the women in *Pregnant by Mistake* saw sex as an inevitability of life. While each sex act might have been more or less voluntary, having sex throughout life was not generally voluntary. People had sex much like they ate; each meal might be voluntary, but eating was not. The women viewed lifelong abstinence as an unrealistic expectation. When Samantha got pregnant with an IUD implanted in her, she explained: "I hadn't even made a *mistake*. And I felt it was very *unfair* that it should happen to *me*. . . . And I think I felt the whole world was kicking me in the teeth for something that I really had nothing to do with. But short of abstinence, this is something of a chance you take" (38).

Antonia, a married woman, reported a similar response: "I used to be pretty rigid in my thinking, until it happened to me. And I realize how easy it is to get pregnant, *even* for people who are very careful and knowledgeable" (24). From these women's perspectives, they necessarily had sex, and sex necessarily meant the possibility of pregnancy. Consequently, they developed a moral maxim holding themselves accountable only for doing everything *possible* to avoid pregnancy while having sex.

Children

The women could excuse themselves from the consequences of their inherent sexuality because they did not value the fetus and future children as absolutely or exclusively as did the public vocabulary. With only one exception, all of the women emphatically stated that they *loved* and valued children, and loved the children they had. However, they also emphasized that children made extreme demands against their own limited resources. Jean said, "I know personally, for myself, that it's better for me not to have more than two children. I—I can give just so much. I feel I've reached my limit" (281). Antonia felt similarly: "They tell you you're so selfish when you don't want a child. Well, God, let them try it! Even if you want them it's still a lot of work. I mean, it takes a lot out of you even if you *willingly* do it" (31). Thus, the women described a limit to the number of children who could be rewarding and desirable, and they noted the many limiting conditions in individual lives that could make children "not wanted."

The Fetus

The women thus balanced the ideal of children and the real pleasures of children against other personal needs and demands. They balanced the implicit "rights" or interests of the fetus in a similar manner. In the first place, many of the women denied that a fetus constituted a "life" similar to that of their children. They did not characterize the fetus in terms of some definitional ideal or principle but rather in accord with its material characteristics. One woman defined the fetus as "a collision between a sperm and an egg" (Annie, 125). Another group of women referred to its physical appearance. Patti noted that "I just saw a pan full of blood with this little blob in it" (198), while Catherine commented that "we conjure up this little thing that you're holding in your arms with its blue eyes and its little face.—This is *not* what you're dealing with, when you're talking about an eight-week pregnancy. . . . I, I talk a great deal about the physical development of this creature. Very vividly, in terms of where it is, week after week" (301).

Yet another group of women characterized the fetus in terms of their relationships with it—its material effect. Carole said: "I didn't consider it a life, that it was a mistake. And it wouldn't be a life until the baby was born" (96). Allison also emphasized the importance of the relationship in making the characterization: "I really don't have strong feelings that when a woman is first pregnant that there's any kind of reality about a 'human being' inside of her. I think that she *makes* it real if she so chooses. I mean I see pregnancy very much as a purely physical state, that's not unrelated to any other physical state. Growing something inside of you—it's no different than a plant, you know. And I really feel that the thing that makes it real is the choice to *have* the child" (85).

For most of the women, time was a crucial variable in the definition. After time, the fetus would begin to define itself; its materiality would become substantial enough to *force* a relationship. Louise recalled that "I had an abortion before I was quite six weeks pregnant. I had no feeling for the child. I could have never waited until the fourth month or so when the child was kicking. I would already have started to have feeling for the child" (327). Antonia also cited the importance of time: "We had nothing against abortion as long as it was done early enough" (5). Less sure of herself, Samantha also saw time as a relevant criterion: "I was very fortunate. I think I may have been eight . . . maybe *just* eight weeks pregnant. So I was very lucky. I mean, you know, it's probably not really very pregnant at all. [Laughs] Well . . . !" (39). The seriousness of these distinctions about time for the women is most evident in Allison's testimony: "He [the abortionist] kept saying, 'you're much more than eight weeks pregnant, you must have just had a false period, you must have just been spotting,' et cetera. And that was really one of the worst—that was the only time that I really had any sense of 'an abortion' in the sense of killing an embryo" (73).

The women thus characterized the fetus in terms of its real historical and material being, as manifested in its relations to other beings.

They did not generally characterize it in the abstract terms of the public discourse, such as genetic structure, personhood, or soul. In fact, they resisted abstract hypotheticals. When asked if she felt guilty about the fact that, if she had had the chance, she might have aborted her first child, Carole answered: "She's—she's really terrific. And it would be a shame if—if rather than being Jenny, she were an abortion. But then again, the second one is fine and terrific; and so I could have had her, probably, again. You know, like right now, if I were just getting married now. So, you know, it's a hard thing to talk about, 'If everything were different.' It's just hypothetical" (107).

Even the women who accepted the personhood of the fetus relied on a direct material base in defining its status. Sandy said, "It's a human being . . . that baby, or that young fetus, or whatever it was, was having a tremendous effect on my body. I mean, there it was, growing" (150). Even when pushed to use more abstract criteria, Sandy tried to make them concrete: "This had all the genes and all the potential of being like us. Not just 'potential' [she struggled against abstraction], it was *going to be*"(150–51).

The women thus defined the fetus in terms of their material experience of it, rather than through the abstractions of the public realm. This material orientation helped them to avoid the digital "yes/no" of the abstract public categories and permitted them to judge the fetus against themselves. It is important to note that whether they viewed the fetus as fully human or less than that, each of the women weighed it as of lesser value than her own life. Betsey concluded that "I do believe there was a child there. And I, you know, *I'm sorry*! I *didn't want to* . . . to kill it. And I think I did. But I—I also—you know, I can't honestly say I regret it at all" (54). Speaking from the same position, Sandy explained further: "I mean, I'm sorry, I'm not going to sacrifice my life for someone I don't even know. And that was the one thing that I did feel most strongly after the abortion: that I did save my life, by sacrificing somebody else's" (151). Carole, with different feelings about the status of the fetus, concurred in the final judgment: "I just feel that my life is more important to me right now" (96).

This stark difference between the women's weighing of the fetus and that of the public discourse arose from the different meanings possible for the public term *mother's life* and the private experience of *my life*. Because the public term *mother's life* had to cover so many women, it could only be reduced to the common denominator of physical survival. However, the women's version of the term *my life* meant identity—the "everything I was." Although for the women, this was necessarily a higher and more differentiated concern, from a male or institutional perspective, the woman's life was just an abstraction to be weighed against the equal abstraction of the fetus. To the extent that women were categorized *essentially* as childbearers, the weighting was necessarily tilted in favor of the fetus. In the dominant view, therefore, it did not make sense for the women to reject this primary role; hence, any refusal to bear a child could only be seen as secondary, a "whim" or temporary "convenience." Women who rejected this role were *selfish because they did not serve the interests of others as others would wish them to do.

Thus though the public and private discourses shared the common denominator of "women's stories" as their core and focused on similar issues, they were divided by crucial differences. The public characterizations of the pregnant women and their purposes were simple and gathered under a narrow heading of socially acceptable grounds, defined by a morality alienated from women's interests and perspectives. The private characterizations were intricate and complex, because they had to counter the public principles and express interests based on understandings of sexuality, the fetus, and children grounded in the material experiences of women's real lives.

These variations probably resulted both from a permanent and general difference in the nature of public and private discourse and from the fact that the public discourse was essentially *male-dominated, while the women's private discourse revealed in Maxtone-Graham's interviews was less so. Public discourse, because it appeals to vaster audiences and interests, may always speak through an abstract, indirect vocabulary, isolated to some extent from material experiences. The distance between that public vocabulary and the private terms of the women seems to have been lengthened by the overwhelming lack of inclusion of female experiences in the existing moral set. Until the concerns of women themselves were part of the social vocabulary, women would be only instruments for others in the social system.

Private Lives Influence Public Discourse

It was precisely the public assimilation of the women's vocabulary that created the conditions for reducing the differences between the public and private realms. Careful examination suggests that untidy and interesting interactions occurred in the assimilation process. The public inclusion of women's stories simultaneously expanded women's "choices" in the public realm, while pruning and shaping the "women's discourse" that pushed the public revision.

The clearest example of the process by which women's discourse was simultaneously included in and altered by the public discourse is the change in the use of the word *want*. The term was translated from an expression of the desires of individual women into "unwanted children," a social concern, and then into Choice—a matter of women's rights.

"What I *want*" was the phrase most frequently used, by the individual women in *Pregnant by Mistake* and in other interviews, to describe the warrant behind their private decisions. While terms such as *freedom* and *I had to* also often appeared, *want* provided the most central explanation why the women chose to have abortions performed. Antonia, for example, said, "It would just have changed my life completely; and not the way I wanted it . . . we [she and her husband] were just not willing" (7). Even the weighing of values was done through a lens of what the pregnant woman *wanted*. Samantha argued that "I wanted the *child*" in a biological way, but "on a purely intellectual level, I didn't *want* the child, didn't want to have it, didn't want to keep it" (36). In the private discourse, personal *want* was the most pervasive claim, and it seemed to sum up other terms when they were used.

As the public discourse opened to women's voices in the period 1960–61, the magazine articles discussed the "wants" of individual women. In contrast to the women's own discourse, however, in the public realm the term did not carry great force. Instead of presenting the woman's "wants" as sufficient justification in themselves, the authors added other social-moral terms. Initially, *want* did not seem to be a comfortable or successful *social* defense of the act of abortion, so its use was relatively infrequent. The use of the root term *want* in the public discourse increased fairly substantially across time. In 1964–65 the term appeared more frequently and in 1970–71 more consistently (see Appendix C). The growth in frequency, however, was coupled with a crucial transformation process. The term *want* was transformed into a concern with "un*want*ed children."

The raw power of acting women provided the material ground for social change. Women's willingness to seek abortion "at any cost" (in Ellie's words, 343)—acting without "care about the danger I was in" (Allison, 70), risking death for what they "wanted"—forced society to allow them to express their interests. The contemporary revision of American law and culture related to abortion, therefore, was a direct consequence of *women's* interests—a fact directly traceable in the discourse trail.[12] Ultimately, however, to be *persuasive* in the public realm, the women's vocabulary—their ways of seeing the issues and speaking about them—had to be transformed. The women's term *want* was able to enter the social vocabulary and to exert public force only when transformed so that it indicated its impact on others. An individual desire—"I didn't want any more children"—became a threat to a well-integrated society. "Unwanted" children, the articles made clear, were *not* socially desirable. The magazines described how such children would be abused, delinquent, ill-educated, and disorderly. Such life-styles negated the social functions for which society had bound women to motherhood (of a traditional sort); such pregnancies were not socially productive (and it was progressive "productivity," not mere reproduction, that was socially preferred). In addition, being "unwanted" was a serious enough condition (given the dependency of human infants) that the term even weighed against the presumed desire of the fetus for its own life. Women were thus able to make their "wants" count, in large part because their wants influenced other social goals and the wants of other social beings.

The expression of women's "wants" as a means for the society to avoid "unwanted children" was not, however, the last step in the process. Had it been, adoption would have provided an adequate public solution. The society and the fetus could have insured their interests by requiring a woman to bear the child and give it to someone who did "want" it. Women, however, resolutely resisted adoption, proclaiming adamantly that it presented the worst possible experience. "Oh God," said Allison, herself an adoptee, "I couldn't even consider doing that!" (84). Betsey agreed, "I don't think I could do that" (53). This response, however, lacked compelling *social* interest and was not frequently heard in the public discourse. In its place, the concern about "overpopulation" provided a *social* justification that quieted the demand for women to continue to produce children.

The "Zero Population Growth" movement made possible the transformation of "unwanted children" into "Choice" by counteracting the force of pro-natalism.[13] The movement deflated the social desirability of women producing children they did not want by eliminating the presumption that the society *wanted* those children, even if their mothers did not. In so doing, it challenged the social grounds on which women's choices had historically been sacrificed. By suggesting the negative consequences of too much "motherhood," the overpopulation rhetoric helped to free women from exclusive assignment to the category of reproductive laborers and thereby created a new opportunity to claim the full range of Choices granted to male workers in a (partially) "free enterprise" economy.

Thus as women's discourse was included in the public vocabulary, it was modified by other forces: individual wants became social Choices. The movement from a woman's desire to "fulfill her wants" by "making her own choices" to an ideographic "Right to Choose" or "Freedom of Choice" was also pruned and transformed in another way. As the private discourse reveals, the public persuasion was directly derived from the articulated demands of real women, both the poor and the rich, the intellectually gifted and the mentally weak. This women's discourse was, in an important sense, a classless, raceless, undifferentiated movement of "women as a whole." In the process of transforming this general demand into a successful public vocabulary, however, the needs of particular groups of women— especially the poor—were pruned out of the discourse.

The desire of all women for greater power to fill their individual wants was cut back to the political option for those already holding economic power to be allowed to make their choices legally.

In part, the translation of this generally shared *want* to economically limited Choice occurred because the American social system and its vocabulary protected only political rights, not economic desires, and hence it did not protect the poor in general (in any of their sub-classifications—e.g., teenagers, stigmatized ethnic groups, the mentally handicapped). In practice, middle-class women were in the position to articulate their private vocabulary as a public one; poor women were not. Because the "articulate" class's primary limits on *their* choices were not economic, but legal, their primary arguments were directed at the single factor that prevented their wants from being realized—the coercive power of the state.

The arrival of the term *Choice* as a representative of women's interests was therefore a complex event. To say that the rhetoric of Choice was merely a middle-class movement would be too simplistic an assessment. The vocabulary of Choice was rooted in the words and "wants" of women across economic lines; however, the transference of the wants of women into public discourse was incomplete. That incompleteness emphasizes the impact of the process of public persuasion—a process which allowed women to articulate their interests, but only through the interests and vocabulary of others, and with the help and limiting influence of other powerful discourses. This same consequential, transformational process was evident in a second crucial component of the women's discourse—the women's narratives as a whole. The women's stories became publicly powerful enough to generate public value change only through translation into the life stories of other more powerful groups.

Between 1960 and 1961 the primary narrative in the public discourse was, at least in outline, the private "women's story." By 1964–65 this public version of the women's story was truncated and partially replaced by a "physicians' story." By 1970–71 an even broader "social story" was most frequently produced in the public realm. A clear set of percentages indicates this change (see Appendix C). In 1960–61 about 50 percent of the discourse in the popular magazines consisted of narratives, primarily about women and the illegal abortions they faced. About 11.5 percent of that discourse consisted of statistics supporting the generalization of these narratives. In 1964–65 these percentages dropped to about 31 and 8 percent respectively. By 1970–71 the numbers were 16 and 7 percent. As the "stories" of women began to take up less space, the number of "histories" (the social story) gradually increased and the focus shifted to legal structure and social institutions (the term *law* was used 81 times in 1960–61, 108 times in 1964–65, and 172 times in 1970–71; see Appendix C on statistics). The change was not merely a replacement but rather a gradual translation of meanings.

The women's story, so prominent in 1960–61, generated the "physicians' story," most prominent in 1964–65. Physicians were among the major leaders of the reform laws. As chapter 2 indicated, they reported that they participated in the debate because they felt trapped between the women's stories and the pre-existing social set defined by the law ("no abortions except to save the woman's life"). Doctors tended to see "woman's life" in a broadening sense that included more than physical being. Alan Guttmacher argued that "a doctor's primary interest must be in preserving life. But is it only the physical life which is to be protected? Or should we also take into consideration the mental and emotional life and health of a patient?"[14] The doctors' sense of duty thus clashed with the law.

Additionally, the doctors saw that women's lives were threatened by the physicians' inability to provide these women with legal/safe abortions; the women turned to illegal unsafe abortions, a fact the doctors often faced when they tried to save the women or repair the damage (to the extent of perhaps 350,000 hospital admissions a year).[15] Here, the law contradicted the doctors' own values and itself, because it made explicit protection for "women's lives" but did not allow operations that would, in effect, save many women's lives (considering incomplete abortions ranged from a third to a half of maternal deaths at the time).[16] Guttmacher protested that "many highly-thought-of hospitals place themselves and their doctors in jeopardy of prosecution many times each year. It is, I feel, unfair for doctors and hospitals to be asked to do this. But what are the alternatives? To refuse therapeutic abortion to the mother of five children who recently has been operated on for cancer? To reject the application of a psychotic woman unable to care for the children she already has? Many women denied therapeutic abortions turn to illegal abortionists. . . ."[17] It was more than a coincidence that the first constitutional challenges to the law were based on its "vagueness" about what constituted a threat to "women's lives."

The women's life stories thus compelled the doctors to tell their own story in the public arena, demanding social attention to their individual needs and desires. The effect of these linking stories told by the doctors was additive—that is, the political and social power of the doctors was added to the force of the women. But it was also multiplicative, for the doctors were more powerful economically, politically, and socially; their rights and privileges were already inscribed in the laws and vocabulary of the land.[18] They were therefore able to help construct and expedite a third level of stories—the "social histories" that told of legal abortion as a social good.

This third level of stories had a complete and variegated *dramatic structure. The social *purposes* for legal abortion included "no unwanted children," "women's lives," basic "rights," and even direct reduction of poverty. The terms conveying these social purposes came to include Freedom, Right to Privacy, "right to control one's own body," and Right to Choose (in 1970–71 each of these terms occurred much more frequently, and the term *right* occurred thirty-four times, whereas it was virtually nonexistent earlier). The *agency* of "legal" abortion as a safe, cost-effective measure was directly contrasted to unsafe, expensive illegal abortion (and this component came directly from the women's stories). The *scene* was a world of overpopulation and expensive social programs and a country in which individuals had certain rights. The *agents* were needy persons. The *act* was fundamentally a political one, removed from moral issues. Through a three-step translation, therefore, the women's narrative, like the vocabulary of want/Choice, was able to infiltrate the public vocabulary and force change, but only in modified form and indirectly, through its impact on other vocabularies.

Public Discourse Impacts Private Lives

To this point, the comparison of public and private discourses has suggested serious tensions between public and private depictions of abortion and indicated the translative devices through which women's talk was restructured to provide the foundation of a new public vocabulary that authorized abortion. As this new public discourse developed, however, it had a reciprocal impact on private lives.

To analyze this impact we must examine private discourse of different periods. I have chosen another set of "almost private" discourse—a set of "stories" about abortion told in *People* magazine in 1984.[19] The set is highly impure because it has been intrusively edited by the reporters, and it contains stories of activists who know they are telling such stories for rhetorical purposes. Nonetheless, it gives us some indicators and guides.

Basically, the stories from 1984 are very similar to the earlier private discourse reported by Maxtone-Graham. Because of their public focus and their activist backgrounds, they are more compact and contain more explicit mention of key terms from both sides of the movement ("affirming Life," "Right to Choose"). They also feature greater diversity (the stories of 1985 include opponents of abortion) and a greater tendency to take into account the lessons of the pro-Life movement. Otherwise, they are very similar to the women's narratives of *Pregnant by Mistake*, told between 1971 and 1972. That is, the basic explanations of purpose and the revelations of character are roughly the same.

This similarity suggests that perhaps the key to the influence of public discourse upon private is not exclusively one of vocabulary. That is, the private discourse was perhaps such a fundamental base of the pro-Choice vocabulary that little new content was added to private talk by the appearance of sustained public discourse supporting abortion. At the most, the prominent public arguments provided a greater certainty—a change of "my choice" and "my wants" to "my Right to Choose." This is not to say that the public discourse had no impact, however. For that impact, we return to the discourse of *Pregnant by Mistake*.

Several of the women interviewed by Maxtone-Graham had earlier borne "unwanted children" and had either kept them or put them up for adoption. The "second time around," however, these women chose abortion, and generally they indicated that they would rather have aborted the first time. Each explained that she had not done so, however, because she had not known of the option. Alex, for example, bore the child of her first unwanted pregnancy because, she said, "I figured that this was the only way out. Abortion was—so *unknown* to me, that I did not pursue the matter" (165). She indicated, however, that "I would do an abortion again. I would not do a pregnancy and give the child up again" (191). Alex's experience suggests that the public discourse about abortion may have only made minor changes in the *way* women made their fertility decisions, or discussed them, but it provided a new option—both by making safe abortion more generally available,[20] and by making the option known to more women. Given the fact that the number of births to unmarried women decreased markedly after abortion was legalized, these stories are probably reasonably typical.[21]

The vital importance of public discourse for creating some places where legalized abortions were available and for informing more women about them was evident in the women's private discourse. There was a distinct class of "fence-sitters"—women who weren't willing to risk illegal or unsafe abortion, even though they didn't really want another child. Antonia indicated the link between safety and legality, and its importance: "Illegal. Yes. Well, it wasn't legal in most cases. . . . But at least he was a doctor. . . . I was really scared, you know, I was really scared about an illegal set-up. . . . I could not afford to risk getting hurt or getting killed. . . . If that was the choice, you know I would certainly not endanger my life" (8). Lynn concurred. She had gone to seek an illegal abortion, but had changed her mind because the abortionist "was the most filthy little woman you have ever seen in your life" (240).

Legality was also directly entwined with knowing about abortion and seriously considering it as an option. Some women did not hear about abortion *because* it was illegal. Carole indicated, "I think that if— if I were eighteen now, and pregnant, I *would* have an abortion. But then there was just no question of it, because it was illegal. Well, that was five years ago and I don't know where it was legal" (106).

The most powerful facet of having the "public discourse" include a group's private discourse may be that it helps the discourse to reach more women, informing them about more options and giving them the opportunity to express themselves about those options. Even if the basic forms of expression do not change (the stories of reasons for offering a child for adoption are very similar to abortion stories), the outcome is markedly different. As Lynn pointed out, carrying a pregnancy to term is different from abortion, "because those months [of carrying the child] were very destructive to *me*. Very destructive. I haven't really ever thought about this—clearly, but uh—(pause). That was the end of my trust in people" (263–64). Spreading a public discourse, even when it is derived from some of a class's own private discourse, thus can make a major difference in private lives.

This does not deny the fact, pointed out by both pro-Choice advocates and the women in their private stories, that many women had illegal abortions before abortion was legal; they just didn't articulate their experiences. It indicates, however, that different channels of attitudes and information are available in different private lives. Where public discourse on a subject is lacking, fewer women will have access to the discourse core because not all channels of private discourse carry that core perspective. Public discourse simply adds one more source from which women can gain an additional vocabulary of potential use in their lives. "Persuasion," then, is not solely a process of changing closed minds but is also the addition of possibilities. Public discourse thus enriches the perspectives or information available to members of a subgroup by better distributing the knowledge to more of the potential users of that knowledge.

Public discourse might also change private lives by confronting women directly with opposing perspectives, providing incentive for them either to modify their actions in the face of new interests or to account for their refusal to modify. The private discourse in 1971–72 and the "mixed" discourse of 1985 (in increased measure) show an effort to respond both to diffuse public sentiment and to the increasingly well-articulated public discourse opposing abortion. In the 1971–72 period, for example, Annie and Louise both expressed their response to the claim that abortion opposed Life. Louise noted the arguments they faced, saying that other people insinuated "that for us to be able to do this we must just be the worst people possible, and have *no feelings*. And it's just really the *opposite*. We feel very—you know—we have very *strong* feelings. We *do* care, we *are* concerned. We don't want to be considered *murderers* in any way. Because we're not. We're *pacifists*—by *every* standard" (334). Annie described how she confronted such arguments and began to articulate a response: "I started to talk a lot about my two children. About how much getting pregnant and being pregnant with them had meant to me. . . . And the next thing that became so obvious to me was the utter respect that I *do* have for human life" (118).

The existence of the public controversy thus exposed more women not only to their own vocabulary but also to a more articulate version of the values and interests opposing them. It thereby encouraged the women to develop their own understandings in more detail and perhaps to modify those understandings as well. If we do not see more actual modification of the decisions, it may well be because the pro-Life discourse had held sway for so long that little additional information was added.

Despite its importance, the public discourse should not be viewed as a magic key that instantly gives access to knowledge on both sides to all members. The women's private discourse of 1971–72 occurred during acrimonious public discussion about abortion, and it reveals a crucial factor—the differential permeability of private discourse to public talk. The women of many of these stories had much contact with the public discourse, others had virtually none. Some of the women interviewed by Maxtone-Graham used a large amount of the public vocabulary ("rights," "control of one's own body," and "Choice"), and they referred to the public controversy; others used it very little. Women who were facing abortion decisions thus responded to the public discourse in a variety of ways. They may have been exposed to more or less of it, and they may have absorbed and used more or less of it. Both the strength of the women's own explanations and the degree to which the "translated" public discourse matched the women's own discursive needs affected the way public discourse came back to private use. This is not to say that public discourse in general has no effect but merely that it had a range of effects because it has different uses for different persons. Articulation of women's interests in public discourse was thus not a complete solution; it was simply one component of a set of solutions to the exclusions, problems, and challenges women faced.

Conclusion

This sample of discourse from the private lives of the women of *Pregnant by Mistake* suggests that, indeed, the torrent of public discourse about abortion in America constituted a "meaningful" change because of its relationship to the real lives of some women. The persuasive force of the public tide was not a coercive revision of women's worldviews but rather an enabling of discursive and pragmatic "choices" made possible by wider dissemination of a wider range of ways of talking about childbearing decisions. Moreover, the public discourse about abortion was materially grounded in women's life experiences. The vocabulary was formed from the inclusion and transformation of the words women spoke—the expression of their "wants," their demands for more "choices," their framing of the concrete realities of childbearing and sexuality and fetuses in their lives.

The transformation of private to public produced a revision, however. What had been a classless *women's* private discourse was publicly articulated by middle- and professional-class American women (because they had the discursive skills and were economically privileged enough to have access to the communicative channels). These women did not share the economic problems and cultural barriers faced by women in poverty or minority groups. The childbearing choices they were likely to emphasize were choices to limit or repudiate childbearing. In addition, these spokeswomen advocated the women's discourse within an American public vocabulary that featured an historically developed commitment to laissez-faire economic liberalism. Finally, they articulated it against competing arguments from the pro-Life interest group. As a consequence of all these limitations, the American *public* version of the vocabulary of Choice evolved in a way that made it fit most closely the demands of middle- and professional-class women. The public meaning of "Choices" for women was thus derived from very broad and multifaceted private desires for the ability to make choices that served women's wants, but it was transformed into the narrower but still important ground of political laissez-faire.

The inclusion in the public realm of women's discourse on the single issue that distinguishes them clearly as a class—their childbearing—was therefore only partly accomplished. The compromise achieved with the reigning public discourse and the Right-to-Life Movement was bought at a cost to the least powerful women—the poor and to some extent the young and minority groups. That cost was, of course, predictable: the unbending problem of poverty remains that those who are unempowered are always those who lack access to articulation and hence have the least opportunity to generate a discourse that will empower them. Because of the nature of the persuasive process, those are the groups upon whose interest it is always easiest for others to "compromise."

Both of the dominant views of the rhetoric of Choice are therefore inappropriate. "Choice" as it is currently instantiated in American public law, discourse, and practice is neither merely a partisan concern of middle-class women nor a fully adequate vocabulary to express all women's interests. The version of the discourse of Choice that dominated the mid-eighties should be understood from a developmental, processual perspective. It constituted a public vocabulary that grew out of a general women's discourse but was shaped by other influences. Our judgments of the resulting public vocabulary and our decisions about what arguments to make in the future ought to be grounded in the realization that the inclusion of women's interests in the public vocabulary through the debate about abortion was merely subject to the unceasing discursive processes that all public argument in America faces. The public and the private, the social and the individual interact in developing new discursive formations. Because human beings are both individuals and creatures of collectivity, they employ both public and private discourses. In a world of limited material resources and billions of human beings, we are destined to influence each other and are both enabled and constrained by that destiny.

NOTES

1. On such theoretical perspectives, compare Phillip K. Tompkins, *Communication as Action: An Introduction to Rhetoric and Communication* (Belmont, Calif.: Wadsworth, 1982), and Shanto Iyengar, Mark D. Peters, and Donald R. Kinder, "Experimental Demonstrations of the 'Not-so-Minimal' Consequences of Television News Programs," in *Mass Communications Review Yearbook*, ed. Ellen Wartella and D. Charles Whitney (Beverly Hills, Calif.: Sage, 1983), pp. 77–87. Carroll Smith-Rosenberg broaches the issue of the relationship between public and private in *Disorderly Conduct: Visions of Gender in Victorian America* (New York: Alfred A. Knopf, 1983), pp. 45–47.

2. Katrina Maxtone-Graham, *Pregnant by Mistake: The Stories of Seventeen Women* (New York: Liveright, 1973), hereafter cited in text by page number only. (A new edition with introduction and new preface was printed in 1989 by Rémi Books, New York). I have compared this set to a similar collection produced by Linda Bird Francke, *The Ambivalence of Abortion* (New York: Dell, 1982 ed.). The latter was not systematically analyzed, but it does not seem to contradict the findings I suggest in this chapter.

3. Two of the seventeen women did not choose to have an abortion. Some chose adopting out a child or keeping it at one point while aborting another at other times. Some were married, some were not.

4. My hypothesis is this: reporters are primarily articulators of a "popular response" to the conditions on which they report. Women reporters who researched the "back-alley abortion" stories were confronted with the multiplicity of details evident in the "women's stories" and desired to convey this "response" to the public. The generic constraints of reportage did not allow them simply to report all these stories, so, in order to faithfully reproduce the "meaning" of illegal abortion, they used their rhetorical skill to come up with the alternative—"worst cases"—to convey the same emotional meaning. Phenomenological studies and historical interview would be needed to confirm this claim.

5. "Abortion and the Law," *Time*, 3 August 1962, p. 30.

6. Charles H. Bayer, "Confessions of an Abortion Counselor," *Christian Century*, 20 May 1970, p. 628.

7. "Abortion Comes Out of the Shadows," *Life*, 27 February 1970, p. 22.

8. Carol Gilligan, *In a Different Voice* (Cambridge: Harvard University Press, 1982), esp. p. 19. For other critiques see "On *In A Different Voice*: An Interdisciplinary Forum," *Signs* 11, no. 2 (Winter 1986), 304–33.

9. "Abortion Laws Should Be Revised," *Christian Century*, 11 January 1961, p. 37.

10. "Abortion Laws Should Be Revised."

11. "Abortion Laws Should Be Revised."

12. I stress this point because the current attack on the term *Choice* and the liberal vocabulary is often grounded in the claim that it was only a middle-/professional-class term, but the discourse in Maxtone-Graham's interviews, from women of different backgrounds, indicates that it was, in its original form, a discourse indigenous to women of multiple classes and backgrounds. See Rosalind Pollack Petchesky, *Abortion and Women's Choice* (Boston, Mass.: Northeastern University Press, 1984), and Beverly Wildung Harrison, *Our Right to Choose* (Boston: Beacon Press, 1983).

13. Feminists have also been skeptical of the male-dominated "population control" movements—on grounds that they are really interested not in women's control of their own reproductivity but in population control by any means necessary and on grounds that they are potentially racist or ethnicist. Those *potentials* should not be allowed to obscure the instrumental role of these public discourses for women's staged liberation within the United States in the past twenty years. The long-standing role of population control groups is described in Colin Francone, *Abortion Freedom: A Worldwide Movement* (Boston and London: George Allen and Unwin, 1984). See also Petchesky and Nanette J. Davis, *From Crime to Choice* (Westport, Conn.: Greenwood Press, 1985).

14. Alan F. Guttmacher, "The Law That Doctors Often Break," *Reader's Digest*, January 1960, p. 52.

15. The statistical estimates of numbers of illegal abortions are, of course, highly problematic. Good records of illegal activities are always impossible to obtain. However, hospital admissions for complications from abortions provide one of the better measures. Cited, for example, in Jack Starr, "Growing Tragedy of Illegal Abortion," *Look*, October 19, 1965, pp. 149–50. See chapter 2, notes 3 and 4.

16. Another good measure of the number and consequences of illegal abortions can be gained by triangulations using birth rates, birth rates for unmarried women, and maternal mortality rates. Before abortion was legalized in New York, such estimates indicated that illegal abortions accounted for about half of maternal mortality. When abortion was legalized, the maternal mortality rate dropped about half. "Abortion: Rhetoric and Reality," *Christian Century*, 21 July 1971. The article reports that after New York's liberalized abortion law was enacted, maternal mortality reached an all-time low of 2.3 per 10,000 live births from 5.2 in the prior year. Other areas, with different characteristics, reported slightly lower figures. See *Vital Statistics of the United States* (Washington, D.C.: U.S. Department of Health, Education and Welfare, Public Health Service, 1967 and following years) and see the Center for Disease Control in Atlanta's accountings reported in Stanley Hensshaw et al., "Abortion in the United States, 1978–79," *Family Planning Perspectives* 13, no. 1 (January/February 1981), p. 7, and Edward Weinstock et al., "Legal Abortions in the United States since the 1973 Supreme Court Decisions," *Family Planning Perspectives* 1 (January/February 1975), pp. 23–25.

17. Guttmacher, p. 53.

18. Linda J. Greenhouse, "Constitutional Question: Is There a Right to Abortion?" *New York Times Magazine*, 25 January 1970, pp. 30–31, 88. Physicians' interests are reflected in state licensing laws and formed the basis for initial appeals in the federal courts.

19. Marilyn Balamaci, Mary A. Fischer, Julie Grenwalt, Eleanor Hoover, Toby Kahn, Irene Neves, and Debbie Zahn, "Eight Other Women's Stories," *People*, 5 August 1985, pp. 82–88.

20. "Abortion: Rhetoric and Reality" reports that after the enactment of New York's liberalized abortion law, births to unmarried women declined (after a period of increase). Recent studies confirm this trend; see notes 16, 17, and recent issues of *Family Planning Perspectives*, especially Susheela Singh, "Adolescent Pregnancy in the United States: An Interstate Analysis" 18 (September/October 1986), pp. 210–20, and "Unwanted Childbearing in United States Declines, But Levels Still High Among Blacks, Singles" 17, no. 6 (November/December 1985), p. 274.

21. For most women abortions are now more available and more safe. Studies by pro-Choice scholars indicate clearly that there is a severe shortage of well-located abortion providers and problems of financial access, but access for most women *is* easier now than before legalization. Pro-Life advocates argue that abortions are not physically safer now, but by and large their evidence is overwhelmingly outweighed by international and national comparisons. (They also tend to conflate first-term and later-term abortions.) This is not to say that all clinics and settings today are adequately safe. The pro-Life rhetors provide strong evidence indicating that physicians performing abortions are frequently no more sensitive to women's needs than other physicians (who, as feminists have long noted, tend to treat women in reprehensible ways) and that there may in fact be an "abortion industry" which puts money ahead of women's health. E.g., Carol Everett, "Abortion: A First-Hand Account," public lecture, University of Illinois, Urbana, April 7, 1988.

As this book went to press, the decision in *Webster* v. *Health Services* was handed down. It substantially alters the consensus and conditions that obtained during the period examined by this book. Four justices seem to argue for the eventual overturn of *Roe* on the grounds that a state's compelling interest in the fetus from the period of conception onward (*not* the Right to Life of the fetus) outweighs women's Liberty. Although the dissents of Blackmun and Stevens seem to me to be legally definitive, as this chapter has noted, the Court is at base motivated by political ideology, and the balance of power has shifted.

The Social Force of Rhetoric

Between 1960 and 1985 substantial social change with regard to abortion occurred: changes in practice made abortion legal, safer, and more common,[1] while changes in discourse described both abortion and motherhood as "choice." The change process was not, however, a simple replacement of old practices and discourses with new ones. An extremely complex interaction occurred in a variety of arenas, producing negotiated compromise between the interests previously represented and those newly empowered in the public, sociopolitical sphere.

The compromise negotiated about abortion framed it as a woman's choice but also as an undesirable moral act. Abortion was to be legally permitted but not publicly financed. It was to be undertaken primarily in the first term of pregnancy. It was to give women new power over reproduction but also to present them with new sets of problems.[2]

These changes cannot be attributed solely to economic factors (e.g. the enhanced position of many women in the labor market). Explaining the willingness of pro-Life women to fill the jails of Atlanta as the simple result of labor-market shifts misses too much of the story. A woman whose personal experience of the abortion system has left her feeling betrayed does not march on behalf of the image of fetus and family either because she expects economic gain or because she has been duped. Her experiences are real, valid, and important in their own right. Likewise, women who chained themselves to statehouse gates to insist on the Right to Choice did not do so merely in expectation of economic gain—the goods they sought were much broader than material security. Many tossed away economic security to leave confining, traditional homes.

The economic explanation is inadequate not only because it ignores crucial inputs long dismissed as illusory or overdetermined but also because it fails to explain the outcomes fully. The current *stasis of the abortion issue in the United States is only partly explicable in economic terms.[3] Other alternatives might have served the economic imperatives equally well. The minor historical accident constituted by the Supreme Court's membership and the haphazard way in which this particular case was apportioned were not economically pre-ordained, and had these things been only slightly different, the Court's decision could have taken other forms.[4] The result might have been an abortion policy which compromised the interests involved along state lines. It might have allocated power to a committee system. It might have set up criteria for cases under which abortion would be permitted. It might have forbidden second-term abortions. Each of these options has been taken at different times in different Western nations because each can be made to serve effectively the constellation of interests that make up the economic system in advanced capitalist states. They may again take form in the United States. There is no doubt that economic factors were a dominant input, but they were not the sole input.

Neither is the social change process in the abortion controversy fully explicable as a rational outcome of a logical debate (e.g., the correctness of allowing women equality and liberty and of protecting fetuses). A fully rational society would have sought to preserve Life through Choice. It would have focused substantial resources on eliminating unwanted pregnancies, both by reducing unplanned pregnancy and by providing resources so that women who wished to raise children were guaranteed civilized conditions in which to do so. That would have protected the birth rate as well as women and fetuses.

To comprehend the full story of the outcome of the controversy, we must also understand its character and features as a communicative process. In part, these resulted from the *general* nature of rhetoric. In order to persuade others whose interests and values are not identical to their own, social movement organizations must find super-ordinate values, narratives, and characterizations that present proposed policies in terms that represent their desirability for other community members. For example, in the abortion debate the women's "want" was transformed to "unwanted children." Such representation, however, carries consequences: it reshapes the precise contours of the policies and terms at issue. In seeking to persuade others, persuaders adapt their case to the audience's interests and are thereby "persuaded" to represent the issue in terms that incorporate more than their own unalloyed experiences. The process of persuasion is thereby inherently a process of compromise, combining interests (including economic dimensions), logic (because of the ideational elements of discourse), and the discourse itself. The abortion controversy resulted in a compromise of Choice because of this feature.

Understanding the process of communicating social change also requires general understandings of the properties of various units of discourse. Narratives have specific features that allow them to open up new public discursive territory and to embody and highlight contradictions. They also have limitations that prevent them from fully resolving social conflicts. Ideographs have different features that give them tremendous social power. In the abortion controversy, the avoidance of other economically adequate solutions such as committee systems or prohibition on second-term abortions has in large part been a result of the power of the term *Choice*. Lastly, characterizations are perhaps the most fundamental and most slippery of discursive units. It seems relatively easy to create forceful characterizations, especially through visual images, and to shade their meanings in partial ways. It seems equally difficult to challenge such characterizations directly. They form the building blocks of narratives, and yet, on their own, no matter how emotionally compact and stirring, they can not generate a full persuasive or rational case for policy. The simultaneous mass consensus and activist polarization resulted from this feature of the image of the fetus.

Finally, understanding the rhetorical process of change requires attention to the *particular* content of a social argument. The particular characteristics of Life and Choice, for example, had consequences beyond their general features as ideographs or as elements in the persuasive process. Life, with its linkage to young children, motivated large numbers of housewives to political action in ways that other terms would not have done. Choice provided a rationale not only for women seeking abortion but also for those who wished not to finance abortions. In studying social processes there is no possibility of adequate explanation solely at the general level. General theories explain much about public controversies, but understanding specific historical outcomes also requires studying the particularities of content. The equivalent of the predictive test of explanations in human science cannot be achieved without accounting for content. Human processes are, at least in part, a matter of meaning, and they cannot be understood adequately when meanings are completely deleted through the process of theoretical abstraction.

Scholars have only begun to scratch the surface in our efforts to understand how social change is communicated. The complexity of these processes sends us tracking after many false leads, and we have difficulty distinguishing between false hopes and concrete gains. We have, further, a long way to go to achieve any general agreement about what methods are appropriate for balancing the objectivity of generalized description with the subjectivity of the meaning-making process.

This account of the public controversy over abortion has attempted to employ methods of rhetorical analysis that bridge the gap between abstracted theory and real and important controversy. It has been motivated by the belief that theories which are not about important social phenomena are as unworthy of pursuit as are unreflective, atheoretical accounts of those phenomena. It has described public discourse as material, fluid, and changeable. The flow that is rhetoric could take up the interests of wage-laboring women, a group with relatively little power in the social system, and through the persuasive process transform their indigenous expression into a public vocabulary that gave them additional social power.

The process began with a narrative—women's story of unwanted pregnancy in a social scene of illegal abortion. The internal contradictions and materially emotional force of this story spurred broader discursive revisions. Although persuasively challenged by hegemony-maintaining historical narratives, the public argumentative space and argumentative criteria still allowed the women continued confidence in their voice. They therefore moved the controversy to the level of fundamental rights—asserting a Right to Choice. This too was challenged, not only by the fundamental value of Life but by the construction of a potent persuasive image of the fetus.

The result of this competition between two powerful, incommensurable discourses was a series of compromises, arrived at indirectly in several realms. Because of the intricate and particular constellation of law and public discourse, Choice was legally legitimated, but only to the extent of removing the coercive force of the state, not to the extent of social support. Choice was also culturally enacted, but only within limited contexts and against moral preference. Gradually, the public settled down to live in the limited new vocabulary, even while extremist ideologues, not content to accept the discursive compromise, continued their impassioned arguments and even abandoned the realm of argument to substitute their own coercive force for that of the state. The private lives of many women were changed by these uneven modifications of the public sphere, occasioned by its assimilation of women's discourse.

To say that "in the United States, public persuasion is the process of social change," therefore, is not to say that Americans make universally shared, rational decisions based on calm, fair, and dispassionate logic and evidence. It is to say that there is a unique communicative process, open in some important ways, which in its own rather lively fashion constructs vocabularies and policies from vivid images, sound arguments, partisan interests, and historically instantiated public warrants. It is a messy, imperfect system, but understanding its workings may give us greater power to improve it and, thereby, to improve what it is we shall come to speak and to be.

NOTES

1. The increase in the number of abortions upon legalization is, of course, a politically loaded issue. However, the precipitous drop in the birth rate in 1971, when legalized abortion in New York allowed women from across the country access to abortion, seems explicable only in terms of an increased rate of abortion. This does not deny the fact that many women were having abortions long before abortion was legalized, but it suggests that the numbers increased, perhaps by about a third. A graph of the relationship of abortion laws to the live birth rates would indicate this impact fairly clearly. From 1965 to 1970 the birth rates in the United States and in the state of New York were declining at a steady rate (almost 3.8 million in 1965 vs. approximately 3.6 million in 1969). Between 1969 and 1970 the U.S. rate increased slightly, but after 1970, when New York legalized abortion, both the U.S. live birth rate and the New York live birth rate dropped more precipitously (from approximately 3.75 million in 1970 to approximately 3.1 million in 1973). (See figures 1 and 2, p. 204.) This difference was very close in size to the legal abortion rate. (As a result of the maturing of a sizable cohort of women, and arguably, as the ironic result of increased sexual activity resulting from the appearance of liberation provided by legalized abortion, this trend bottomed out around 1974.) See *Vital Statistics of the United States* (Washington, D.C.: U.S. Department of Health, Education and Welfare, Public Health Service, 1967).

2. Some of these new problems, for example, revolved around the responsibility for one's sexuality, including the responsibility for resistance to male demands on one's own desires as well as responsibility for children if women chose not to abort, in contravention of the male progenitor's preferences.

3. Celeste Michelle Condit, "TV Articulates Abortion in America: Competition and the Production of a Cultural Repertoire," *Journal of Communication Inquiry* 11 (Summer 1987), 47–59.

4. For an account of the happenstances surrounding the Supreme Court decision, see Bob Woodward and Scott Armstrong, *The Brethren: Inside the Supreme Court* (New York: Simon and Schuster, 1979).

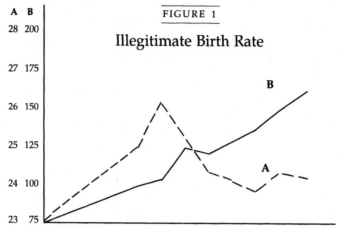

FIGURE 1

Illegitimate Birth Rate

A. Rate of Illegitimate births in the United States per 1000 unmarried women ages 15-44.

B. Rate of Illegitimate births in the United States per 1000 live births.

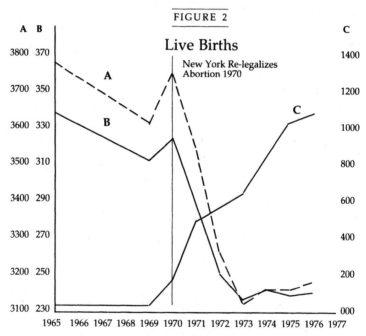

FIGURE 2

Live Births

New York Re-legalizes Abortion 1970

A. Live births (in thousands) in the United States.

B. Live births (in thousands) in New York state.

C. Number of legal abortions (in thousands) in the United States.

A "Right to Life"?

The issue of whether or not a fetus has a Right to Life and the implications of such a right for the abortion debate are important but have been dealt with only indirectly to this point (i.e., with regard to the image of the fetus, chapter 5). This issue must be more fully addressed because the Right-to-Life movement has made it a central question on the public agenda. They have been able to do so, in part, because the persuasive value of their pictures and films derives from a real material entity with more or less substantial being—the fetus. Deciding the status of the fetus is, therefore, a real question that has colored the story I have told here (for I have tried to be non-judgmental in describing the path of the public argument , whereas one who accepted the Right to Life of the fetus probably would have condemned the path of the controversy between 1960 and 1985).[1] I believe it is an issue yet unresolved, and since its full impact on the abortion controversy is yet to be unraveled, I can analyze only the current stasis of the issue.

Life vs. Choice

The first substantive question might seem to be, Does the fetus have the Right to Life? Before addressing that issue, however, I wish to make clear that this question is not itself simple or decisive. As several feminists have pointed out, the Right to Life does not entail the right to use the body of another human being.[2] Few would want to endorse the principle that the state can coerce some people to allow others to use their bodies (e.g., kidneys, bone marrow, blood), even to maintain the life of the others. Such a principle would leave us the nightmarish possibility of a state that decides which of us shall be sliced up for the benefit of others.[3] Thus, even if the fetus has a Right to Life, the pregnant woman does not necessarily lose the right to abort the fetus. Numerous concerns affect the final outcome of this issue,

205

including the special responsibility a woman may or may not have to a fetus—an issue which entails one's view of sexuality—and the active nature of abortion as opposed to the more passive character of most other types of refusal to support others. Further, the fact that many pro-Life advocates support exceptions to a ban on abortion (usually for cases of rape, incest, and threat to the pregnant woman's life) indicates clearly that they also believe that the existence of the Right to Life of the fetus is not determinative.

Therefore, even if we were to find that a fetus has a Right to Life, this would not necessarily mean that a fetus had the right to use the body of a woman. A fetus's right does not necessarily outweigh a woman's Right to Choice, even though the Life of the fetus may seem to some to be a more serious value than the Choice of the woman. In a legal system built on principle and individual rights, we cannot reach judgment by choosing which of two entities the society weighs as more serious (the woman's Choice or the fetal Life). Instead, judgments are based on the spheres covered by individual rights. In this case, the fetal right may not reach far enough to abrogate the woman's right. Nonetheless, we ought to examine the claim that a fetus has a Right to Life.

A Right to Life?

After examining the arguments presented by pro-Life activists on the status of the fetus, I believe that there is an important core to this argument. Pro-Life arguments contend that the human fetus is a being of value, deserving consideration in the abortion issue. Because of this value, an abortion always contains morally undesirable elements. There are, however, incontrovertible differences between fetuses and human persons, and therefore the pro-Life movement's claim that a fetus is identical to a *human being/person from the period of conception is not true. Moreover, the advocates have yet to establish the lesser claim that, in spite of the differences between a human fetus and a human person, we should *weigh* a fetus as a full human being (although this is a proposition that they might someday be able to establish with added grounds and *warrants). To explain these conclusions, I will review here the argument about the status of the fetus in some detail.

Because the fetus has characteristics both like and unlike those of a human being, the classification of the fetus is a contingent matter, *rationally undecidable and rhetorically constructed, rather than a basic fact of nature. As a consequence, rather than relying on some natural, logical classification, we must *choose* how to count the fetus.

Such classifications can be a matter of social *choice* rather than grammatical or logical necessity. This is not the case in all classifications (I am not maintaining an utter relativism here); for example, the classification of "red" as a "color" is a necessary one.[4] Natural and necessary classifications are usually either tautologies or built on analogies that are fundamentally profound, meaning that no overriding differences generate inconsistencies and that to deny the essentiality of the similarities of the compared objects would result in evident contradictions. Some definitional sets operate like that. If we define color with reference to blue and yellow, the analogy between red and blue and yellow makes it impossible to deny that red is a color. More formal definitions, focusing on wavelengths of light, similarly entail that red is a color because of the way both *red* and *color* are defined in terms of wavelengths of light. Such neat classifications are usually found in science, but some are also found in social language use.

In social life, however, many classifications are not so neat. The choices made in these cases (e.g., whether people are "adults" and so to be permitted adult rights such as drinking at age eighteen or at twenty-one) are precisely that—social choices. They are not "mere rhetoric" in the sense that journalists fling that term around, for the choices are based on the careful weighing of a host of relevant facts and values through public discussion ("rhetoric" in the classical sense). Because such social definitions are subject to a "weighing" process, they will be decided differently by different groups who must, quite rationally, weigh things through their own ideologies and conditions. Wherever there are both significant similarities and significant differences, therefore, we are thrown back on social choices rather than upon natural, logical, or necessary classifications. Clearly, if the fetus has major characteristics both like "human beings/persons" and unlike "human beings/persons," the classification of a fetus is such a matter of rational, deliberative choice (either for individuals or for the society).

Before analyzing the characteristics of the fetus, the contest over labels must be clarified. Pro-Choice advocates prefer the term *person* and pro-Life rhetors prefer the label *human being*. Even after arguing for hours over the status of the "personhood" of the fetus, pro-Life rhetors will charge that their opponents "never disagree with us that the fetus is a human being"; therefore, we will have to explore the implications of both labels. However, neither label establishes that fetuses before *viability have, by grammatical, logical, biological, or historical *necessity,* a Right to Life.

The fetus clearly does not have, and cannot have, status as a full person on legal grounds. The Supreme Court's ruling that the constitutional usages of "person" have not included the unborn is convincing. Most simply, the constitutional protections spoken about usually refer to things that can only apply to those "persons *born* or naturalized in the United States of America." More important, the legal problems that would be generated by declaring a fetus a person are legion. Fetuses would have to be counted as dependents for tax purposes, covered by the census and apportionment, and treated as "persons" in dozens of other ways where it is simply not possible to treat them "the same as" persons (e.g., in assault laws). Although exceptions and modifications or special bills could be written on issues such as inheritance, taxes, and assault laws, the very fact that exceptional laws would *have* to be written indicates quite clearly that the fetus cannot share *the same legal status* as "persons." The law *must* treat the fetus differently from other persons because of the objective material differences between persons and the fetus. Legally, then, a fetus cannot be "a full human person" to be treated exactly as all human persons. Even a legal declaration that a fetus was a human person by the Supreme Court, a constitutional amendment, or Congress could not make it fully true, for exceptional laws that denied the claim would also have to be written.

This legal limitation arises from a biological fact. Legally, to have a "right" requires that one be an individual, and until birth, or until a viable separation from the mother, the fetus has not been individuated; biologically, it remains, absolutely, physiologically, a part of the mother. One cannot have a right *to life* unless one is capable of life, and the fetus before viability is not individually capable of life. Pro-Life advocates object to this standard of viability on two grounds—that the period of viability is changing to an ever-earlier stage and that no human being lives "independently," so the presumed independence of the fetus at viability is a chimera.

The first objection—that medical science can alter the point of viability—is valid only if we believe that some unalterable, permanent time-line determines the status of the fetus. The general pro-Life worldview maintains such a view—that things "are" permanently.[5] Essence cannot change. But this Platonic view offers only one possible set of criteria. A broad range of scholars in the twentieth century have pointed out the contingency of language as well as the radical changes in meanings of terms over time.[6] For those able to see that words unceasingly change *some* elements of their denotations through time, the fact that the numerical referent of viability may change does not invalidate it as a logically necessary standard for a Right to Life.

The second objection to viability arises from the concept of "independence." Viability provides an appealing standard for demarcating the transition from mere fetus to "person" because at that point the fetus is capable of independent life. In response, pro-Life advocates point out that no human being can really live independently; we all depend on others at some point in our lives. But, of course, this is not the kind of dependence at issue. To survive, a nonviable fetus must depend on precisely one other person's body; no other human being can offer the fetus what it needs. Moreover, what the fetus requires is *the substance* of the mother's body. That clearly is a unique kind of dependence, to which human beings are not otherwise subject. That difference is recognized in the law: even when a given person is dependent on precisely one other human being for a donated organ (e.g., a kidney) because only one other person can provide a good and timely match, the law and society refuse to compel that potential donor to give up the kidney for another, even if the donor is dead. The fetus thus has at least one substantial biological difference from the rest of us (others will be explored in the discussion of "human beings").

Therefore it is viability—the point at which the fetus can survive *without* absolute dependence on precisely one other person—not conception, that marks the biological point at which it is reasonable to conclude that, like all human beings, the fetus has a Right to Life because it is capable of sustaining life in the same way all human persons are capable of sustaining independent life. This statement might be taken to imply that, once medical science can keep a fetus alive from conception to viability outside the womb, the fetus may have a biologically based Right to Life from conception. The fact that personal physical independence is a necessary condition for a Right to Life does not mean that it is also a sufficient condition and that issue has not yet been much explored.

If the standard of viability is taken to be a sufficient condition, there are serious implications. A woman does not have the Right to Choose the death of a technologically viable human just because she does not want to have it in her body any longer.[7] Therefore, if technology allows removal of a fetus, even at very early stages of pregnancy, without killing the fetus, then, assuming that the physical risk to the woman is the same, she should forego abortion for removal. Some women will not like this requirement because they may continue to feel more responsibility and want legal control. In addition to creating moral dilemmas, this technological capability will generate a whole host of new policy problems—including issues of overpopulation and of financial responsibility for such children (and I believe that the state cannot coerce such artificial births AND require the woman to assume financial responsibility for it NOR place the fetus in an "orphanage" situation). If viability is accepted as a logically necessary *and* sufficient standard, however, we will have eventually to face such issues.

Currently, however, on both legal and biological grounds, there are clear differences between fetuses and human persons which deny the statement "The fetus IS a person" status as a simple, non-problematic fact. The final grounds on this issue are historical. For indeed, language is an historical entity, and if our culture had always said "the fetus is a person," then the claim, although not a necessary natural fact, would have presumption as a true statement because it would reflect a prior classification, made through history by the society. But this also is not the case.

American society has systematically treated a fetus as different from a person. Aside from the legal factors mentioned above, custom has treated the fetus differently. Persons in our society have names, and we have never given fetuses names. The naming as a unique individual person occurs at birth. Additionally, persons in our society are given ritualized burials, but outside of the Catholic church (and even here, by necessity, the fetus is treated somewhat differently), miscarriages have not generally been given the same funeral and burial customary in the society. This, of course, is especially true for the thousands of early miscarriages that occur each year. Moreover, in terms of the response of individuals, an early miscarriage is generally not as crushing a blow as the death of a newborn infant. Thus, our culture has not, historically, treated the fetus as a person.

On historical, legal, and biological grounds, therefore, the statement that a fetus is a person from the moment of conception is not apparently a simple statement of fact. Rather, it is a rhetorical suggestion, an urging that we make such a classification. The tactic used is "classification by denial of classification." Pro-Life rhetors seek to get their classification accepted as a fact by "naturalizing" the issue; denying that they are proposing a classification, they pretend instead that the "fact" is self-evident and inescapable. Instead of claiming that the fetus should be classified or treated as a human person, they claim that the fetus IS a human person. By mere assertion of factual status, they gain the persuasiveness of factual status.

The pro-Life movement, however, prefers to rest its case not on the claim that the fetus is a person but rather on the grounds that the fetus is a human being. Arguing to the effect that the fetus is both human and a being, they indicate that the conclusion is inescapable that the fetus is a human being. Here, we should begin with Abe Lincoln's caution that just because you have a chestnut and you have a horse does not mean that you have a chestnut horse. In a fallacy of composition and division, pro-Life rhetors elide the non-technical meaning of "human" and "being" with the richly embedded cultural meanings of "human being." This move once again relies on careful rhetorical construction.

The core of the pro-Life argument in this area has been vivid pictures of fetuses and the claim that science has discovered that the fetus is a human being *from the moment of conception.* The "discoveries" are the early-nineteenth-century finding that the fetus begins to grow after the joining of sperm and egg, nine months before its birth, and the twentieth-century investigations into the genetic makeup of the fetus from conception.

Although science has indeed discovered that the fetus has a unique, human set of chromosomes from the moment of conception, a problem arises when we try to link this fact with the larger claim that, therefore, because of its chromosomes, a blastocyst, embryo, or fetus is a human being. For example, after conception the "human being" may turn into twins, which might even recombine or dissolve later. According to the pro-Life definition, we have *a* unique person suddenly constituting two unique individuals and then, perhaps, back to one again. In addition, studies suggest that, for perfectly natural causes, as many as a third of all conceptions do not come to term. It seems extremely awkward to our conceptual system to suggest that a third of all "human beings" never get even to the developmental stage of viability. Finally, in addition to genetics other factors determine the characteristics of a fetus carried to term. What the pregnant woman ingests—food, drugs, germs, cigarette smoke, industrial chemicals—and what she does—physical activity, listening to music, natural vs. caesarean birth—will have a huge impact on the specific human being the fetus becomes. A conceptus with chromosomes that would allow musical brilliance or mathematical facility might be born grossly incompetent in these areas if its mother is deprived of a few small vitamins. Consequently, nourishment and history are as crucial as chromosomes in shaping the human personality.

One of the major reasons that genetics appears determinative for pro-Life advocates, even though it provides only a partial account, derives from their underlying belief structure. For different belief groups, the essence or "being" of a thing has been identified with its "substance" (physical or material), with its "spirit" (or "idea"), or with the unique fusion of substance, idea, and, perhaps, history. Because of their religious ideology, pro-Life advocates work from a rhetorical system in which "spirit" or "idea" is the sole important element. Genetic structure, taken as a "code" with information possibilities at its core, fits the concept of "idea" or "spirit" reasonably well. Consequently, the point at which this "idea" is fixed appears to pro-Life advocates to be the point at which the fetus has its "essential" element. All other characteristics are merely accidental. Hence their statement that "anything with a human set of chromosomes is a human being."

Again, however, such a rhetorical structure is not a necessary one. Others view material being as more important or consider idea and material as of equal importance. From either of these alternate perspectives, unless the fetus has a certain material being, it cannot be a human being. The pro-Life claim that once conception has occurred "all that is added is nutrition" thus glosses a major issue. For "mere nutrition" (i.e., physical substance), along with the substance of a personal history, might well be considered necessary components of human nature. This, of course, is a common element of the layperson's objection to anti-abortion laws. The lay statement that the fetus is just a "small blob of cells" captures the sense in which the materiality and history of the fetus are too insubstantial to allow it to count as a human being. The women in chapter 9 directly responded to the fetus in this way. In sum, the conclusion that the fetus is a human being *because* it has a full set of human chromosomes is logical only for those who constitute being solely through "idea" or spirit, supplied in this case by genes.

The pro-Life rhetors have other arguments, however, which attempt to address the issue of "substance" to some extent. In pictures and verbal descriptions they emphasize the substantial elements of the fetus, citing the developmental stages at which its "heart" begins to function, when it has "brain waves," and so on. Here too, however, the pro-Life rhetoric uses metaphorical language that pretends to be literal. When they say that "the heartbeat begins between the eighteenth to twenty-fifth day,"[8] they refer to the early fetal "pulse" which, while definitely an analogy and forerunner of the human heart, does not have the four developed major compartments of the human heart or the developed arteries and veins and pumps at a tenth of the relative force. Therefore, when they say an early fetus has a "heartbeat," they conjure up the image of a beating human heart, but the *substance* of a "human heart" is not really there. Even when referencing material acts, the pro-Life rhetors refer to idea alone.

The same is true of "brain waves." Although electrical impulses can be measured in the embryo as early as forty days, these do not have the full complex patterns of adult brain waves, nor does the embryo have the substantial parts of a human brain. Not until somewhere between the twentieth and fortieth weeks do fetuses even begin to have the kind of brain development that would allow perceptions such as awareness of pain. Once again, the pro-Life rhetoric effectively asserts an analogy as a literal identity. This elision occurs because they take "idea" or "potential" as subsuming substance.

The genetic argument for claiming a fetus to be a human being is therefore internally sound but inadequate because it is incomplete: human beings are not mere chromosome content or "spirit."

The other major pro-Life argument derives from the pictures of fetuses. As chapter 5 indicated, on their own visual grounds the pictures demonstrate that until at least eight to twelve weeks, and perhaps even later, the fetus does not look much like a human being or have much substance. It is difficult to draw lines here—another woman might not be deterred by the appearance of the fetus until as late as sixteen to twenty weeks—but clearly, if visual evidence is the grounds for decision, the early fetus does not meet the criterion required of a full human being. The fact that the pictures circulated in the early eighties by pro-Life rhetors in national magazines were of nineteen-week-old fetuses, not two-week-old fetuses, is a clear sign of their partisanship here.

The pro-Life position that the fetus is a human being from the moment of conception is not a simple statement of natural fact but a highly constructed claim. However, this does not mean that we have no rational grounds for *choosing* to count the fetus as a human being/ person, for the partial grounds of the pro-Life rhetors are nonetheless strong grounds. Ultimately, then, we may *choose* to classify the fetus as a human. Our choice to do so, however, will be based on the weighing of the similarities between "fetus" and "human being/person" against the differences. To this point, there has been no public consensus (nor much discussion) about this weighing process.

One last argument is of interest on the pro-Life side. In public, especially on a national scale, pro-Life rhetors are usually careful to avoid citing religious tradition as a reason for their claims; in fact, pro-Life advocates generally deny the religious foundations of their beliefs

in public. However, since these religious foundations are an absolutely essential component motivating the movement, it is important
to address the Christian Bible.[9]

I do not wish to suggest that the Bible is an adequate authority in
the *public* controversy. Although this nation was founded as a set of
Christian theocracies, we have evolved past such city-state tyrannies
into a secular state in which Moslems, Jews, deists, Hindus, Bud-
dhists, and atheists all have their rights, and arguments based on the
Bible can hold no public authority over these groups. The pro-Life
rhetors recognize this fact in their vehement denials of a religious base
to their arguments.

Nonetheless, in spite of vehement in-group assertions by pro-Life
activists to the contrary, the Bible itself does not explicitly ban abortion. To support their claim, pro-Life advocates cite only the general
commandment against killing, vague and metaphorical passages
about the beginning of life in the womb, and one ambiguous passage
about accidentally induced miscarriage. These proofs are surprising
for the conspicuousness of their weakness and indirection. None
mentions abortion explicitly. The religious proscription of abortion is
not, therefore, the result of clear Biblical commandment but a by-
product of Catholic tradition and the recent fundamentalist politics
that have combined to construct a set of interpretations that cast moral
and religious opprobrium on abortion.

On a multiplicity of grounds, the pro-Life advocates' assertion that
the "fetus is a human being and therefore abortion is murder" is not a
"true" claim but a rhetorical tactic—an effort to establish the claim as a
social choice *disguised* as a statement of fact. There is slippage between
the solid grounds employed by the pro-Life movement and the over-
claiming they do on the basis of those grounds, and this slippage may
be part of the reason that their position has not been fully successful
in legal and other realms.

Until recently the pro-Choice movement has been reticent in addressing this issue. Because they argue that the issue is a matter of
individual Choice, they have refused to "take a position" on the status
of the fetus. While ideologically consistent, that refusal allows the
pro-Life claims to go uncontested. In the long run, this may result in
the adoption of the pro-Life "choice" about the status of the fetus by a
majority of individuals. This could lead to legislative coercion to
compel all individuals to act on the pro-Life definition. The pro-
Choice movement's discursive choice may, therefore, also form part of
the long-term outcome of the controversy.

Even if we dismiss, at least for now, the pro-Life claim that a fetus is a person with a Right to Life, we should not dismiss the grounds they offer us (that kind of either/or response is as partisan as the pro-Life over-claiming). If, indeed, we block out their partisan overstatement and concentrate on the substance of what is left, the pro-Life rhetoric indicates with gleaming clarity that the fetus has value in its material being, its potential, and its "spirit." It seems inhumane to look at the pro-Life pictures, watch their movies, listen to their descriptions of fetal development, and conclude that a fetus is, throughout its development, nothing but a blob of tissue. The human fetus is a living, growing thing, increasingly precious as it develops, gains substance, and builds relationships to the pregnant woman and, through her, to the social world. The pro-Life argument forces us to face the real violence in abortion, and their truths are necessary to keep us morally responsible. They prevent us from seeing abortion as a casual act of birth control; they remind us, powerfully, that we ought to take serious measures as individuals and as a society to reduce or eliminate abortions, even if we must do so through means that do not violate the rights of women.[10]

NOTES

1. My analysis of this still-current political issue of the status of the fetus is influenced by my own predispositions, and so I will indicate what my assumptions and premises are. I define myself as a "substantive liberal": I believe in a balance between the rights of the "individual" and the good of a community or social system. Ultimately, however, I place individuals as primary because they are discrete material entities, while the community is always a non-discrete hodge-podge of material, discursive, and ideal components. I believe, therefore, that a society should endeavor to provide the substance necessary for individuals to exercise their fundamental rights. The fact that I focus on a "balance" point predisposes me toward openness to all arguments, because I am constantly trying to adjust rather than to defend a singular side of the equation. The roots in individualism predispose me toward egalitarianism, which, in this particular historical situation, means I am also predisposed to feminism. I am predisposed against using a religious base for public policy and toward definitions that include both material and ideal elements. I tend further to oppose the use of state power for enforcing morality.

My background influences the way I interpret the issues in the abortion debate, but my position is a centrist position in the United States today. Hence, the "bias" in this analysis is one that is probably the most generally taken one. There is, however, one crucial caveat. One fundamental stumbling stone in the abortion debate is the issue of religious worldviews. As the preceding chapters have indicated, religion has been the underlying motivation and worldview of most pro-Life activists, but religious discourse has not formed the overt center-post of their public argumentation. The following analyses do not accept any overt or covert assumptions deriving from religious views. Consequently, those who look at the issues from a religious foundation will not find these suggestions comforting. The same, however, is true on the other side of the issue for feminists. Although some of the feminist worldview has been part of the public argument, and I share it, that view has not been willing to incorporate the contributions of the pro-Life argument, and I have attempted to do so. In sum, my position ends up pleasing neither pro-Choice nor pro-Life activists, but it probably will end up offering alternatives least acceptable to religious activists.

2. For example, see Beverly Wildung Harrison, *Our Right to Choose: Toward a New Abortion Ethic* (Boston: Beacon Press, 1983).

3. Our government does, in fact, take it upon itself to act coercively, in disregard for individual rights in some instances, most notably for the draft and for taxation. I am partially convinced that it should not do so in these cases. However, I believe that a simple distinction between such cases and those of the fetus vs. the woman is that in these other cases the "social good" done is a tangible one for the person whose rights are deprived as well as for others. Taxes provide services directly to the individual taxed. Even the draft, in theory at least, is undertaken to protect the Freedom of the individual drafted as well as others. This is clearly not the case in the abortion controversy. The reason for the abrogation of the woman's right is not a social good but the competing individual interest of the fetus (except where criminalization of abortion is justified on explicitly pro-natalist grounds, but that would raise an entirely different frame for the issue).

4. For the theoretical underpinnings of this view, see Celeste Condit Railsback, "Beyond Rhetorical Relativism: A Structural-Material Model of Truth and Objective Reality," *Quarterly Journal of Speech* 69 (1983), 351–63.

5. There is not yet published an adequate description of the philosophical pinnings of the pro-Life view, but for partial development see Celeste Condit Railsback, "Pro-Life, Pro-Choice: Different Conceptions of Value," *Women's Studies in Communication* 5 (Spring 1982), 16–28; Randall Lake, "Order and Disorder in Anti-Abortion Rhetoric: A Logological View," *Quarterly Journal of Speech* 70 (1984), 425–43; Kristin Luker, *Abortion and the Politics of Motherhood* (Berkeley: University of California Press, 1984).

6. For example, Ludwig Wittgenstein, *Philosophical Investigations*, trans. C. E. M. Anscombe (Oxford: Basil Blackwell, 1963), pp. 83, 31e-32e; Alfred Korzybski, *Science and Sanity*, 4th ed. (Lakeville, Conn.: The Institute of General Semantics, 1958); Jacques Derrida, *Of Grammatology* (Baltimore: Johns Hopkins University Press, 1976); Jean-François Lyotard, *The Postmodern Condition: A Report on Knowledge*, trans. Geoff Bennington and Brian Massumi (Minneapolis: University of Minnesota Press, 1984). For a concrete example see Michael Calvin McGee, "The Origins of 'Liberty': A Feminization of Power," *Communication Monographs* 47 (1980), 23–45, or McGee, "An Essay on

the Flip Side of Privacy," *Argument in Transition: Proceedings of the Third Summer Conference on Argumentation*, ed. David Zarefsky, Malcolm O. Sillars, and Jack Rhodes (Annandale, Va.: Speech Communication Association, 1983), pp. 105–15.

7. The reason for this has been eloquently implied by women who argue against the destruction of disabled fetuses or female fetuses (femicide). Clearly implied in their arguments is the assumption of the unique value even of pre-humans. See, for example, Anne Finger, "Claiming All Our Bodies: Reproductive Rights and Disabilities," and Viola Rogencamp, "Abortion of a Special Kind: Male Sex Selection in India," both in *Test Tube Women*, ed. Rita Arditti, Renate Duelli-Klein, and Shelley Minden (London, Boston: Pandora Press, 1984), pp. 281–97 and 266–78.

8. For an example of such claims, see Dr. and Mrs. J. C. Willke, *Handbook on Abortion* (Cincinnati, Ohio: Hayes, 1979), p. 18.

9. I have already cited several examples of this, but consider, for example, the case of Joseph M. Scheidler. In public media he argues pointedly that his position is based not on religion but on science. "Discussion," *Christian Century*, 18 July 1979, p. 738. In *in-group rhetoric, however, Scheidler's discourse is some of the most thoroughgoingly Christian I have seen. He argues the necessity of saving the *souls* of women and abortionists *for God*, even against their own will; for example, "We want the abortionists to be converted, returned to God, and be saved," or "We do not want anyone to lose his soul. We do not want the abortionists to be punished in hell for eternity." Scheidler, *Abortion: Opposing Viewpoints* (St. Paul, Minn.: Greenhaven Press, 1986), pp. 171–75.

10. Policies which would protect Life through Choice would include intensified education, especially for young males, about the consequences of intercourse, the reasons for abstinence, the available contraceptive options, along with the provision of more attractive alternatives than young, unwed motherhood to economically deprived teenagers and the provision of maternal care, day care, and other child-raising support mechanisms to women who desire to have children.

Text of Anonymous Letter Claiming Responsibility for Pensacola Clinic Bombings

Dear Editor:

So you want to know who bombed the 3 abortion clinics, huh? I did.

Let me tell you why.

When I was stationed here in the waves, before I got married, I got pregnant. Everyone had told me that a fetus was just a little shapeless blob anyway, so I got an abortion. I was almost 6 months pregnant by then.

Later, after it was too late, a friend gave me some literature one day showing how the baby developed at different stages. I never realized that at that stage, a fetus is so much a baby that some of them have been born at that point and LIVED!

Well, you cannot imagine what that did to me, knowing that I had not just "had an unwanted intra-uterine growth "removed", [sic] but had KILLED MY BABY ! It just about ruined my life. Even today, several years later, I lay awake at nights sometimes crying about it.

So maybe you can undertand my reason for doing what I did.

It was not because of religious fanaticism . . . I don't even go to church.

It was because I have seen for myself what the psychological effects of an abortion can do to a woman, and I didn't want what happened to me to happen to anyone else.

I did not act alone. And if these clinics reopen, we will see that they are closed again.

Some will say that it is wrong to use violent means to put an end to the killing. Well, we used a lot of violence in World War II to stop the killing of the Jews.

It is a well-established principal [sic] of justice that force, even deadly force, is justified in order to save innocent lives if necessary. So, I do not feel that I have done anything wrong.

We will stop the slaughter of the innocents. We WILL put an end to the murder of babies. And we WILL prevent any more lives from being ruined.

Signed,
A Woman Who Knew
What She Was Doing

Printed in the *Pensacola Journal*, 28 December 1984, p. 1, and the *Pensacola News*, "Writer Makes Claim," 27 December 1984, p. 1. I have retained the original layout, punctuation, and emphasis as much as possible.

Methodological Issues
from Chapter 9

The unique task undertaken in Chapter 9—the comparison of public and private discourse—generates at least two serious methodological problems. The first is simply gaining access to any real data base of "private talk." The second is determining how such unique data might be compared. This appendix addresses these issues.

"Private" Discourse

A full comparison of public discourse and private talk requires a broad set of private discussions about abortions—decisions about whether to have abortions and whether to perform abortions, and probably gossip about one's neighbors' abortions as well. Further, to grant perfect understanding these texts would have to be spaced through time to precede, parallel, and follow the public discussion of abortion. Of course, such a fantasy data base is simply not available. All that talk has occurred but has now disappeared into the atmosphere, inaccessible to us. Moreover, to collect private discourse on a topic before it becomes a controversial public issue, we would require rather impressive predictive powers. We are driven, then, to obtain any scrap of material we can use to make what few comparisons can be made. We cannot discover irrefutable laws of cause and effect through less full sets of discourse, but we may seek useful suggestions about similarities, differences, and interactions.

The discourse set offered by Katrina Maxtone-Graham's *Pregnant by Mistake* is imperfect in many ways. In the first place, it is partially edited. Fortunately, the editor appears sincerely to have removed as little as possible and to have carefully avoided adding or altering. Secondly, these women are "justifying" their decisions after the fact, rather than actually talking about a decision in progress. While this does not give us an accurate data source for determining how public discourse influences private discussion in making abortion decisions, it does give us a basis for comparing that public discourse to the ways women talk about their childbearing decisions in their own lives. Finally, the women are not a "representative sample." If such a thing could be assembled, it cannot be achieved in seventeen case histories.

Some of these women are unusually aware of abortion issues (two had made a study of the public discourse before having their abortions, as part of their decision processes). Many became abortion counselors after their own abortions. Many joined women's groups or what they call "Women's Lib." However, not all of the women fit these models, and there is great diversity among them. Clearly, some of the women are well-educated, some have worked outside the home, and some are older. Others, however, are young, immature, or, in their own words, unstable. One woman is black; the others are white. Some are Catholic; some are not. If there is a serious bias to the sample, it is simply the fact that all of these women found themselves with "unwanted pregnancies." That leaves us unable to guess at how public discourse on abortions affects women who do not have to decide about unwanted pregnancies. Nonetheless, even given the limitations of the texts available, the issue of the inter-relationship of public discourse and private lives deserves our willingness to make a first effort and to see what comparisons might be made.

Critical Coding Procedures

The comparison of a large number of texts on a micro-analytic scale presents some challenging problems. The first issue is one of comparison sets. I selected three sets of arguments from mass distribution magazines for comparison with the private discourse from *Pregnant by Mistake*. For the years 1960–61, 1964–65, and 1970–71, I examined all the articles listed in the *Reader's Guide to Periodical Literature* that made a fairly direct and directed argument in favor of legalized abortion (thereby excluding arguments against abortion, "How to get an abortion" articles, foreign comparisons, etc.). I expected these articles to resemble most closely the private discourse that favored the abortion choice. The three time periods represented roughly the "beginning" of this round of the public discourse, the point at which the private discourse was made, and a mid-point in the development of the argument (which earlier work had indicated was a turning point).

The second procedural issue is what to compare and how. In order to assess this, I first made a preliminary critical reading of the texts, drawing on standard procedures in rhetorical criticism. This reading, of course, ultimately depended on the categories I have been trained to notice, but during the readings I attempted to maintain at least one open eye. This critical reading suggested to me fifteen bases of comparison between and among the sets of texts. These formed a set of internal hypotheses and coding categories:

Categories Coded and Counted
in Public and Private Abortion Discourse

Structure (organizational plan)
Number of lines of
    Statistics
    Narratives (abortion stories)
    Histories (social narratives)
    Examples (comparisons to other countries)
Statements of
    Principles
    Responsibility
    Opposition to criminal abortion
    Response to issue
        Abortion as killing/murder
        Universalization
        Generalization
        Normalization
    Response to narratives
        Identity
        Sympathy
    Purpose of abortion
        Eugenics
        Rape
        Incest
        Economics
        Life-style
Characterizations
    Method of determining
        Adjectives applied about subject
        History of actions
        Manner of expression
            Grammar
            Word choice
        Goals stated
        Purposes characterized
        Social roles

   Demographic profiles
      Age
      Number of children
      Marital status
   Groups
      Pregnant women
      Opponents of reform
      Supporters of reform
Word counts
   Law, legal, illegal
   Life, mother's life, fetal/child's life
   Wanted/unwanted, needed, had to
   Fair, choice, equality, discrimination, freedom, rights

I then returned to the texts, this time coding and counting the fifteen elements. This coding effort does not match current social scientific standards for quantitative work. There are no "reliability" tests for my coding to compare with that of someone else. In addition, given the complexity of the amount of data I was coding for, I certainly missed some factors and elements at some times. Thus, this semi-quantitative effort is not "content analysis" but rather a more rigorous verification of initial critical insights. Some portions of it might later be subjected to quantitative verification if the benefits proved worth the costs.

Following, I present a summary of the numerical findings of this coding and counting. These are not presented in statistical form because I believe this material does not fit the standard assumptions for statistical tests. The discourse does not accurately represent a sample from a population. The public discourse is all of the locatable discourse of this form. The private discourse and public discourse are both influenced by unique formal characteristics that make statistical tests misleading. Consequently, the author and reader are required to substitute judgment for statistical tests in assessing the significance of these numerical variations. In the text I have cited those numerical variations that seem to me to be of importance. They remain open to debate.

Appendix C

RESULTS OF CODING AND COUNTING
OF PUBLIC AND PRIVATE ABORTION DISCOURSE*

Category Coded	Private Discourse		Public Discourse					
			1960/61		1964/65		1970/71	
	C**	S/R***	C	S/R	C	S/R	C	S/R
#1 Statistics	1/15	<1%	7/9	12%	9/10	8%	6/8	7%
Narratives	15/15	90%	8/9	50%	9/10	31%	6/8	16%
#5 Word Count—Law								
Raw score		2	7/9	81	8/10	108	8/8	172
Use/line of text				.231		.328		.343
#7 Word Count—								
Life		2	5/9	9	3/10	16	7/8	81
my/mother's life		91	7/9	29	7/10	29	5/8	20
fetal/child's life		2	5/9	10	5/10	13	6/8	21
#8 Word Count—								
wanted/unwanted		77	5/9	13	6/10	17	6/8	21
choice		12	1/9	2	4/10	4	6/8	9
rights		4		1		3		34

*Private discourse is from *Pregnant By Mistake;* public discourse are all articles arguing in favor of change in abortion laws indexed in the *Reader's Guide* for the indicated years
**C is the consistency score—that is the number of articles that used that item out of the total number of articles available
***S/R is either a percentage (where % appears) or a raw number of times the item appears in the indicated sample

GLOSSARY

ALI. The American Law Institute—sponsor of a revised "model" penal code that would have legalized abortion in cases of rape, incest, fetal deformity, or threat to the physical health or life of the pregnant woman.

Articulate. Able to persuasively speak one's interests. After using this term, I discovered a related usage by Stuart Hall, but Hall seems not to recognize the way in which the material instantiation of articulations in individual speaking subjects is crucial to social processes; he abstracts "articulation" from the process of articulating individuals and groups.

Articulation. The expression of a group's interests in public in such a way that it is, or seeks to be, persuasively related to the public vocabulary. See also "double articulation."

Catholics. In general I refer to the church hierarchy and those members who identify with a given dogma, rather than the entire membership of the church. The role of the church in the abortion controversy is large, and so any account of the debate must describe this role. I believe it important to distinguish opposition to the church hierarchy and its political activities from prejudice against individual members as human beings.

Characterization. A universalized depiction of a class of concrete agents, acts, scenes, or purposes that are culturally current (positive and negative forms of "stereotypes").

Character-type. Technical term for a characterization.

Classes. Multiple individuals who share with each other important characteristics—e.g., gender, wealth, role in productive processes, race, etc. See groups.

Commentary. One of the three rhetorical processes that influence the persuasiveness of a visual image; the words that describe, name, or associate a visual image used persuasively.

Constitutive values. See Ideograph.

Continuity. One of the three rhetorical processes that influence the persuasiveness of a visual image; the use of a series of images to link image "A" and "B" wherein each element of the series takes on more and more similarities of the opposite image (or character-type).

Culture. The collection of discourses, artistic objects, behavioral norms, etc. that constitute the boundaries within which individuals structure the meaning of the experiences of their lives in any social network (e.g., nation, community, family, tribe, polis, section, etc.).

Diachronic. Across time rather than static; opposite of synchronic; history is a subset of diachronic studies.

Differentiation.   A rhetorical tactic which draws distinctions between related or similar groups in order to control by sanctioning some and praising others.

Dominant elites.   Individuals and groups who have their interests and organizations explicitly and implicitly recognized in the legal and cultural systems of society, currently in a disproportionate manner at the expense of unrecognized groups.

Double articulation (of rhetoric).   A characteristic of persuasive discourse, which allows it to be read on two levels—manifest interest and rhetorical tactics. This new application of the linguistic term *double articulation* is my own, but it should be noted that Murray Edelman has clearly pointed out the ability of discourse to have both a "universal" symbolic dimension and a partisan, functional dimension. I suggest here two things. First, both levels of this discourse are both symbolic and functional. Second, such an evaluation eliminates the "dismissive" response toward public discourse suggested by Edelman and others. Merely because there is an interest component to a discourse does not disqualify our attention to the public, universal components that may be served by the discourse. See Murray Edelman, *The Symbolic Uses of Politics* (Urbana, Ill.: University of Illinois Press, 1964).

Dramatic structure.   Kenneth Burke's dramatistic pentad—the act, agent, agency, purpose, and scene that constitutes any narrative—discursive depiction of human situations and events.

Enthymeme.   Inferential structure in discourse, generally taken to require the audience's participation in reasoning about probabilities; sometimes described as a rhetorical syllogism.

Epideictic.   One of Aristotle's three macro-genres of public discourse; ceremonial address (as opposed to deliberative and forensic address).

Framing.   The use of ambiguity and multiple interlocking themes to construct a simple, singular square that limits and controls the meaning of some significant object or event.

Grounding images.   Visual representations that provide original support for argumentative claims by adding information that is not fully carried through verbal grounds or verbal commentary on the image.

Groups.   Members of a class that are organized to protect their interests through public action.

Hegemony.   Control of vocabulary and practices by dominant elites, achieved rhetorically, hence, not by direct demand but rather through compromise of competing interests; often functions by making alternatives unspeakable, i.e., unpersuasive.

Heritage.   A social myth constructed about a shared past, which gives that past a unified set of meanings, endorses the social formations represented as existing in that past, and thereby constructs a description of what the future should be.

Human being/person.   In order to avoid taking sides in this technical dispute, I combine the preferred terms of each side of the controversy.

Hyperbole.   Figure of speech in which the words or other symbols chosen deliberately overstate some characteristics of the entity they supposedly represent.

Ideograph.   A word or short phrase that sums up key social commitments and thereby constitutes a society.

Ideology.   The set of beliefs, values, and ways of communicating of a social group; always more or less partial and preferring.

Image.   Visualization or actual visual representation; especially of a character-type.

In-group rhetoric.   Discourse directed to those audiences already committed to the central vocabulary of any group.

Inter-textualized.   Gaining meaning through relationships with other texts or sets of texts.

Male-dominated.   Any culture, institution or the like in which political, economic, and social power is held disproportionately by males or in which those values, narratives, and characterizations traditionally associated with the male gender in Western industrial societies are disproportionately reproduced.

Maximal human reproduction.   The birthing and raising of human offspring in a manner that insures an optimal balance between a high quantity and a functional quantity of people, especially from the perspective of capitalists.

Metaphor.   A figure of speech in which the connotations and sometimes denotations of the name for one item are transferred to another item, "renaming" it, at least in part; e.g., the "leg" of a chair was once a metaphor transferring the meaning of an animal's body part to a support in a piece of furniture.

Metonymy.   Figure of speech in which one technical, precise, or denotative name for some class of things is replaced by a different name that relates to a quality, attribute, or characteristic of a thing.

Motherhood.   The culturally prescribed relations between female parents and their children; varies widely; dominant in American mass culture before 1960, the "myth of motherhood" prescribed this role as the primary or sole identity of women and idealized it.

Myth.   A narrative or component of a narrative that has become a commonplace in a culture and carries great social force.

Mythic commonplace.   A portion of a social myth or a truncated version of that myth (a "commonplace" is a classical rhetorical term for a set-piece of discourse, repeatable in a variety of situations).

Narrative.   A story; the recounting of the actions of an agent for a purpose in
a scene with a method.

Out-group rhetoric.   Discourse, usually persuasive, directed to those not
already committed to the discursive core of an organized social group.

Performative.   A speech act which creates a condition through its utterance;
e.g., a "promise" creates an obligation through being spoken; as opposed
to expressive or referential functions of language usage.

Popular opinion.   The range of beliefs held by all of the citizens of a nation.
See also public opinion.

Presence.   Technical term formulated by Chaim Perelman and L. Olbrechts-
Tyteca in *The New Rhetoric* to describe the ability of rhetoric to give more
force to particular symbols, acts, agents, etc., or to make them more salient
simply by repetition in a discursive arena.

Presumption.   A formal term in argumentation theory (deriving primarily
from Whately) that indicates which side of a controversy must only defend
their case (holding presumption) and which side must attack (carrying the
'burden of proof'); the side of a case that has either history, majority, least
cost, or prior agreement on its side.

Pro-Choice.   Supporters of re-legalization of abortion laws, motivated by the
rhetoric of "right to choose."

Pro-Life.   Supporters of a ban on abortion, publicly motivated by a concern
for the "right to life" of the human conceptus.

Pro-reform.   Supporters of liberalization of abortion laws who promoted
ALI-type laws or were motivated by the "myth of illegal abortion."

Public.   The social formation constituted through the interests *and voices* of
all "active" or potentially active members of a social group. The dominant
elite is the most active subset of the public. The public is an active subset
of all members of a social group; "the people" is the self-ascribed identity
of any public and it is constituted through the discourse of a leader or
leader-system.

Public opinion.   The range of beliefs held by the articulated members of a
populace.

Public vocabulary.   The acceptable words, myths, and characterizations used
for warranting social behavior in a community.

Quickening.   The point at which a woman feels a fetus move inside herself.

Rationally undecidable.   A question for which, although there are relevant,
objective facts, there can be no single "correct" answer because different
groups must weigh the facts in ways that lead to disparate conclusions.

Regulative ideographs.   A constitutive value which mediates between substantive constitutional commitments; a means term.

Rhetoric.   The use of language to persuade; the persuasive dimensions of a
communicative act; the study of public discourse in its persuasive dimen-

sions; that element of a discourse which makes it appear truthful and therefore compelling; persuasive discourse. The social process of governance through mutual persuasion.

Rhetorical conditions. The sum of rhetorical positions of all individuals and groups in a social system.

Rhetorical position. The social group counterpart to the "rhetorical situation"—the place in the social system-network held by a group, especially with regard to the policies and vocabulary they wish to support and the factors which create resistance; such a place interacts with the arguments available to the group.

Rhetorical tactic. The particular approach used to make a persuasive case; generalized lists of such approaches are never definitive but heuristic because of the interaction between form and content.

Selection. One of the three rhetorical processes that influence the persuasiveness of visual images as metaphors; the choice of particular images to stand for a given character-type.

Selfish. The desire to serve one's own interests before those of others; significantly, the term is ascribed to women more frequently than men, presumably because greater self-sacrifice has historically been expected of women than of men.

Stasis. A technical term of classical rhetoric signifying the point on which an issue or cause rests; the heart of a contested matter at a given point in time; also the development of an issue at a given point in time.

Substantive ideograph. A constitutive value term that serves as an end in itself; a reason for the constitution of a people.

Summarizing image. A visual depiction of a narrative that is widely used by a social group; generally adds force through graphic and shorthand portrayal of the "point" of a narrative but has primary value as reminder that unifies.

Synecdoche. The figure of speech which substitutes a part of an item for the whole of another.

Thematization. The rhetorical definition of an event or issue by indicating that its meaning is captured in a single principle or maxim.

Traditional family. The social myth that describes the ideal life as being conducted within the bounds of a social formation consisting of a mother, father, and children living under the same roof, with the father as economic support and final decision authority.

Universality. Having application to all members of the culture.

Universalization. The increase in universality of participation in a social process.

Universalizing. The attempt to demonstrate that an action or value serves the interests of all members of the culture; frequently used to mis-identify particular interests as general interests; also universalization.

Viability.   The ability of a developing human to survive outside the womb of
   the woman who gestated it for a substantial period of time without permanent damage arising from early separation from the womb.
Vocabulary.   Especially "public vocabulary" but also a group or class vocabulary; the words, phrases, narratives, ideographs, images, and characterizations used habitually in the public arena—i.e., in public argument.

Wage-laboring woman.   Any female human being who works for a direct
   cash income usually paid on a weekly or monthly basis. The *needs* of this
   particular group constituted the impetus behind the move for abortion
   reform. This struggle simultaneously constituted them as one of the
   groups to be represented in the system-network. May include professional, middle-, and working-class women (some of whom are also or
   instead poverty class).
Warrants.   Underlying generalizations that constitute the link between a
   claim and its argumentative support. Something like a "major premise" in
   classical logic. Derived from Stephen Toulmin's model of argumentation as
   consisting of claims, grounds, and warrants.

INDEX

Abortion(s): allowance of, 67; analogy to slavery or murder, 49–50, 89–90, 164; changes in practice and meaning of, 1, 199; definition of, xiv; legalization of, 22, 99, 100–104; Medicaid funding for, 112–15, 122n; medical insurance coverage of, 37n; medical risks of, 37n, 77n, 112, 198n; as personal choice, 28–31, 35–36, 174–76; portrayal of, on television, 125–42; pro-Life portrayal of, 44–45; as public concern, 1, 22–36, 176–77; rhetorical articulation of, 23–24. *See also* Abortion law; Illegal abortion; Legal abortion, *Roe v. Wade*

Abortion clinics: bombing of, 151–63, 218–19; comparison to "Nazi ovens," 51; picketing of, 151, 153

Abortion controversy: characterizations of women and motherhood as central to, 14; emergence of new vocabulary in, 15; narratives as discursive units in, 13–14, 31

Abortion culture, creation of, 123–24

Abortionists: characterization of, in abortion narrative, 33–34; and class structure, 34

Abortion law: discrimination in, 66–67; history of, 100–102; public advocacy on need for reform of, 24; role of doctors in controlling, 22–23, 38n, 39n; studies on changes in, 2

Abortion narrative: audience in, 26, 34–35; class differences in, 26, 35–36; controversy in, 31; creation of mythic commonplace in, 27–28; depiction of abortion victims in, 32; depictions of agents involved, 32–34; description of illegal abortion in, 26–27, 33–34; image of motherhood in, 25, 29, 31; legal and medical need for, 23–24; persuasiveness of, 27–28, 30–31, 36; portrayal of women in, 23, 25, 26; prostitution and gambling in, 27; of

Sherri Finkbine, 25, 28–31, 35–36, 177; stories about individual women in, 35, 173–96; tension between old beliefs and new conditions in, 31–34; vocabulary used in, 35. *See also* Pro-Life heritage narrative; Persuasive narrative

Abortion reform, responses of pro-Life forces to, 60–61

Abortion study: focus on abstract ideas, 3; inclusion of discursive forces, 3; politics of, xi–xiii

Adoption, as alternative to illegal abortion, 60

Alaska, abortion law in, 65

ALI. *See* American Law Institute

ALI-type reform laws, 65, 74n

American Law Institute (ALI), 225; "model law" on abortion, 23, 24, 35, 43, 60

American Medical Association, 43

Anti-abortion forces: Catholic church as early visible, 52–53; financing of, 66; *Life* as major constitutive value grounding, 59–63; organization of, 66

Arguments: construction of, 10–11, 19n

Aristotle, 48

Arkansas, abortion law in, 60

Articulation, 4, 23, 225; of abortion problem, 23; access to, by powerful groups, 8; double, 9, 226

"Assignment Abortion," 157

Basil, 54

Birth control: effectiveness of, 69–70; rhetorical features of, 69

Blackmun, Harry A., 98, 100–101, 103, 108, 109, 110–11

Brown v. Board of Education, 111

Buffalo Bill, portrayal of abortion on, 125

Cagney and Lacey, portrayal of abortion on, 125, 126–33, 137, 139, 140

California, abortion law in, 60